Gulliver's Travels

A Critical Study

By

WILLIAM A. EDDY, PH. D.

Submitted in Partial Fulfillment of the Requirements for the Degree of Doctor
of Philosophy, to the Faculty
of English, Princeton
University

GLOUCESTER, MASS.
PETER SMITH
1963

"In this city (Keba) there is established an Academy in which the liberal arts are taught. My landlord conducted me, one solemn festival day, to the college auditory, at the time of creating a MADIK, or Doctor of Philosophy. The business proceeded without the least ceremony, except in so far that the candidate held a neat and well-grounded discourse on a certain physical problem; whereupon he became inscribed, . . . and received a license to teach publicly. After our return home, when my landlord asked me how I liked this manner of obtaining promotion, I answered him, that it appeared to me, much too dry and insipid. I related to him, that with us the *magistri* and doctors were obliged to wrangle previous to their being created to those dignities; at which information he wrinkled up his nose in a very strange sort of way. He then inquired of me, not without a degree of contemptuousness, regarding the nature of these disputations; in what manner they were maintained; and wherein they differed from others. I told him, that they in general treated on matters of the greatest importance; particularly on such as regarded the manners, language, and dress, of two ancient nations, which had flourished in Europe in days of yore. I assured him that I, myself, had maintained in three learned disputations all that I conceived could be said respecting the slippers belonging to these said two ancient nations. On hearing me utter these words, he burst into so immoderate a fit of laughter, that it echoed through the whole house."

("Journey of Klimius to the World Underground.")

Preface

The investigation of the literary relations of *Gulliver's Travels* falls naturally and inevitably into three parts. In the first, I shall attempt to distinguish the philosophic type of *Imaginary Voyage* literature, and discuss briefly the most important of *Gulliver's* fore-runners. I shall note the various narrative forms of the *Philosophic Voyage,* and indicate the general trend of its satiric and utopian content. This survey of the field will be followed by a concise statement of the sources used by Swift in the composition of *Gulliver's Travels.*

In the second and most substantial part of the present work a detailed study will be made of each one of the voyages of Gulliver. The four voyages present such a variety of adventure and criticism that it will be convenient to think of them as four separate *Philosophic Voyages* instead of one. Each one of the *Voyages* will be related to its own special tradition in fiction and satire.

The third and last part will be devoted to the influence of *Gulliver's Travels* on subsequent literature of the eighteenth century: the immediate popularity of the work; a bibliography of keys, commentaries, sequels, and imitations that appeared in large numbers; and a statement of the significance of *Gulliver* in the history of English literature.

The present study was undertaken, originally, to fulfil the requirements of the degree of Doctor of Philosophy. It has been executed, nevertheless, with unexpected interest and pleasure. Neither Swift himself, nor his many readers, I dare say, would care to read a prosaic analysis of *Gulliver's Travels.* Wit dies promptly, when it is laid out and dissected. An edition of *Gulliver,* annotated like this book, would forfeit forever its willing readers. No labor, however, is misspent, which discloses to an unsuspecting public a rich vein of humor and imagination. This intensive study of *Gulliver* has revealed other works of similar interest, now almost entirely forgotten. I doubt if more than one of the ten readers of this book have read the comic *Voyages* of Cyrano de Bergerac, or the *Journey of Klimius to the World Underground,* by Baron Holberg, or any one of a dozen other masterpieces of fancy, related in one way or another to the *Travels* of the famous Captain Gulliver. These, I maintain, are worth preserving. Man may be a Yahoo, but he has also been called an animal gifted with the sense of humor. The saint and the cynic agree at least in this: that wit is the divine gift, which must not be hidden in the ground. The justification for this present work is that it unearths a valuable portion of that treasure.

The limitations apparent throughout the book are my own. Its merits are in no small part due to the generous assistance rendered by others: to the untiring patience and professional skill of Mr. Howard Leach, the Reference Librarian of Princeton University; to the sympathetic interest and invaluable advice of Dr. Geoffroy Atkinson of Amherst College, upon whose scholarship I have leaned heavily; to my esteemed teacher and friend, Dr. Robert Kilburn Root, of Princeton University, who has guided my steps in this task, and whose rare gift of attracting students to literature by lectures which themselves are delightful works of art, first turned my ambitions toward his own profession; and, finally, to Mary Garvin Eddy, whose sacrifices of time and labor made this work possible, and whose enthusiastic and discriminating appreciation of the literature of the eighteenth century turned the task into a mutual pleasure.

WILLIAM A. EDDY.

Princeton, 1922.

Contents

Part I
The Fore-runners of *Gulliver's Travels*

Part II
The Travels of Lemuel Gulliver

Part III
The Influence of *Gulliver's Travels*

BIBLIOGRAPHICAL NOTE

Gulliver's Travels

The text which has formed the basis for this study, and which is quoted throughout, is the edition by G. Ravenscroft Dennis, 1899, Vol. VIII of the *Prose Works of Jonathan Swift*, edited by Temple Scott. London, 1897-1907. 12 vols. in-8.

In the footnotes, the text is referred to as *Gulliver*, without further description. In the case of all other editions, the editor's name is given.

In the footnotes to the individual voyages in part two of this book, the text of Dennis is sometimes referred to by name of sub-division; for example, *Lilliput*, 32.

The very complicated matter of the bibliography of the editions of *Gulliver* is discussed by Dennis, *Gulliver*, xxx-xxxi, and by Temple Scott, *Prose Works of Jonathan Swift*, XII, 225 ff.

Swift

The edition used and quoted throughout is the one by Temple Scott, *The Prose Works of Jonathan Swift, D.D.* London. George Bell and Sons. 1897-1907. 12 vols. in-8. The references in the notes to this edition are given as follows: *Prose Works*, X, 337 (*etc.*)

The text for Swift's poems is the following:

> *The Poems of Jonathan Swift, D.D.*, Edited by William Ernst Browning. London, George Bell and Sons, 1910. 2 vols. in-8. (Uniform binding with *Prose Works*.)

References to this edition are to *Poems*, II, 38, (*etc.*)

The text for Swift's letters is the following:

> *The Correspondence of Jonathan Swift, D.D.*, Edited by F. Elrington Ball. London, George Bell and Sons, 1910-1914. 6 vols. in-4.

References to this edition are to *Correspondence*, III, 337, (*etc.*)

Part I

The Fore-runners

of

Gulliver's Travels

"(Rabelais)—I would as soon undertake to measure the difference between the height and bulk of the giant Gargantua and his Brobdingnagian Majesty, as the difference in merit between my writings and Swift's. If anyone takes a fancy to like my book, let him freely enjoy the entertainment it gives him. . . . If another person likes *Gulliver*, let him toast Dr. Swift. If a third likes neither of us, let him silently pass the bottle and be quiet.

(Lucian)—But what if he will not be quiet? A critick is an unquiet creature.

(Rabelais)—Why then he will disturb himself, not me."

(Lyttleton's, "Dialogue Between Lucian and Rabelais.")

Introduction

(Which the reader will find uninteresting but necessary)

All accounts of travel are either authentic or fictitious. Those of the former class may be, and frequently are, embroidered by the writer's imagination. This does not, however, alter the fact that in every case the narrative is an account of, either a voyage that has actually been made, or of a voyage that never had any existence outside of the writer's imagination. All *Voyages* of the latter class will be described in this book by the term *Imaginary Voyages*.

The term *Philosophic Voyage* is employed in this study to designate a didactic treatise in which the author's criticism of society is set forth in the parable form of an *Imaginary Voyage* made by one or more Europeans to a non-existent or little known country, including an account of the traveler's journey and adventures, together with a description of the imaginary society visited.

This definition will enable us to emerge at once from the outer darkness of voyage literature. Two classes of *Voyages* are obviously eliminated from further consideration: first, all accounts of actual travel; second, all books of travel whose chief purpose is to entertain the reader. The *Philosophic Voyage* is wholly fictitious and primarily didactic.

One obvious difficulty must be disposed of at once. It becomes apparent upon reflection that a great deal of voyage literature is to some extent didactic. The tired business man does not return from his two-hundred dollar trip to the Bermudas without telling of the better way in which things are done down there. Tourists in general, whether relating experiences or inventing their accounts, are much given to describing the superior customs of some remote race unknown to their audience. *Robinson Crusoe*, certainly not a *Philosophic Voyage*, does not lack passages and even chapters designed to admonish the reader and inform him of the workings of Providence (1). All of this is true, but the object of this study is not to trace

---

(1) *Robinson Crusoe*, 1719. It has even been argued that "Defoe wrote it primarily for the edification rather than for the delectation of his readers." (W. P. Trent, *Cambridge Hist. of Eng. Lit.*, IX, 1913, 22.) This is, I believe, a mistake, but there can be no question of Defoe's didactic purpose, which is evident at many points in the narrative. See especially the unreadable sequel, *Serious Reflections of Robinson Crusoe*, 1720.

the didactic element in voyage literature. It is rather to discuss those *Voyages,* which, like *Gulliver,* were written primarily to expound a philosophical position, and in which the narrative is simply a vehicle for instruction.

It should be evident, then, that the *Philosophic Voyage* is an artificial and sophisticated form of literature. It is employed only by educated writers, who, seeking new mediums for instruction, borrow the popular forms of travel literature in order that they may attract readers to a serious theme. The *Philosophic Voyage* is a form of novel, analogous to the modern novel of propaganda, that deals with a social "Problem"; analogous also to the dramatized sermons of Bernard Shaw. So *Gulliver's Travels,* and all *Philosophic Voyages,* are critical works disguised as fiction, one way in which society's pills have been sugar-coated.

On the other hand, the *Philosophic Voyage* must not be a mere homily; the story element must be genuine and considerable. There must be the adventures and discoveries characteristic of a voyage. Harrington's *Oceana* (2), and More's *Utopia* (3), in which the imaginary countries are created in a few paragraphs and described in several hundred pages, are not genuine *Philosophic Voyages.* These and other works designated by Morley as *Ideal Commonwealths* do not possess any considerable account of adventure; the voyage element is either very negligible or else wholly lacking. They belong, essentially, not to voyage literature but to the purely philosophic form of treatise best represented by Plato's *Republic.* That these *Ideal Commonwealths* are closely related to the *Philosophic Voyage* will become clear as we proceed to study its relation to other forms of expression.

Classification of *Philosophic Voyages*

Philosophic Voyages might be classified into groups according to the nature of the philosophy they contain, but I have not found that convenient. Each author has his own peculiar purpose in writing, and selects his favorite objects of satire.

---

(2) James Harrington, *The Commonwealth of Oceana,* 1656. (Morley's Universal Library, Vol. 53.) Oceana, representing England, is a Utopia characterized by an idealized political economy. There is no voyage or story of adventure at all. The imaginary country is gratuitously assumed to exist.

(3) Sir Thomas More, *Utopia.* (Written in Latin about 1516.) The narrative thread is slight and soon lost. *Utopia* is described by the seaman Raphael, who is said to have visited it in the course of his voyages. These voyages, however, are in the past, not a part of the account itself. See further below, chapter 2.

Many of the works that come under this type are separated
from each other by long intervals of time, and by the differing
culture and environment of the writers. The various *Philosophic Voyages* are not bound to each other by a community of
theme, but rather by their common story forms, in respect to
which certain definite lines of influence and imitation can be
distinguished. The classification here used, therefore, is made
on the basis of narrative forms. These same narrative forms
exist, it should be remembered, in *Voyages* that are purely
romantic and fictional, as well as in those that are didactic.
Confusion will be avoided, however, if the reader will keep in
mind the fact that this investigation is limited to those
Voyages, of each narrative type, that are *Philosophic*.

(a) *Fantastic Voyages*

The phrase *Fantastic Voyage* is employed throughout this
work to designate a narrative of a chimerical voyage made by
one or more Europeans to a fabulous country, in which the
marvelous or supernatural elements are sufficiently prominent
to make the account obviously unreal.

The fundamental distinction of *Fantastic Voyages* is their
admittedly marvelous character, the fact that they are not
credible and not intended to be accepted by readers as authentic. Realistic strokes may abound, as they do in *Gulliver's
Travels*, but if so they are only a part of the narrator's art,
calculated to insure the reader's interest rather than to impose
upon his credulity.

Fantastic Voyages may be sub-divided for convenience as
follows:

(1) *Extra-terrestrial*. Example, Cyrano de Bergerac's *Histoire
comique de la lune.* (4)
(2) *Sub-terrestrial*. Example, Holberg's *Journey of Klimius to
the World Underground.*
(3) *Terrestrial*. Example, *Gulliver's Travels*.

(b) *Realistic Voyages*

The phrase *Realistic Voyage* is employed throughout this
study to designate a fictitious narrative purporting to be the
veritable account of a voyage made by one or more Europeans
to an existent country, or one that might easily exist, in which
the mode of travel and the adventures are restricted to the
possibilities of an actual voyage.

---

(4) See further below, chapter 1. All *Voyages* hereafter mentioned
in the text are *Philosophic*, unless it is otherwise stated. Unnecessary
repetition will thus be avoided.

In determining the "possibilities of an actual voyage" the knowledge possessed by the author's contemporaries must be taken into account. A seventeenth century *Voyage* describing unicorns and hermaphrodites (5) does not on that account fail to be a *Realistic Voyage,* however prodigious such features may seem to a modern scientist.

It is not necessary for our purpose to distinguish the degrees of realism within this type. Whether a voyage be to Australia or to Utopia makes no material difference, so long as the account was credible when written. An example of a *Realistic Voyage* of didactic content is the *Histoire des Sévarambes* (6), by Denis Vairasse d'Alais.

The above classification of *Imaginary Voyages* into *Fantastic* and *Realistic,* with convenient sub-divisions, will be found exhaustive and satisfactory. These terms will cover every *Imaginary Voyage,* not alone those of didactic content. The *Voyages of Sindbad the Sailor,* Jules Verne, and Baron Munchausen, are *Fantastic;* Sterne's *Sentimental Journey,* and Defoe's matchless imitations of real travel, are *Realistic.* The classification is made on the basis of form and is therefore indisputable. Readers may differ about the purpose for which a book is written, but there can be no question about the form in which it is published.

Of the application of the other method of classification, made on the basis of the author's purpose in writing, I am not so sure. It may be that some *Voyages* will elude classification as *Philosophic* or *Romantic.* Certainly it is true that entertainment and instruction are frequently combined in baffling proportions. Whether or not this grouping will account for every *Imaginary Voyage,* there will be no difficulty in recognizing as *Philosophic* all those *Voyages* which, like *Gulliver,* are primarily works of criticism rather than works of fiction. Indeed there is no single work so likely to defy this classification as *Gulliver's Travels,* a classic of juvenile fiction that has been reprinted times without number for the delectation of

---

(5) See P. Justel, *Recueil de divers voyages faits en Afrique et en l'Amérique qui n'ont point esté encore publiez.* Paris 1674, where there is a long discussion on the unicorn (pp. 220-223) under the title, *De la fameuse licorne, des lieux où elle est nourrie et comme elle est formée.* This description appears side by side with detailed accounts of plants and animals common in Africa and elsewhere.

Foigny, in *Jacques Sadeur,* 1676 (see further chapter 2) describes a race of hermaphrodites in Australia.

(6) Published, 1677. See further, chapter 2.

the lovers of romance. If I can succeed in establishing my point with regard to *Gulliver,* there will be no difficulty about any of the other works classed as *Philosophic Voyages.*

Classification Used by Other Critics

No thorough or consistent classification of *Imaginary Voyages* ever has been made. Four or five of the most important *Philosophic Voyages* are called by Dunlop in his *History of Prose Fiction* (7), *Voyages Imaginaires,* a phrase loosely used by various writers, especially French ones (8). The trouble with this term is that it has been employed to describe all sorts and conditions of "Voyages" from Sterne's *Sentimental Journey,* and Montesquieu's *Troglodytes,* to the *Golden Ass* of Apuleius and the erotic dreams of Boccaccio; and it has become, consequently, worse than useless for a critical study.

Voyages Imaginaires is the title of a collection of *Imaginary Voyages* in thirty-six volumes, 1787, in which types are hopelessly confused. The set has been of great value to me in rendering accessible a variety of *Voyages,* some of which are now unobtainable in any other edition. The collection lacks any introduction (10), but a sub-division into groups is made that will illustrate the confusion that must have existed in the minds of the editors. The *Voyages Imaginaires* are printed in four divisions, entitled, 1.—*Romanesque;* 2.—*Merveilleux;* 3.—*Allégoriques;* and 4.—*Amusans.* The futility of such a classification must be obvious; form has been confused with content. A marvelous *Voyage* may be amusing and allegorical at the same time; there is nothing in fact to prevent any one *Voyage* from belonging to all four groups at the same time. It is like saying that all men are either 1.—Tall, 2.—Good-natured, or 3.—Clean-shaven. If this study accomplishes nothing else, it is to be hoped that a consistent division will bring order out of the chaos in which *Imaginary Voyages* have been allowed to remain.

(7) First edition, 1814. See edition by Henry Wilson, 1911, Vol. II, pp. 518-538. Criticism of *Imaginary Voyage* literature began with, and must always be dependent upon, Dunlop's excellent review of a few of the most significant *Voyages.*

(8) *Voyages Imaginaires, Amsterdam et se trouve a Paris MDCCLXXXVII* (1787). The phrase is employed by French writers. See, for example, G. Lanson, *Manuel de la littérature française,* 1914, p. 519.

(10) Introductions, of four or five pages, often less, are prefixed to each volume, giving brief accounts of the individual authors and remarks about the various *Voyages.* There is no discussion of the field as a whole.

The *Voyages* to planets, by Cyrano and his imitators (11), have been variously described as *Marvelous* (12) and *Fantastic* (13), of which I have selected the latter term, extending its meaning to include all chimerical *Voyages* whether confined to the surface of the earth or not.

Quite recently Geoffroy Atkinson has employed the phrase *Extraordinary Voyage* (14) in a very specialized sense to describe a limited group of *Realistic Voyages* written in France between 1675 and 1720, which reflect the growth of French rationalism. This use ·of the adjective, *Extraordinary* (15), is to my mind unfortunate, in view of the fact that the *Voyages* in question are selected on the basis of their realistic setting. In fact the term would be more aptly applied to the class of *Voyages* that I have called *Fantastic*. The connexion made by Atkinson between his *Extraordinary Voyages* and contemporary rationalism, renders the term unsuitable for a more inclusive classification, even were it a desirable one. Apart from this point of mere terminology, however, Atkinson's book is by far the most valuable contribution to the study of *Imaginary Voyages* that has yet appeared. In it he has traced the beginnings in one country of the novel in voyage form, and has analyzed in a most scholarly and fruitful fashion a closely related group of French *Philosophic Voyages*.

The survey of the history of the *Philosophic Voyage* in the three chapters that follow is not an exhaustive study, except in so far as *Gulliver's Travels* is concerned. A great deal remains to be done in the way of specialized investigation of certain *Voyages*, a work to which I hope this study of *Gulliver's Travels* may prove an incentive.

---

(11) See further, chapter 1.

(12) By Pietro Toldo, *Revue des études Rabelaisiennes*, 1906-7. Vols. 4 and 5.

(13) See Ferdinand Lotheissen, *Geschichte der Französischen Literatur im XVII Jahrhundert*. 1877, pp. 453-462.
Also, Heinrich Körting, *Geschichte des Französischen Romans im XVII Jahrhundert*. 1891, pp. 169-205.

(14) *The Extraordinary Voyage in French Literature* (before 1720) in two volumes. Vol. I, Columbia University Press, 1920. Vol. II, in preparation.

(15) Atkinson follows M. Gustave Lanson who first applied to the same group of *Voyages* the title, *Voyages extraordinaires*. *op. cit.* (note 8 above), pp. 518-519.

CHAPTER 1

Narrative Types of the *Philosophic Voyage.*

I. *Fantastic Voyages.*

In its mature form the *Philosophic Voyage* represents a
blend of two distinct literary types: a story of adventurous
travel, and a didactic account of some imaginary commonwealth. Historically, both of these literary types preceded
the *Philosophic Voyages.* The *Odyssey* is a *Fantastic Voyage*
of the non-philosophic variety. Plato's *Republic* and his
description of the submarine country, Atlantis (1), are philosophic accounts of imaginary commonwealths, lacking any
narrative of adventure. Each of these types has its lineal
descendants. Certain ones of the *Arabian Nights* stories,
Baron Münchausen, and the romances of Jules Verne, belong
to the Homeric category; Campanella's *Civitas Solis* (2),
More's *Utopia* (3), and Andreae's *Christianopolis* (4), to the
Platonic. Although works of the types just mentioned contributed materially to the development of the *Philosophic* type
of *Voyage,* they do not enter directly into the field of the
present study. This is not a thorough study of the *Philosophic
Voyage* closing arbitrarily with the publication of *Gulliver's
Travels* in 1726. *Gulliver* is our starting point in the consideration of certain important fore-runners, which, by virtue of
their influence upon, or their resemblance to, the work of
Swift, make its significance in the history of literature more
clear. *Philosophic Voyages* not vitally related to *Gulliver* are,
for the sake of unity, omitted altogether from the text. Such
Voyages may be consulted in the appendix.

These opening chapters may seem inadequate, furthermore,
on account of the very cursory remarks to which the discussion

(1) See Plato's *Timaeus* and *Critias. Works of Plato,* translated by
Henry Davis, 1894, vol. II, pp. 325-9, 420-9. The people of Atlantis are
described as possessing "true and altogether lofty ideas," and practising
"mildness united with wisdom." The fiction of the Atlantis was revived
by Francis Bacon in his *New Atlantis,* 1622-4, and in Mrs. Manley's
work with the same title, 1709.

(2) By Thomas Campanella, *circa* 1632. Translation in Morley's *Ideal
Commonwealths,* 1896.

(3) Written in Latin, 1515-16. Translation in Morley, *op. cit.*

(4) Johann Valentin Andreae, 1619 (Latin). Translation by F. E.
Held, 1914 (University of Illinois, *Studies*).

of each *Voyage* is limited. In this connexion I wish to emphasize the point that the first part of this study is restricted
to considerations of *Gulliver's Travels* as a whole. Relation-
ships between fore-runners and individual voyages of Gulliver,
including nearly all the definite parallels, are reserved for the
detailed study of the various situations in the second part of
this work.

The earliest known *Philosophic Voyage* is Lucian's *True
History* (5), written about 170 A. D., for our purposes one
of the most important if not the most important of all *Fantastic Voyages* before *Gulliver's Travels*. We have no example
of a *Realistic Voyage*, on the other hand, earlier than Foigny's
Jacques Sadeur (6), 1676, by which time at least eleven *Fantastic Voyages* had appeared (7). The reason for this is not
hard to find. Realism in travel literature was a late development, a result of the increased knowledge of the world brought
about by geographical discovery in the sixteenth and seventeenth centuries. *Jacques Sadeur* differs from the *True History* in the same way that the authentic *Voyages* of Dampier
differ from the *Travels* of Mandeville. The *Philosophic
Voyage* grew up rapidly in the atmosphere of magic long
before the forbidding hand of science waved the imaginary
travellers back to earth. In his preface to the *True History*
Lucian insists that his story is no exaggeration of the supernatural accounts given out by contemporary travellers as true
history. Later, the marvellous features of medieval literature
furnished the writers of *Philosophic Voyages* with models for
their fantastic narratives. The whole cycle of dream visions
and spiritual allegories, including the *Divine Comedy* itself,
reflects medieval preference for fantastic travel and disregard
for geographical realism. The legend of *St. Patrick's Purga-
tory* (8) is a good example. *Sir Owain* is dragged about the
universe by grinning devils. Praying for escape from a pit
into which he has been cast, he is expelled by a blast of wind
which comes in answer to his petition. The *Marvellous*

---

(5) The text upon which this study is based is the translation by
Tom Brown in the *Dryden Lucian*, 1711, vol. III, a text with which
Swift himself was probably familiar (see chapter 4). The best critical
studies of Lucian's *True History*, are the following:
    1. Pietro Toldo, *Revue des Etudes Rabelaisiennes*, vol. 4, 1906, con-
tinued in vol. 5.
    2. H. W. Hime, *Lucian, The Syrian Satirist*, 1900.
(6) See further below, chapter 2.
(7) See the chronological list of *Fantastic Voyages* in the appendix.
(8) For bibliography and synopsis of this medieval legend see J. E.
Wells, *A Manual of the Writings in Middle English*, 1916, pp. 334-5,
806, 815.

Voyages of St. Brandan (9) are even more fantastic. The travellers visit an island inhabited by sheep, another ruled by birds. They celebrate Mass on the back of a whale, and pass through many other adventures no less grotesque. There is no need here to do more than illustrate the proverbial fondness of the medieval mind for the marvellous, and to point out that it was largely responsible for the fantastic form of the earliest *Philosophic Voyages*.

Lucian wrote two *Fantastic Voyages*. One of these, *Icaro-menippus, or a Voyage to Heaven,* is interesting chiefly on account of its influence upon the *Voyage to Lilliput,* and it will be considered in chapters four and six, below. The other one, the *True History,* may be regarded as the real beginning of *Philosophic Voyage* literature. The *True History* is so essential to an understanding of the fore-runners of *Gulliver,* and we shall have occasion to refer to it so frequently in the chapters that follow, that it will be well to become familiar with its contents at once.

Lucian's "Gulliver" begins by setting sail with fifty companions and a trusty pilot to discover what lies beyond the western ocean. After encountering a storm which lasts eighty days they arrive at a hilly and richly wooded island, where they find a pillar of brass, with an inscription in Greek, "Thus far came Bacchus and Hercules." Two footprints, one of enormous size, mark the farthest step of god and hero. The rivers of the island flow with wine instead of water. The women there below the waist are mere vines. When two of the travellers attempt to kiss them, they are clasped tight in their tendrils and transformed into vines. These vines scream with pain when any twig is broken off.

Sailing away from the island, the ship is caught by a whirlwind which carries it three thousand stadia into the air. The real adventures of the crew now begin. They sail to the moon, are hospitably received by King Endymion, and enlist in the war which he is about to wage with King Phaëton. Endymion's forces consist of eighty thousand warriors who bestride vultures, each with three heads, so huge that every feather is as big as a ship's mast. The battle ends in the total discomfiture of Endymion. The inhabitants of the moon live a strange life. They do not die, but vanish when the time of death approaches. Their only nourishment is the odor of roasted frogs. They extract oil from onions, get pure water from their grapes, wear garments of glass, and drink air squeezed into a goblet. To preserve their sight they take out their eyes, using them but rarely, the rich buying up the spare eyes of the poor.

Leaving the moon, the travellers come next to the City of Lanterns (Compare Rabelais, V, ch. 32) where they land and see many curious things. After several other adventures they are swallowed up by an enormous whale, three hundred miles long, at one gulp, ship and all. (Compare Rabelais, I, ch. 38.) Once inside they

---

(9) *Les Voyages Merveilleux de Saint Brandan, Légende en vers de XIIe siècle.* Paris, 1878. (Introduction by F. Xavier Michel.)

can at first see nothing at all, but gradually perceive that they are in a vast cavity. All about them lie bones of fish and men, and ships with their cargoes. Sailing farther on, they arrive at a small island, forty-five miles round. On landing they come upon an old man and his son, the last survivors of a mishap exactly like their own, who have lived upon the island for twenty years. After a long imprisonment, the idea occurs to them to effect their escape by setting fire to the forest which covers the island. After the wood has burned for a few days, the whale sickens rapidly and dies. The travellers prop his jaws open with beams of timber and sail out onto the open sea.

Other adventures do equal credit to Lucian's imagination. The travellers get into a frozen sea, where they dig a cave and live in the ice. They arrive at the sea of milk with its island of cheese, and also at the salt sea where men have feet made of cork and skate about without sinking. A long stay is made at the Island of the Blessed, governed by Rhadamanthus. The city has palaces of gold and pavements of ivory; there are crystal baths, and round the city flows a stream of rose water. The people lie in beds of flowers, while nightingales drop roses on their heads and choirs of sweet-faced boys sing to them. All the demigods and old philosophers are there. Socrates is in temporary disgrace, having carried his levities too far. Diogenes is married and has taken to drink. Plato is marooned on an island by himself, where he makes laws forever. The Stoics are not admitted, but are kept busy climbing the steep slopes of the Hill of Virtue, while the Academicians, who would like to enter, are excluded on account of their having denied the existence of the place.

The travellers meet with many other adventures of the most fantastic type imaginable, after which the story closes abruptly with the promise of more next time.

Direct imitation of Lucian is evident in the *Fantastic Voyages* (10) of Rabelais, Cyrano de Bergerac, Baron Holberg, and Swift, writers, who, together with Lucian, wrote the greatest of all *Fantastic Voyages*, without whose work there would be no excuse for the time spent in writing this chapter. The most influential part of the *True History* is the description of the voyage to the moon, where the travellers are received among a people of strange customs and novel government. Unlike the theme of the lunar commonwealths of Godwin, Cyrano, and Defoe, described later in this chapter, Lucian's interest is not so much in the new civilization as in

(10) For Rabelais' debt to the *True History* see Walter Besant, *The French Humorists*, 1877, chapter 5; P. Toldo, *op. cit.* Cyrano's debt to the *True History* is indicated by Dunlop, *History of Prose Fiction*, 1814, edition by Wilson, 1911, II, 530 ff. Holberg, in his *Autobiography* (see below, note 34) admits following Lucian in his *Journey of Klimius to the World Underground;* the imitation is obvious in several situations, notably in the circumstance of the human trees which bleed when twigs are broken off. The influence of the *True History* on *Gulliver's Travels* is summed up in chapter 4 of this study.

the marvellous character of the adventures, all of which are
purposely exaggerated. The reason for the excess of wonders,
and the total lack of any appearance of probability in the narrative, is that Lucian is here writing a parody on the supernatural accounts of poets and historians. The title, *A True
History*, indicates the limits of his purpose, which is to ridicule
the forgeries of all historians "who write untruly" (11), of
whom Lucian names Ctesias and Herodotus as conspicuous
offenders. The *True History* with its single aim of parody is
thus a long way from *Gulliver's Travels*, where the voyage is
the medium for an extended commentary on life in general.
In the history of the *Philosophic Voyage*, however, the *True
History* occupies a significant place, and for three reasons. In
it were combined for the first time the travel of adventure and
the satirical representation of an imaginary commonwealth.
Furthermore, the exaggerated character of the fantastic adventures established a precedent of unreality which persisted into
nearly every *Voyage* of the *Fantastic* class. Finally, the *True
History* is of significance because it supplied a rich mine of
material for fiction and satire alike to a host of writers from
Rabelais to Fielding (12).

The *Philosophic Voyage* was revived, near the middle of the
sixteenth century, in the work of Rabelais, in unmistakable
imitation of Lucian. The fourth and fifth books (13) of
Rabelais are occupied with the voyage of Panurge, accompanied by Pantagruel, from the World of Error to search after
Truth, which Rabelais represents as located in a bottle, alluding to the well-known effects of intoxication.

> The travellers visit many lands, each of which is made the vehicle
> of some new satire. They sojourn first in the island of Medamothy
> (Nowhere), which with its rarities and prodigies, is, like the *True
> History*, a satire on the improbable fictions of travellers. The
> Land of Pettifogging is a satire upon inferior officers of justice.
> The travellers are caught and nearly wrecked in a storm, which
> typifies the persecution raised in France against the Huguenots.
> The travellers escape the storm by taking refuge in the Islands of
> the Macreons (British Isles) where they are safe from Popish
> persecution. They visit the Island of Pope-figgland, the inhabitants
> of which, though once rich are now poor, wretched, and subject
> to the Papimanes. These latter worship not God but the Pope,
> who is referred to by Panurge with most obscene disrespect. They

---

(11) Quoted from Lucian's introductory essay, *How to Write History*,
prefixed to the *True History*, where he explains his satiric purpose at
unnecessary length. *Dryden Lucian*, IV, 12-34.

(12) See Fielding's *Journey from this World to the Next*, 1743.

(13) Written about 1547. This study is based on the Motteux translation, 1694, reprinted and edited by W. E. Henley in *The Tudor Translations*, 1900, vol. XXVI.

go to the court of the great inventor, Gaster, the first Master of Arts in the world. There, Rabelais shows, by means of most ingenious allegory, how necessity and self-preservation are the parents of all arts and sciences. Six chapters are devoted to an account of the Ringing Island in which, without the least disguise, the Church is described. There the single Pope-hawk lives with priest-hawks, bishop-hawks, abbot-hawks, and cardinal-hawks. These birds are all of strange birth, having been imported from the land of Lack-bread to which they never return. Their only duty is to sing at the ringing of the bells. In the Island of the Apedefers (Ignoramuses) the travellers pass through terrible adventures with monsters of prodigious sorts. The Queendom of Whims is, like Laputa, which was modelled in part upon it, a satire upon academic learning. Many other lands are visited, including that of Gripe-men-all (Inquisitor) and Lanternland (borrowed from the *True History*) before the travellers finally reach the Oracle of the Bottle.

Although much of Rabelais' satire is obscure and incoherent, it is not difficult to distinguish the four principal objects of his ridicule: 1.—The crooked politics of his time; 2.—The vices of degenerate clergymen, and religious superstitions then prevalent; 3.—The lying and extravagant tales circulated by travellers; 4.—The pedantry of the age. The narrative of the voyage made in the last two books is a loose and disconnected one; the travellers arrive and leave capriciously, and the motivation throughout is poor. The reader is frequently at a loss to account for the itinerary, for Pantagruel is an adept at annihilating space. We shall have occasion to return to Rabelais in subsequent chapters. For the present we do not need to consider his works any further than is necessary to note that the *Fantastic* form of the *Philosophic Voyage* was revived in France where it was destined to find its richest growth, and in a form in which the narrative is ruinously subordinated to rambling satire.

In the year 1638 Bishop Francis Godwin published the *Voyage of Domingo Gonzales, or The Man in the Moon* (14), a work not so important for itself as for its influence upon the romances of Cyrano de Bergerac, beyond all question the greatest *Fantastic Voyages* in French literature. Godwin's narrative, a matter of less than thirty pages, is in brief as follows:

Returning from the Indies, where he had amassed great wealth, Gonzales is taken dangerously ill and is set ashore upon a desert island by the heartless captain. Upon recovering his health Gonzales busies himself with the task of domesticating the animals

---

(14) The first edition of this work is very rare. The text is reprinted in the *Harleian Miscellanies*, 1808-11, XI, 511-534. Also in *Anglia*, X, 328-356.

on the island, especially a kind of wild swan that breeds there in
large numbers. He conceives and puts into execution the idea of
harnessing a flock of these wild geese to an improvised chariot,
and thus making his escape. The geese are difficult to train, but
after one unsuccessful attempt to fly they carry Gonzales away,
not to Spain, however, but to the moon. As he approaches the
moon Gonzales notices that it is in all respects like another earth,
while our own world, conversely, assumes a "kind of brightness
like another moon." The journey occupies eleven days, during
which time Gonzales feels neither hunger nor thirst. The inhabitants of the moon turn out to be men of differing size, varying from
a little above the normal human stature to the prodigious height
of one hundred and twenty feet. Mental and moral excellence is
possessed in direct proportion to physical stature. Many of the
Lunarians live above a thousand years, longevity also being a
function of height. "The taller the people are of stature, the more
excellent are their endowments of mind and the longer they live."
The moon-men detest lying and falsehood; their rulers are models
of justice and virtue. Their language consists, not of words but
of tunes, a circumstance copied by Cyrano in his description of
the moon people. Everyone on the moon is happy and contented
because there are no lawyers or physicians there to create disorder. At the end of a year, Gonzales, having become homesick,
takes his leave, trims his flying-machine, and returns to the earth.

Certain features of the *Voyage of Gonzales* will demand
close study in connexion with Gulliver's *Voyage to Brobdingnag,* chapters seven and eight of this study.

In 1648 a French translation of Godwin's romance, by Jean
Baudouin, appeared under the title, *l'Homme dans la lune,*
under the influence of which Cyrano de Bergerac commenced
to write, in the following year, the *Histoire comique de la
lune* (15), the romance about which criticism of the *Philosophic Voyage* must ever center. A work of intrinsic excellence, full of independent interest, it deserves our attention in
addition because of its manifold relations to other *Philosophic
Voyages* (16). Cyrano borrowed and incorporated into the
work much that he had learned from Plato, Lucian (17), and
Godwin (18); giving in turn numerous ideas to Holberg, and
to Swift. In the story Cyrano himself is the adventurer. On
reaching the moon by means of a device as impractical as that
employed by Godwin, he meets there both Gonzales and
Socrates, whose names suggest the two-fold nature of the
work. Cyrano imitates Godwin's story of a trip to the moon,

---

(15) *Histoire comique des états et empires de la lune. Nouvelle edition
par P. L. Jacob (Paul Lacroix)* 1858. The introduction is excellent.

(16) By far the best critical study is by Pierre Brun, *Savinien de
Cyrano Bergerac,* Paris, 1909.

(17) P. Toldo, *op. cit.*

(18) The influence of Godwin's romance upon the works of Cyrano
is exhaustively treated by Hönncher, *Anglia* X.

elaborating the astonishing adventures, but he also follows Socrates (or rather Plato) in the construction of an imaginary commonwealth of an ideal character. As will be seen by referring to my study of Gulliver's second voyage, the adventures of Cyrano in the moon correspond very closely to those of Gulliver in Brobdingnag, for which they were the direct source.

Following a discussion with several friends of the possibility that the moon be inhabited, Cyrano resolves to make a journey thither himself. He fills bottles with morning dew and attaches them to his person, in the hope that the dew will be attracted by the sun. The experiment is only partially successful, for with the help of the bottles he does actually rise into the air only to subside again upon the earth, landing not in France but in Canada, due to the revolution of the earth. Here he makes new experiments, and succeeds finally by rubbing the marrow of certain animals on his body, which the moon sucks up. On his arrival he is met by the inhabitants, giants twelve cubits high. He is appropriated by a mountebank who shows him for money, making him perform as a dwarf in a circus, turn somersets, make faces, and jump at the end of a rope. Cyrano meets Socrates with whom he is able to converse in Greek. He complains to Socrates of the treatment to which he has been subjected, but Socrates reminds him that it is no worse than the lot which would befall a moon-man if he should come to the earth and claim to be a human being.

Socrates brings Cyrano to the court, where he becomes the pet of queen and courtiers in general. The philosophers disagree about his species, but conclude at length that he must be an ill-formed specimen of the genus to which the queen's dwarf belongs. When he meets this dwarf, Cyrano recognizes him as Domingo Gonzales, the Spaniard who had flown to the moon by the aid of birds. Both are confined in a cage where they converse together at night on philosophy, and pass the daytime on exhibition before curious crowds of spectators. They pick up a smattering of the moon-language, the result of which is that some free-thinkers in the moon hold them to be endowed with reason. This opinion is combated on the ground that nature would never have wasted intelligence upon such mis-shapen creatures. The quarrel becomes so violent that Cyrano is ordered to appear before a public assembly which is to pass upon his rationality. The verdict is in the negative, and Cyrano is again confined to his cage. A young giantess falls desperately in love with Cyrano and begs him to take her away with him when he goes back to the earth. Cyrano nearly loses his life by asserting that the moon is in reality only a moon and not an earth, a statement which he is compelled to retract in public. After becoming further acquainted with the customs and manners of the moon-people, Cyrano escapes with the aid of Socrates, who carries him to Italy whence he returns home.

Cyrano's second romance, *Histoire comique des états et empires du soleil* (19) is an inferior account of a somewhat similar trip

(19) Bound with the lunar romance in the edition noted, above, in note 15. Both romances were published posthumously in 1657.

to the sun, not so well known as the other, but very important
for its influence upon the satire in Gulliver's fourth voyage,
for which see, further, chapters four and twelve. I give here
only the barest outline of the story.

> After a journey of four months Cyrano reaches one of the small
> stars which circle about the sun. There he makes the acquaintance
> of a small, naked man who lets him into the profound secrets of
> nature. Cyrano understands him because the native speaks a
> mother language akin to all other languages. Cyrano leaves the
> star and goes to the sun itself, where he finds a race of people
> who are able to assume any shape they please. A nightingale
> leads him to the province where the people have assumed the
> shape of birds. There Cyrano has most humiliating experiences.
> On the moon he was not credited with human intelligence. Here
> the fault with him is that he is human, and hence a miserable
> wretch, unfit to live. He is sentenced to death, but manages to
> escape.
>
> Other adventures include the marvellous forest, the trees of
> which can speak; and the Lake of Sleep into which five rivers
> fall, the rivers of the five senses. Cyrano meets Campanella and
> Descartes, at which point the story breaks off, uncompleted.

The importance of the romances of Cyrano for our study is a
two-fold one. In the first place, they furnished more material
for the composition of *Gulliver's Travels* than did the works
of any other author (20) ; and in the second place, Cyrano was
the first to employ the form of the *Fantastic Voyage* as a device
for setting forth under a fictional disguise a serious condemnation of human nature (21).

The mind of the reading public in the seventeenth century
was filled with speculation about the possible habitation of the
planets, a curiosity for which the Philosophers were largely
responsible, as is illustrated by the treatise of Fontenelle,
Entretiens sur la pluralité des mondes, 1686 (22). Earlier
than that, in 1647, Pierre Borel wrote his *Discours nouveau
prouvant que les astres sont des terres habitées, et la terre une
estoile* (23). Going back further yet we find *The Discovery*

---

(20) For the study of the sources of *Gulliver*, see chapter 4.

(21) Lucian and Rabelais had satirized human weaknesses and human
institutions, but Cyrano degrades the race itself to a position below the
animals.

(22) Fontenelle, *Oeuvres*, Paris, 1790. II, pp. 1-176.

(23) P. L. Jacob, *op cit.* pp.xxx-xxxi of the prefactory *Notice Historique*.

of a World in the Moone, 1638 (24), by the eminent scientist and theologian, John Wilkins. About the middle of the eighteenth century two *Philosophic Voyages* were published in France, which, though they do not properly belong to this study since they were subsequent to *Gulliver*, should nevertheless be mentioned here as probable imitations of the romances of Cyrano, and as examples of the popularity of the extra-terrestrial *Fantastic Voyage*. These are, first, a work of unknown authorship entitled *Relation du monde de mercure*, 1750 (25), a very readable account of a curious civilization and of comic adventures on the planet Mercury, occupying something over three hundred pages. The other one is a more ambitious work, *Voyages de Milord Céton dans les sept planettes* (26), written by Marie Anne de Roumier, some time before 1771. It is an account of an English nobleman who is carried by a friendly genius through the moon and seven planets. The author accommodates the character of the inhabitants of each star to the name it bears on earth. Venus is the abode of physical passion; Mercury is characterized by avarice; Mars is peopled by warriors whose only concern is to kill each other; Jupiter is the home of pride; the Sun is a land of enlightenment and reason, etc., etc.

Daniel DeFoe's *Consolidator*, 1705 (27), is the story of a trip to the moon, of the conventional type, with a good deal of uninteresting political and religious satire mixed in. It represents Defoe at just about his worst.

> After referring contemptuously to the crude devices employed by Bishop Wilkins and the "learned Spaniard" (Gonzales), the author describes at great length his own excellent contrivance for reaching the moon. This is accomplished by means of an engine called a Consolidator being in shape like a chariot mounted on two

(24) A work frequently referred to by contemporary writers, notably by Defoe in the *Consolidator*. (See below p. 24.) It is not a *Fantastic Voyage* so much as a conjectural description from the scientific point of view of a possible civilization on the moon. The last chapter is devoted to a serious discussion of possible methods for reaching the moon. Wilkins argues that man may yet devise an aeroplane capable of making the trip.

(25) *Voyages Imaginaires*, 1787, XVI. See also Gilbert Chinard, *L'Amérique et le rêve exotique dans la littérature française au XVIIe et au XVIIIe Siècle*, 1913, p. 443.

(26) *Voyages Imaginaires*, XVII-XVIII. See Dunlop, *op. cit.*, II, 536-7.

(27) *The Consolidator, or Memoirs of Sundry Transactions from the World in the Moon. Translated out of the Lunar Language by the Author of "The True Born Englishman."* This early work by Defoe is practically unknown, and has never been mentioned in connexion with *Gulliver's Tavels*.

bodies furnished with vast wings, composed of feathers nicely put together. When the engine is started, these wings take on a regular motion by which the Consolidator is propelled upward into the air. The passenger drinks a sleeping potion and never wakes until he reaches the moon.

On the moon Defoe discovers men and women, knaves and whores, nations and political parties, in all respects like those of his own world. The philosophy of the moon people is explained at great length by the Man in the Moon. The provinces of the moon represent satirically human factions in church and state, Deists, High and Low Churchmen, Whigs and Tories, etc. The folly of dissension is exposed by the account of the numerous unnecessary wars waged among the lunar provinces. The first one hundred pages are fairly readable, but in the remaining two hundred and sixty the allegory becomes tiresomely repetitious, unrelieved by any adventures. The book closes without any account of the return trip to earth.

As a fore-runner of *Gulliver's Travels* the *Consolidator* is of interest chiefly because of the tongue-twisting language spoken by the Lunarians, the invention of which by Defoe is one of the rare anticipations of the languages which Gulliver has to learn in the course of his travels (28). Thus in the *Consolidator* the vocabulary acquired by the traveller includes the following:

Abogratziarian	Anti-every-body-arian
Dullobardian	Priest
Upogyla	Religion
Hecato	Penny
Lazognians	Magistrates
Bloutegondegours	Stock-brokers

In addition the reader is treated to a stanza of native poetry which is, in origin and in quality, really lunatic.

"Wondelis Idulasim Perizola Metartos
Srigunia Crolias Xerin Hytale Fylos
Farnicos Galvare Orpto Sonamel Egonsbersch
Sih Lona Sipos Gullia Ropta Tylos" (29).

While busy exploring the planets, the imaginary voyagers did not neglect the earth. Sub-terrestrial *Fantastic Voyages* were not uncommon in the seventeenth and eighteenth cen-

(28) Another fore-runner of *Gulliver*, Joseph Hall's *Mundus Alter et Idem* contains a similar account of a meaningless language. See below, chapter 3.

(29) *Consolidator*, p. 306. The stanza is translated by Defoe as follows:

"Caesar, you trifle with the world in vain;
Think rather now of Germany than Spain.
He's hardly fit to fill the eagle's throne
Who gives new crowns, and can't protect his own."

turies, though most of these are not *Philosophic* as that term
has been here defined. In 1665 was published the scientific
romance, *Mundus Subterraneus* (30), by the celebrated German scientist, Athanasius Kircher. The *Voyage du pôle
arctique au pôle antarctique par le centre du monde*, 1723 (31).
is a story done with vivid imagination, replete with physical
and geographical wonders, but free from any didactic purpose.
Of the same type is *Lamékis, ou les voyages d'un égyptien dans
la terre, intérieure*, 1735 (32), by the Chevalier Mouhy, a work
of no great merit. By far the most ingenious and fascinating
sub-terrestrial *Voyage* is *The Journey of Nicholas Klimius to
the World Underground* (33), written by the Danish drama-
tist, Baron Holberg, in Danish, but soon afterwards translated
into German, French, Latin, and English, in all of which translations it is now obtainable. The date of composition of
Klimius is unknown. The earliest notice of the work is a
review in the *Hamburg Gazette*, 1732, but Holberg states in
his autobiography (34), that the work was completed "several
years" before it was given to the press. Since *Gulliver's
Travels* was published in 1726, it would be difficult to establish
any influence either way. Be that as it may, with the single
exception of the romances of Cyrano, there is no other known
work which affords such a close parallel to the general types
of adventure found in *Gulliver,* and no other *Philosophic
Voyage* which so rewards the reader as does this story of
Holberg.

After winning for himself the highest academic degrees to be
obtained in the universities of Denmark, Klimius proceeds on his
vacation to explore a haunted cave not far from his native village.
There he has the misfortune to fall down a bottomless pit out of
which he drops into a subterranean universe filled with solar sys-
tems not unlike the real universe except that the scale is much
reduced. Klimius is astonished to find himself revolving about a
planet whose inhabitants regard him as their moon. His pride
knows no bounds when he discovers that a piece of bread, which
falls out of his pocket, circles about him as his own satellite.
making him no less important than any other planet. Klimius

(30) Written in Latin. A romance of an imaginary world underground, written from the scientific point of view.

(31) Anonymous. *Voyages Imaginaires*, Vol. XIX. See also Chinard,
op. cit., p. 441.

(32) *Ibid.*, XX.

(33) *Ibid.*, XIX. Obtainable in a number of editions, including an
anonymous English translation, London, 1828.

(34) See, *Memoirs of Lewis Holberg, written by himself in Latin and
now first translated into English*. London, 1827. p. 175 ff.

manages at last to make a landing, and proceeds to tour the
provinces of the new world. There is in this story a definite
attempt to throw an atmosphere of authenticity about the narrative, not found elsewhere in any other *Fantastic Voyage* before
Gulliver's Tavels. Thus Klimius is careful to state that certain
prodigies described by the natives are only rumors for which he
refuses to vouch. Again he confesses in another place that one
of his adventures may have been slightly exaggerated by his vivid
imagination. At still another point the narrative is interrupted
by a gap, which Klimius explains is due to the loss of several
pages from his diary. During his visit in Potua, Klimius attempts
to elicit admiration by discussing his doctoral thesis on *The Slippers of the Ancients*, but the Potuans are not impressed. To the
traveller's further chagrin he discovers that scholars and pedants
are employed solely to debate before spectators in the theatres
for the amusement of the public. He himself, though treated
with kindness, is rated as an inferior being, not endowed with
reason. He orates at length to the King on the glories of European civilization, but the latter is only disgusted, especially with
the accounts of lawyers and court procedure. (Compare Brobdingnag.) In this underworld there is a reversal of our moral ideas,
not unlike that described by Samuel Butler in *Erewhon*. For
example, the social rating begins with the laborer at the top and
descends to the less useful occupations of king, priest, and scholar.
In another province, the young rule over the old, and mischievous
fathers obey their wiser children. In the state of Cambara, the
span of life is four years, and the inhabitants are models of
virtue. In Spelek, on the contrary, where they live four hundred
years, vice is rampant and suicide frequent. (Compare with the
Struldbruggs.) In Kilak the term of each one's life is marked
on his fore-head at birth; here repentance is always put off until
the eleventh hour. Passing through the land of animated musical
instruments, Klimius is wrecked and cast adrift in Guama, where
he manufactures gun-powder and fire-arms (previously unknown)
and assists the emperor against the Tanaquians. He discovers in
the public library an account of his own world written by a Tana-
quian who had visited it. Klimius is eventually made emperor
and founds the fifth monarchy, but is overthrown by a revolution,
provoked by his tyranny. Seeking to escape, he tumbles down a
cleft in the hills, which proves to be the hole through which he
had fallen originally, and he lands once more on the familiar
mountain near his own home. The narrative of Holberg is unusual, not only for the originality of its conception, but also for
the constant variety of the numerous adventures. As will be
pointed out later, the *Journey of Klimius* at one point or another,
bears some close and interesting relation to each of the voyages
of Gulliver.

Entirely apart from the interest in the voyage of fanciful
exploration which reached its most artistic form in the romances of Cyrano and Holberg, fiction was supplied with a
renewed interest in pure marvels through the introduction
into western Europe in the latter part of the seventeenth
century of the oriental tale, especially through the translation

into English of the *Arabian Nights,* in 1724 (35). This new interest is reflected not only in the numerous *Contes des Fées* (36) of Perrault and others, and in the literature of the The Oriental Traveller of Du Fresne (37), Montesquieu (38) and their school (39), but in the increased fondness for prodigy manifested in *Fantastic Voyages.* To the interest in the extravagant life of the eastern civilization and to its grotesque mythology of genii, giants, ogres, and magical agencies, must be attributed the luxurious life of the peoples visited by the imaginary travellers, as well as the giants, roc, and the magic island described in *Gulliver.*

In this brief review it must have become clear that *Gulliver's Travels* belongs to the type of *Philosophic Voyage* which I have defined as *Fantastic,* though as I shall show in the next chapter it is something else as well. The consistency and the realism with which Swift works out his fictions does not make them any the less fantastic in conception. No one of Gulliver's voyages, excepting the brief stay in Japan (40), is made to an existent country or to one that could exist. The romances of Cyrano and Lucian seem more improbable than *Gulliver,* but this is a difference in style only. It would be hard to find, within the limits of any other *Fantastic Voyage,* a list of marvellous races equal to those in *Gulliver:* six-inch pygmies, seventy-foot giants, the flying island Laputa, deathless Stuldbruggs, the magicians and the departed spirits of Glubdubdrib, and finally a race of speaking, thinking, and self-governing horses. The narrative of Swift is more coherent than were most of its fore-runners. The several voyages are clear in outline and consistent in detail. The reader will search in vain for any earlier voyage in which the illusion of size is maintained as it is in the first two voyages of Gulliver, where with scrupulous art Swift has shaped every detail to the unusual scale of life, until he has created a pygmy and a giant world, which satisfy the most critical tests of consistency (41).

---

(35) This was a translation, not from the original Arabic, but from the French of Galland, whose version of the *Arabian Nights* in twelve volumes was in circulation by the year 1704 twenty years before it was done into English.

(36) A favorite of Swift. See *Journal to Stella, Letter XL,* Jan. 26, 1711-12. *Prose Works,* II, 327. The collection, *Le Cabinet des Fées* (41 vols. 1785) consists largely of oriental tales written before 1720.

(37) *Amusements sèrieux et comiques,* 1699.

(38) *Lettres Persanes,* 1721.

(39) Imitations of these authors appeared in the works of Tom Brown, Lyttleton, Goldsmith, Saint-Foix, etc. See under their names in the general bibliography.

(40) *Voyage to Laputa,* part of chapter XI.

(41) With two or three minor exceptions noted in chapter 5, below.

Barring the initial miracle of size, the reader is deprived of any further hint of unreality. In *Gulliver's Travels* a fairy world is visualized in which the traveller himself is the only monstrosity and his conception of life alone eccentric. In point of interest the first two voyages excel anything produced by the narrative art of the writers of *Imaginary Voyages*. In its total variety of adventure, *Gulliver's Travels* has more to offer than any of its fore-runners, excepting the *Journey of Klimius* alone. Granting the relative dullness of the third voyage, the book remains a masterpiece of wit and invention, its comparative merit as a romantic tale attested by its survival of the deluge of modern fiction, while its predecessors have been lost to all but the professional student of literature.

Chapter 2

Narrative Types of the *Philosophic Voyage.*

II. *Realistic Voyages.*

The method of study followed in this chapter differs radically from that of the preceding one. A number of *Fantastic Voyages* are individually important because of their respective contributions and relations to *Gulliver's Travels,* and because of the varied types of adventure they represent. As forerunners of *Gulliver,* the *Realistic Voyages,* on the contrary, are individually of no significance at all, inasmuch as no direct relation to any one of them can be traced (1), and inasmuch as the narrative form of all is the same. The *Fantastic Voyages* varied; the *Realistic Voyages* conformed to a type: the type of the narrative of actual travel, distinguished by the standard, invariable experiences of an ordinary seaman (2). This *Realistic* type of narrative is important, because it is the narrative form of *Gulliver's Travels,* in substance a *Fantastic Voyage* (2-b). We shall consider, therefore, not individual fore-runners, but the *Realistic Voyage* in its formal relation to *Gulliver.*

---

(1) This does not mean that parallels cannot be found in incident and idea, but only that no single *Realistic Voyage* as a whole bears any distinctive relation to *Gulliver's Travels.*

(2) It is surprising to see how little variation there is in the various accounts of embarkation, storm, shipwreck, and landing on the strange shore. The countries visited differ widely in many respects, but the mode of travel and the adventures are usually about the same.

(2-b) The fantastic nature of *Gulliver's Travels* is frequently understated. Dennis expresses a view commonly held, when he writes (concerning the first two voyages),

"If we once accept the scale on which the countries and their inhabitants are drawn, there is nothing in what follows to throw any strain on our credulity." (*Gulliver, Introduction,* xxiv.)

A moment's reflection will expose the absurdity of this statement. If, for example, we accept the Lilliputian scale, then Gulliver becomes a prodigy, and his actions must be viewed, as they appeared to the Lilliputians, as monstrous. Accept the Brobdingnagian scale, if you will, and then try to account for the tiny dwarf Gulliver, who can be thrust into a marrow bone, without straining your credulity. The only escape from this dilemma would be through the simultaneous acceptance of both scales as normal, a feat that is beyond the powers of the human mind. Whether the reader bears in mind the point of view of the traveller, or that of the natives, he will find every adventure fantastic and incredible.

To this plan it might be objected that, whether individually
related to *Gulliver* or not, the various *Realistic Voyages*
deserve study along with *Philosophic Voyages* of the *Fantastic*
type. To this there is a two-fold answer. In the first place,
let me repeat that this work is a thorough study only of *Gulliver's Travels*, (chapter headings to the contrary notwithstanding.) In the second place, the important *Realistic Voyages*
before 1726 have already been studied with respect to their
philosophic content, by other critics, whose works are easily
accessible (3). The leading French *Voyages* of this type have
been analyzed in detail and considered collectively as a form
of rationalistic novel by Geoffroy Atkinson, in his thorough
and scholarly two-volume work, *The Extraordinary Voyage in
French Literature (before 1720)*, 1920-2 (4).

The present chapter will, consequently be very brief, no
longer, in fact, than is necessary to place *Gulliver* in its relation to the realistic trend of voyage literature, bringing into
the discussion for the purpose of illustration but two *Philosophic Voyages* of the *Realistic* type, the two selected being of
special interest, first, because they are the earliest examples
of fully-developed *Realistic Voyages;* second, because they are
works which previously, though on insufficient grounds, have
been claimed as sources for *Gulliver* (5).

I.

With the sole exception of a few realistic strokes in the
Journey of Klimius, previously noted (6), the *Fantastic
Voyages*, before *Gulliver*, were admittedly fabulous. The
authors invited the reader to follow their heroes to another
world, the route to which was marked out by fancy, not by the
mariner's chart. The only determining factor in the adventures was the writer's imagination, which was employed to
lift science into the rarer atmosphere of romance and to sur-
round the curious traveller with such prodigies as dreams are
made of. From the traveller's departure to his final adven-

---

(3) Gilbert Chinard *L'Amérique et le rêve exotique dans la littérature
française au XVIIe et au XVIIIe siècle*. Paris 1913.

Gustave Lanson, *Origines et premières manifestations de l'esprit phil-
osophique.* (*Revue des Cours et Conférences* Dec. 1907-Dec. 1909.) See
also Lanson's article in *Revue du Mois, tome IX*, 1910.

The philosophic content of utopian *Voyages* other than French, is
discussed at length by F. E. Held, in his *Introduction* to Andreae's
Christianopolis (1914) pp. 1-128.

(4) Vol. I, Columbia University Press, 1920. Vol. II, Champion, Paris,
1922.

(5) See the discussion of doubtful sources of *Gulliver*, chapter 4, below.

(6) Above, chapter 1, p. 26.

ture, the authors intended it to be obvious that they were inventing. The narrative of *Gulliver's Travels* is of a very different type. However much the countries visited, or the adventures narrated, may find their analogues in the *Fantastic Voyages*, the form of the story is that of an authentic history. Gulliver claims membership in the fraternity of discoverers, who, like Dampier, were reclaiming for civilization the unknown lands to the west and south of the Pacific Ocean. He reaches his destinations, not by means of a flying machine, but by the ordinary means of compass and North Star. I am writing here with reference to the prevailing mode of travel; neglecting for the time being *Gulliver's* supernatural adventure on the flying island, Laputa (7), and his departure from Brobdingnag by means of an eagle (8).

No pains are spared to authenticate the narrative. In a *Letter to the Reader*, the publisher vouches for the truth of the voyages and the veracity of Mr. Gulliver, his personal friend. In *A Letter to His Cousin Sympson*, Gulliver casually compares his *Voyages* to those of his "cousin" Dampier (10), whose *Voyage round the World* had recently passed through its sixth edition (11), and expresses irritation at the blunders of the printer, by which the perfect accuracy of his work was marred. Each *Voyage* was furnished with a map, showing the geographical position of the countries visited. Within the narrative, Gulliver includes unimportant details of his early life, the circumstances of embarkation, a matter-of-fact account of his voyages, storms, latitude and longitude, place names of no significance, and a host of circumstantial trifles that serve to disarm the reader's suspicion. This inclusion alike of irrelevant as well as essential detail suggests the inconsistent and undramatic plot of real life, of which ninety per cent leads to nothing. That this intentional artlessness was successful in its aim was demonstrated by the old English gentleman who went immediately to his map to search for Lilliput (12), as well as by the Irish bishop who concluded, after mature deliberation, that the book was full of lies (13).

---

(7) *Laputa*, pp. 160-2; 170-9.

(8) *Brob.*, 146.

(10) These letters will be found prefixed to every edition of *Gulliver*. See edition by Dennis, pp. 3-9.

(11) *A New Voyage Round the World by Captain William Dampier, Sixth Edition, 1717.* (2 vols.)

(12) Arbuthnot to Swift, Nov. 8, 1726. *Correspondence*, III, 358.

(13) Swift to Pope, Nov. 27, 1726. *Correspondence*, III, 368. To a Spanish version of *Gulliver* is prefixed an *Aviso al Lector* in which the reader is warned that the work was written by a heretic dean, which accounts for the glaring deviations from truth to be found in the narrative. (*Notes & Queries*, 1831, Ser. VI, vol. vi, p. 128. W. E. Axon.)

In adopting the authentic style, Swift was merely taking advantage of the popular craze for discovery. In 1725 very few Englishmen were reading Cyrano's account of the moon (14), but many were reading Defoe's descriptions of Africa and Virginia. The discovery of the New World by the Elizabethan voyagers had stimulated curiosity, and at the same time, limited credulity. A Mandeville or a Marco Polo could no longer pose as the only authority on the remote regions of the world, and tell what he pleased. Competition was keen, not to see who could astonish the most, but to win a reputation for reliability. Rumors of undiscovered islands to the west and south of the Pacific, were still big with possibilities as huge as Brobdingnag, and as curious as Lilliput. Those possibilities do not exist for us today; our superstitions have migrated from the South Seas to Mars. It is well to remember, however, that it is due in part to Swift's clever appeal to those superstitions, that "several thousand" copies of *Gulliver's Travels* were sold the first week (15).

Even when the novelty of geographical discovery was spent, there remained a steady interest in strange manners and customs. The continents had been mapped, but their inhabitants were still strangers. Throughout the seventeenth century the influx of foreign ideas was received in Europe with increasing interest. The *Voyages* ceased to advertise the extraordinary wonders and monstrosities of the new worlds in their pages, assuming instead the style of a Baedeker's *Guide*. Transoceanic commerce, especially as carried on by the enterprising Dutch, became a matter of routine. The style of the typical *Voyage* took another turn toward realism, and shifted the emphasis from adventure to ideas. Readers were asking what these strange races thought and how they lived. The *Voyages* of Dampier, to which Gulliver refers as his model, carried a title-page very different from the *Travels* of Mandeville. Instead of being tempted with "Marvellous Adventures," or the "Marvels of Ind," the reader is promised a faithful account of the various countries with a minute description of "Their Soil,

---

(14) There is no record of any eighteenth century English writer who connected *Gulliver* with the works of Cyrano. As a matter of fact, the latter seems to have been virtually unknown to English readers before 1800.

(15) Quoted from the tract *Gulliver Decypher'd* (*Arbuthnot Miscellany*, 1751). See also the following from the letter of Pope and Gay to Swift, Nov. 17, 1726, *Correspondence*, III 258: "The whole impression sold in a week." In the preface to an anonymous French translation, printed at the Hague, 1727, it is stated that ten thousand copies were sold in three weeks.

Rivers, Harbors, Plants, Fruits, Animals, Inhabitants, Customs, Religions, Government, Trade," etc. These works of Dampier represent the very height of realism, according to which things too remarkable, even though true, are omitted, lest the narrative be discredited. The style is expository, unadorned, and free from the most distant suggestion of invention. This is the style in which Gulliver relates his fantastic adventures, the style of the chronicler whose sole business is to record the facts (16).

II

However much *Gulliver* may resemble the authentic narratives of men like Dampier, this difference remains, that the latter were written by real travellers, while *Gulliver* was composed by a clergyman in his study. Its realism, then, is only pseudo-realism, and the apparent truth nothing but a clever counterfeit. The question arises, what precedent was there for this composition, with the aid of the imagination alone, of a *Realistic Voyage,* for which there was no basis in fact? I refer now, not to *Philosophic Voyages* in particular, but to any fictitious *Voyages* written in the authentic style.

To begin with, it should be remembered that a large proportion of real *Voyages* of the time were filled out by the writers' imagination. Atkinson has traced the fictitious element in seventeenth century books of travel, but with this we are not here concerned (17). Here I shall merely illustrate from two or three works, which like *Gulliver* are complete forgeries. Conspicuous among these is the *Histoire des Sévarambes* (18), by Denis Vairasse d'Alais, 1677-9, itself a *Philosophic Voyage.* Our interest in this work as a fore-runner of *Gulliver* is increased by the fact that the two were associated in the minds of the early readers of *Gulliver's Travels.* In 1727, an English translation of the *Sévarambes* was published as volume III of *Gulliver's Travels,* which had appeared the year before in two

---

(16) "It may be noticed that the style of 'Gulliver' is evidently founded on Dampier." (Footnote, *Gulliver,* 5.)

(17) *Op. cit.* Atkinson is now preparing a third volume, dealing with the philosophic content of *Real Voyage* literature, in which the compound of fact and imagination in the *Voyages* of the period will be treated in full.

(18) The date given is that of the first known French edition, the first part of which appeared in 1677 (2 vols. in-12), and the second part in 1779 (3 vols in-12) Paris. The first part had appeared two years earlier in English, with the title, *The History of the Sevarites* or *Sevarambi. London, 1675,* followed in 1679 by a Part II, which, however, does not correspond to the French at all, and was probably not written by Vairasse. See Atkinson, *Op. cit.* I, 87-9, 167-170.

volumes (19). The imposture was soon detected. Also, in a very rare Dutch translation of *Gulliver*, 1728, there are two engravings, one of Brobdingnag and one of Sévarambes (20). From beginning to end the *Sévarambes* is fictitious; the important point here is the laboured attempt by the author to establish the authenticity of the account. Evidence is not lacking to show that the story was accepted generally as a true account (21).

> The preface (*Avis au Lecteur*) contains a history of the documents, which the author pretends simply to be editing. He begins by drawing a sharp contrast between this work, and imaginary *Utopias*, etc. According to the preface, the documents here published were committed by Captain Siden when on his death bed to the attendant physician, with instructions to have them published verbatim or not at all. The doctor, unable to read the languages in which the account was written (22), turned them over to the present editor, who has not departed from the wish of Siden to have the papers published as they were written by himself.
>
> Before publishing, the editor satisfied himself of the authenticity of the *Voyages,* being unwilling to cheat the public with what might prove to be a forgery. He visited Siden's native town, where neighbors of the late captain verified the facts about his early life which appear in his work. Not yet satisfied, the editor wrote to the Dutch trade commissioner in India, who confirmed the movements of Siden's ship.
>
> The editor is, of course, Vairasse himself. It might be noted in addition that SIDEN, the name of the traveller, is an anagram for DENIS, the author's first name. Similarly, SEVARIAS, the law-giver of the Sévarambes, is an anagram of VAIRASSE.

In this preface will be recognized the devices used by Swift in the letters of the publisher to the reader, and of Gulliver to his cousin Sympson. The *Histoire des Sévarambes* is the most striking fore-runner of *Gulliver's Travels* in the matter of introductory attempts to throw an air of truth about the narrative.

The above devices, however, are mechanical ones; they imply that the narrative is of a suspicious character, else why so

---

(19) *Gulliver, Bibliographical Note,* xxxi. Also the following in the edition of W. Cooke-Taylor, 1864, p. 63:

> "His (Desfontaines') continuation called *Le Nouveau Gulliver* I have never met with, but another published as the third volume of his *Travels* in 1727 was stolen from a French work called *L'Histoire des Sévarambes.*

(20) Dunlop, *Op. cit.* II, 536n.

(21) Prosper Marchand, *Dictionnaire historique,* 1758-9, p. 12. For further evidence of contemporary credence in the authenticity of the *Sévarambes,* see Atkinson, *Op. cit.* I, 89-92.

(22) "Après sa mort, le médecin examina ses papiers, et trouva qu'ils étoient écrits en latin, en françois, en italien, et en provençal." (*Voy. Imag.* V, xix.)

much trouble to defend it? In the pseudo-realistic narratives
of Defoe, all defence is ignored. In the plain, blunt manner of
familiar history, Defoe simply retells the "Life" of Robinson
Crusoe, or of Captain Singleton. Impartial treatment of
strange, commonplace, and irrelevant details, the apparent
absence of any moulding or selective art, disarms suspicion.
The realistic narrative of Defoe, at its best, is not distinguish-
able from a book of authentic biography or travel. It is interesting to note that this is the achievement of the man who had
failed signally to produce a *Fantastic Voyage* of merit (23).
Truly there is a diversity of gifts. A good example of Defoe's
pseudo-realistic style is to be found in *The Life of the Famous
Captain Singleton*, 1720. One-third of the story is located on
familiar ground, which is readily recognized by the reader as
a part of his own world. Here Defoe is careful to invent
nothing which does not echo the common experiences of
mariners. When the reader has ceased to suspect the history
of any departure from fact, then, and not until then, does
Defoe start Singleton on a trip across Africa. The descriptions of the "dreary deserts" and "frightful forests," the long-
lost Englishman who has become a tribal chief in the Sudan,
are very convincing; but Defoe had no first hand information
about the interior of Africa. He has *camouflaged* his imaginary deserts and forests with familiar colors, until they merge
imperceptibly into the real landscape on each side. Somewhere in the heart of Africa, Singleton discovers a beast "of
an ill-gendered kind, between a tiger and a leopard." The
reader recognizes the tiger and the leopard and so accepts the
fiction thus compounded. This incident, trivial though it be,
illustrates to perfection the realistic method of Defoe. The
real voyage is from fact to fiction, and then back again to
fact, and the journey is agreeable because there are no jolts
in transition. The method used by Defoe is also the method of
Swift, who sends Gulliver from England to Lilliput, and from
Luggnag to Japan. The device is that of surrounding a few
important lies with a multitude of insignificant truths.

III

The wholly fictitious narratives of Defoe, with their ingenious imitation of the actual voyage, leave us still a long way
from *Gulliver's Travels*. *Captain Singleton* is only an entertaining book of travel, hence not a *Philosophic Voyage*. The
artificial use of the *Realistic Voyage* form for didactic pur-

---

(23) Defoe's *Consolidator*, 1705. See chapter 1 above.

poses has been made the subject of learned investigations (24) of such a scope that it would be vain to attempt a review of the subject within the limits of this chapter, especially, since the only connexion with *Gulliver* is the geographical setting common to the *Realistic Voyages* as a whole. I will therefore close this chapter with references to critical works covering the subject, a brief statement of the main currents of this philosophic movement, and a summary of the two earliest *Philosophic Voyages* of any importance, with which the reader may wish to be familiar, inasmuch as they enter into the discussion of the sources of *Gulliver*, chapter four, below.

Didactic works of the straight utopian type (25) must be considered as closely related to the *Realistic Voyage* even though there be no narrative of adventure, properly speaking. The authors usually connected their imaginary world with the discoveries of contemporary voyagers. To this there are exceptions. Harrington's *Oceana*, and Campanella's *Civitas Solis*, lack any geographical adventure whatsoever. More and Andreae, on the other hand, assert that their realms were discovered in the course of a voyage, though the device is transparent and merely prefatory to the main exposition in hand. In his *New Atlantis*, Bacon gives a much more substantial setting, but it can hardly be called an attempt at realism. About ten pages are devoted to an account of the voyage and reception of the travellers.

One of the most popular uses of foreign travel for the purpose of satire consisted of a device, the reverse of the voyage abroad, by which a foreigner was brought to Europe to comment on Western usage. The Oriental Traveller in Europe became a favorite mouthpiece for satire, popular, partly, no doubt, because it is easier to walk about one's own country, finding fault, than it is to invent a better world abroad. The *Lettres Persanes* of Montesquieu (26), the *Amusements sérieux et comiques* of DuFresne (27), and many other works of the same type (28), differ, further, from the *Realistic Voyage* in the subordination of the element of adventure. The interest is not centered on how the Oriental gets to Europe, but only on his reactions to the new civilization, the character of which is discussed further in the next chapter. Yet these

---

(24) See references in note 3 above, and especially Atkinson, *Op. cit.*

(25) See the Introduction to Morley's *Ideal Commonwealths*, 1896, and to F. E. Held's translation, 1914, of Andreae's *Christianopolis*.

(26) 1721.

(27) 1699.

(28) See, M. P. Conant, *The Oriental Tale in England in the 18th Century.* 1908.

works bear a distinct relation to *Gulliver's Travels*. In two of Gulliver's voyages, the adventure is succeeded by an interview between Gulliver (who is a foreign if not an oriental traveller) and the natives, the purpose of which is the ridicule of the natives. This is true especially of *Lilliput* and *Laputa* (29). Gulliver's impressions of the professors at Lagado is a distinct echo of the impressions of the Indian who visits the Academies of England in Tom Brown's *Amusements Serious and Comical* (30), a work from which Swift borrowed several hints for the composition of *Gulliver* (31). The *Voyage to the Houyhnhnms*, on the other hand, is true to the type of the *Philosophic Voyage*, in which the ideas of the traveller, not of the natives, are discredited (32).

The *Realistic Voyage*, employed as a "Document of Ideas" (33) was a French product of the seventeenth century. For an account of its development, the reader is referred to the study by Atkinson, already cited, and to the earlier critics cited by him. The earliest, mature example of a *Philosophic Voyage* of this type is *La terre, australe connue par Jacques Sadeur*, 1676 (34), by Gabriel Foigny, a work that passed through numerous editions, appearing in English as *A New Discovery of terra incognita Australis, by Mr. Sadeur*, London, 1693 (35).

After a series of remarkable adventures and shipwrecks, bordering on the fantastic, Sadeur is received among a race of hermaphrodites in Australia. The country is divided into areas named Hust, Hump, Hued, etc. Within this commonwealth there is perfect harmony of customs and beliefs. To know one native is to know all, for they were born without that European desire to quarrel and disagree. The children attend a community school, where their studies are useful and adapted to the respective ages of the pupils. These Australians are free from all the diseases so common to the Western World. The natives argue that Sadeur cannot be of a perfect race because, possessing but one sex, his nature is imperfect. Sadeur argues from analogy with the beasts who have but one sex, and the native grants him his point, namely, the intelligence of the beasts but no more. Perfect liberty in all matters

(29) In Laputa especially Gulliver tours the provinces, exposing the folly of the inhabitants, very much in the manner of the Oriental Traveller.

(30) 1702. The title is copied from Dufresne. See *Works of Mr. Thomas Brown*, 1760, III, 1-136. Especially, *Amusement X*, 86-88.

(31) See my source study, below, chapter 4.

(32) The satiric method that prevails in the fore-runners of *Gulliver* is discussed in the next chapter.

(33) Phrase borrowed from Atkinson, who uses it to indicate the didactic content of his *Extraordinary Voyages, Op. cit.*, II, 8.

(34) *Voyages Imaginaires*, XXIV, 246-400.

(35) For complete list of editions see Bibliography.

is the law of the natives. Not only must there be no compulsion in
matters of faith, but no one dares to attempt any missionary work.
Their religion is vague and deistic. The inhabitants, free from all
sickness, live more than one hundred years. Avarice and lust are
unknown. The native tradition regarding the Europeans is a
parody on the account of the creation given in the Scriptures.
Sadeur at length manages to tame and train one of the huge native
birds (Urgs) which carries him off to Madagascar.

It would be difficult to generalize about the purpose of the
work, as the objects of satire are so varied. It represents a
rather confused attack on the tyranny of European traditions
by a free-thinker who had himself suffered through his violation of the social code (36). As a narrative, *Sadeur* may seem
to some a *Fantastic* rather than a *Realistic Voyage*. Hermaphrodites and Urgs do not, however, render a *Voyage* of the
seventeenth century necessarily *Fantastic*, as they were matters of common report at that time (37). On the other hand,
there is a great deal of effective pseudo-realism *in Sadeur;*
nearly one-fourth of the book is devoted to Sadeur's earlier
voyages to less remote lands. Its importance for our study
lies in the fact that the *Sadeur* is the earliest instance of a
Realistic Voyage in which there is a balance between adventure
and satire, absent in works of the *Utopia* type, but characteristic of *Gulliver* and of all typical *Philosophic Voyages*.

The next *Voyage* of this type, in point of time, is the *Histoire
des Sévarambes*, already discussed as an authenticated
fiction, the didactic content of which may be summarized as
follows (38) :

> "The religion of the Sévarambes is Deism, with external features
> resembling the religion of the Incas. A satire on the miracles of
> the Old and New Testaments is found in the long digression con-
> cerning the imposter Omigas. The priesthood of Europe is criti-
> cized in the story of the love of Dionistar and Ahinome.
>
> The government of the country is despotic, but the despot is
> elected democratically. The despot is responsible, through his rep-
> resentatives, for the feeding, clothing, and housing of his subjects.
> Equality of education, of clothing, . . . and of food is required
> by law. Marriage is compulsory. Children are educated and
> housed in public schools from the age of seven. Military service

---

(36) Foigny was a notorious rake. Beginning as a Franciscan monk
he later became a paid singer in a Protestant Church near Geneva.
Appearing one day drunk in church, he was discharged from this position and became a private tutor. He seduced more than one woman,
including his maid-servant whom he deserted in disgrace. (See Bayle,
Dictionnaire critique, ed. 1715. Article, *Sadeur*.)

(37) Atkinson, *Op. cit.*, I, 49-50, 57-8. The folk-lore of the Ruk, or
great bird that carried off men and elephants is briefly discussed in
chapter 7 below.

(38) The synopsis is quoted from Atkinson, *Op. cit.*, I, 138-9.

is obligatory for both sexes . . . The clergy are not exempted from civic duties.

The language of the country is a 'created' language, and is based on logical principles, rather than on tradition. Rimed verse is not in use, and is considered barbaric."

The *Sévarambes* is a great improvement over the *Sadeur*. The author knows what he is about and does not contradict himself in his satiric method as Foigny does in the earlier work (39). As a *Realistic Voyage*, too, the *Sévarambes* is a success, in fact there is nothing in the least extraordinary about the narrative, excepting only the general superlative excellence of the civilization discovered, which, of course, did not exist in Australia at that time. This its readers did not know. Both of these *Voyages* offer incidental parallels to *Gulliver*, on account of which they have been included in the list of Swift's sources by recent critics (40).

---

(39) After asserting the superiority of the Australians to Europeans throughout his narrative, Sadeur leaves the country voluntarily, complaining that the excessive virtue of the inhabitants was unbearable.

(40) See below, chapter 4.

CHAPTER 3

Didactic Content of the *Philosophic Voyage*.

Turning now from the story form of the *Philosophic Voyage* and from its interest as a romantic tale, let us examine the author's purpose in writing. In its fully developed form the *Philosophic Voyage* was always a vehicle for ideas, never an end in itself. Swift's avowed aim in writing *Gulliver* was "to vex, not to divert, the world" (1). The survey of the motives, satiric and philosophic, which run through the fore-runners of *Gulliver* must be here very brief. The four *Voyages* of *Gulliver* present so many different criticisms of life that it would be impossible to bring the study to a definite focus as was done with the narrative form. The distinct purpose and satiric method used by Swift in each voyage will be discussed later when the situations are studied in turn.

As has been already suggested, a number of the *Fantastic Voyages*, concerned themselves with fanciful, and wholly impossible, trips of exploration, in the interests of speculative science. Cyrano de Bergerac and his imitators (2) sent their travellers to the moon, the sun, or to the center of the earth, where conversation with the better informed inhabitants disclosed new theories about the constitution of matter, the laws of physics, and the habitation of the planets. In this connexion it is to be noted simply that this motive of scientific speculation is almost wholly absent from Gulliver (3).

Obviously the connection is to be sought, not in abstract philosophy but in satire. No one of the fore-runners is so exclusively a work of satire as is *Gulliver*, and yet satire is usually included; sometimes it is incidental, again it is organic. In quality it ranges from the mild ridicule heaped upon the Lilliputians to the intense misanthropy represented in the picture of the Yahoos. It has been a notable blunder of criticism

(1) Swift to Pope, Sept. 29, 1725. *Correspondence*, III, 276.

(2) Holberg's, *Klimius;* the anonymous *Voyage du Pôle Arctique au Pôle Antarctique*, and *Relation du Monde de Mercure;* Mouhy's *Lamékis;* and Roumier's *Voyages de Céton dans les Sept Planettes.* See Bibliography.

(3) I say "almost" because there is, in the second voyage, a reminiscence of the debate on biology that takes place in Cyrano's *Histoire de la Lune*, in the argument over Gulliver's origin and species. *Gulliver*, 106. See further chapter 7, below.

to suppose that the latter was peculiar to Swift. The satiric method employed by Swift's predecessors was almost invariably that of a contrast between the degenerate state of Western civilization, represented by the traveller, and the ideal life of the people visited. Gulliver's fourth voyage, to the land of the Houyhnhnms, and the latter portion of his second voyage, to Brobdingnag, conform to this type. It is not necessary to seek the elaboration of this method in the pure Utopian literature of Plato's *Republic*, Campanella's *Civitas Solis*, More's *Utopia*, or Bacon's *New Atlantis*. The ideal commonwealth appeared frequently in combination with imaginary adventures as in *Gulliver*. These ideal commonwealths are of two general types. A race, living in a state of innocence, is found to be the product of ideal government, unselfish customs, and benevolent religion, subject to the laws of charity and justice alone. Such are the Lunarians of Cyrano's first romance, *L'Histoire Comique de la Lune*, and the Potuans whom Klimius encounters underground. The satire in *Voyages* of this type is implied in the contrast with European practices, or it is brought out more directly by the surprise with which the natives receive the traveller's account of kings, priests, and lawyers, in his own world. On the whole, however, the stress is placed upon the objective description of the Utopia, in the organization of which there is a wearisome repetition of the formula, charity and justice, which shows the literature to be a phase of the deistic trend of contemporary thought (4).

A variation of this satiric method only a little less popular, is a contrast between European civilization and a superior race of animals, just as in the fourth voyage of Gulliver. Here the accent is shifted from the Utopian quality of the new civilization to a direct satire on mankind. This use of animals is much older than Aesop himself. In general, however, the fable literature, including the cycle of *Reynard the Fox*, presents an allegory in which the vices and foibles of the human race are identified with, or disguised under, the actions of the animals. For the contrast between man and beast, resulting in the humiliation of man, there was plenty of precedent. The tradition of Ulysses and the beasts (5), popularized by

(4) Atkinson has made a careful and detailed study of the deistic and rationalistic content of the *Realistic Voyages* in French. *op. cit.*

(5) Based on the *Odyssey*. The tradition first took an independent form in Plutarch's dialogue entitled, "That Brute Beasts Make Use of Reason," in which Ulysses vainly argues with Gryllus to reassume his human shape. (*Plutarch's Morals, translated from the Greek by several eminent hands, London, 1704*, V, 203-216.) Plutarch was one of Swift's favorite authors. *Prose Works*, XII, 364.

Giovanni Gelli in his *Circe* (6) and by Howell in the *Parley
of the Beasts* (7), represents the beasts refusing to return
to their human shape, and perfectly contented with their
animal life.   In d'Ablancourt's *Sequel* to Lucian's *True
History*, and in Cyrano's second romance, *L'Histoire comique
du soleil*, both known to Swift (8), the traveller finds himself
despised by a race of animals who refuse to confirm his claim
to the status of a reasonable creature.   As will appear in my
study of the sources, the satire on man in Cyrano is not less
brutal than in Gulliver's fourth voyage.

According to Swift, Gulliver does not have to go to the
moon, or to the center of the earth to find ideal beings.   His
travels are confined to this world, in the remote regions of
which live the amiable Houyhnhnms and the gentle Brobdingnagians.   It is a point very much to the credit of Swift
that his ideal races are after all creatures of his imagination,
giants and horses, and not natives of India or China.   The
Utopias of the *Philosophic Voyages*, the voluminous literature
of the Oriental Traveller (9), of Montesquieu, DuFresne, Tom
Brown, Lyttleton, and Goldsmith, all are marked by cheap
sentimentality,—that of the "long distance" illusion.   The
Australian, Chinaman, Hindoo, or whatnot, is represented as
nature's unspoiled child, a sort of Israelite in whom there is
no guile, who cannot comprehend the diseases, tyrannies, and
vices of the Christian world.   The illusion seemed to spring
from a theorem that virtue increased as the square of the
distance from Europe.   It is the sort of sentimentality
familiar enough to us today in the writings of H. G. Wells (10)
and in the pages of the so-called "liberal" magazines where we

---

(6) Translated into English by Tom Brown, 1702, and very likely a
part of the latter's works which Swift had "read entire." (See *Prose
Works*, XI, 221. *Introduction to "Polite Conversation."*)

(7) 1660.   The complete title reads, *The Parley of the Beasts; or
Morphandra, Queen of the Enchanted Island.   Wherein Men were found,
who being transmuted to Beasts, though proffered to be disenchanted,
and to become Men again; yet in regard of the crying sins and rebellious
humors of the times, they prefer the life of a brute animal before that
of a rational creature.   Which fancy consists of various philosophical
discussions . . . touching the declinings of the world, and late deprava-
tion of human nature.   With reflexes upon the present state of most
countries in Christendom.   Divided into XI sections.   By Jam. Howell,
Esq.* In the preface the author alludes to Gelli as the one who "taught
the beasts their grammar."

(8) See further, chapter 4, below.

(9) See Bibliography under these names.   Also, M. P. Conant, *op. cit.*

(10) Especially Wells' articles written after his visit to Russia in
1920, in which he contrasts the "sincerity" and "highmindedness" of the
Soviet demagogues with the corruption of the Allied statesmen.

find it written that Trotsky of all statesmen is alone sincere, and China, an untainted nation of peaceable villages. It is the illusion which has started a wave of sympathy in favor of the "much abused" Turk, for the wrongs he has suffered at the hand of Christendom, a sympathy never felt by those who have lived under the shadow of the Crescent. From the charge of such nonsense, of which most of his predecessors were more or less guilty, the author of *Gulliver* can be acquitted.

In *Gulliver* another method is followed besides that of contrast between civilizations, and that is the allegorical device of representing the life of the Western world under a disguise. This is the case in Lilliput, Laputa, and the earlier chapters of Brobdingnag (11), where the animal called man is made to appear ridiculous, stupid, or disgusting. While this method of satire seems simple enough, it is exceedingly hard to manage, and was actually very rarely employed (12) in the *Philosophic Voyage* before *Gulliver*. Once made famous by Swift, the idea was copied in a dozen imitations (13), in which Lilliput was England; Blefuscu, Ireland; Flimnap, the prime minister; Nardac, a nobleman; and so forth.

Since *Gulliver's Travels* owed so much of its immediate popularity to this allegorical representation of human society, it will be of interest to notice two examples of it in the *Philosophic Voyage* before Swift. In Baron Holberg's *Journey of Klimius to the World Underground*, a work which Swift in all probability did not know (14), the traveller visits a number of subterranean countries, most of which are contrasted with our world, but two of which are identified with conditions above ground. Lalac is a land inhabited by an idle aristocracy, whose uninterrupted luxury is attended by consequent misery (15). This is very obviously a picture of court life in Europe. Mascathia is the land of the philosophers. The coun-

---

(11) The two-fold nature of the satire of the second voyage is discussed in chapter 8 below.

(12) This sort of allegory seems not to have occurred to most of the writers of *Philosophic Voyages*. Their tendency was rather to have the traveller discover something new and different from European custom, hence the predominance of utopian contrast instead of allegory. There were, however, purely allegorical works which do not concern us here directly because of their lack of genuine adventure. So-called *Voyages* were written describing "fake" countries, not located anywhere. See Fontaines' *Pays de Jansénie*, 1664; Tallemant's *Isle d'Amour*, 1663; and other allegories of the Bunyan type, listed together in the Bibliography.

(13) See the list of imitations, appended to Part III, below.

(14) For a more general description of the work, see chapter 1, above. The possibility of its influence upon *Gulliver* is discussed in chapter 4.

(15) *Klimius*, 147-150.

try is filthy and uncultivated, the philosophers are indistinguishable from pigs. So busy have they been in devising a way to reach the sun and the stars, that they have had no time to improve their own world. To the traveller's practical questions they return absurd and incoherent answers. The author makes it plain that Mascathia is a satire upon academicians, of the same type that we find in Gulliver's voyage to Laputa (16).

Another instance of this satiric method is to be found in an obscure Latin satire by Joseph Hall, *Mundus Alter et Idem* (17), which has never been mentioned in connection with *Gulliver,,* even though, as I shall show in the next chapter, it is not unlikely that it was known to Swift. This work, written about the year 1610, is the reverse of the *Utopia*. The author embarks on the good ship Phantasy for a new world located somewhere in Australia, which is conceived of as the duplicate of the Western world, except that the vices and weaknesses of human nature are assigned to separate provinces instead of being spread out over the entire country as in Europe. As the satire has never been translated in full, and is practically unknown, I will give a brief account of it to bring out the unique relation which it bears to the satiric method of Swift in a part of *Gulliver's Travels*.

> The first country to be visited is Crapula, the land of inebriate excess. It is divided into two provinces, Pamphagonia (or Gluttony) and Yvronia (or Drunkenness). In the capital cities, Livona and Roncara (Snort and Snore), the people sleep continually. The natives are all monks who worship their God, Time, because he eats everything. Adjacent to Crapula is the desert Terra Sancta (Holy Land) which is uninhabited and unexplored. Moronia (Foolsland) is at once the most populous and the most uncultivated of all. There the natives go about naked in winter that the warmth may enter their bodies readily, whereas in mid-summer they wear heavy coats to shut out the heat. Moronia is inhabited by a stupid Philistine class who are subject to the rule of the aristocratic Laverians, or thieves. In Moronia there is an academy of innovators, not unlike the one visited by Gulliver at Lagado, where the single idea is to invent something new, no matter how useless it may be. The innovators have replaced language by a mystical speech, of which several pages of sample vocabulary are given. For example, "ointment," in this language is simplified to

---

(16) *Ibid*, 167-177.

(17) The only edition I have seen is one dated 1643, 1 vol. in-12, in which the *Mundus* is bound with Bacon's *New Atlantis*, and Campanella's *Civitas Solis*, all in Latin. The first six chapters of the *Mundus* were translated into English by Swift's friend, Dr. William King, sometime before 1711. (See further, chapter 4, below.) This fragmentary translation may be found in Morley's *Ideal Commonwealths*, 1896.

"Oppodeltoch;" "spirit" to Nenufarenicaballi;" "health" to "Zeninephidei;" "Mercury" to "Diatessdelton;" etc. The intellectual wizard who invented this Honorificabilitudinitatibus is none other than Bustius Hohenheimus—the headmaster. The treatment is throughout light and witty, and the satire, very obvious. But the method of holding up to ridicule the achievements of the western world is the rare method employed in Gulliver's voyages to Lilliput and Laputa.

So much for the general method and setting for satire in the *Philosophic Voyage*. In regard to the specific objects of satire, there does not seem to be any important development to note. While the choice of subject varies slightly from one author to another, for the most part the range is the same. From Lucian to Swift, the offensive is directed at historians, academicians, lawyers and court procedure, physicians, kings, priests and religion. In *Gulliver* the list is quite as long as in any of the earlier works, but the omission of religion is a conspicuous departure from precedent. The allusion made in passing to the High Church and Low Church parties in Lilliput (19) involves no question of religion, but only a reflection upon the motives of expediency which determined the piety of King George I, and the Prince of Wales. If Swift had followed the tradition of his predecessors he could, like Rabelais (20), have charged Christianity with the guilt of the world's insincerity and disease; and in the manner of the French deists (21) he could have portrayed the sweet and charming piety of the Hindoos or Confucianists as the ideal. That we do not find this in *Gulliver* might be adequately explained by the assumption that Swift knew something about the "gentle" practices of the Hindoos, but this is not necessary. From other of his writings it is clear enough that Swift was not one of those who deny the power of Christianity because they find its obligations inconvenient. In fact, the Christian Gulliver, though bad enough, is ranked by the Houyhnhnms above the Yahoos (22), who unquestionably represent the destiny of a race ruled by instinct and passion alone. Swift is not a Platonist. Man left to his own devices will not discover the eternal pattern of truth in the stars, for he is loath to look up. At best he may discover its blurred reflection in the mud.

---

(19) *Gulliver*, 48. (*Lilliput*, chapter 4.)

(20) See synopsis of Rabelais in chapter 1, above.

(21) See Montesquieu, DuFresne, *etc.*, works listed in the Bibliography under "Oriental Traveller."

(22) That Gulliver was a Christian is stated in *Laputa*, chapter XI. *Gulliver*, 226. Gulliver's superiority to the Yahoos is repeatedly stated by the Houyhnhnms, see especially, *Houyhnhnms*, chapter VIII, first paragraph.

This is perhaps the best place to consider some of the more general features of the satiric style of *Gulliver's Travels*, a style famous for its sustained irony and biting wit, in its relation to its fore-runners. In most of the *Philosophic Voyages* there is no great merit of style and seldom anything that is even consistent. The styles of Lucian, Cyrano and their imitators are for the most part nondescript. One chapter is in the ironic vein, another purely comic, and still another of a straight narrative character. Where there is real art, it is of an eclectic and variable type. Two authors, however, have contributed materially to the method of Swift in *Gulliver*. To an imitation of the works of Rabelais (23), which Swift knew well and quoted from memory, must be assigned the fondness for the filth of the body with its odors, excrements, and pollutions, which appears in *Gulliver* (24). In Rabelais this element of obscenity is drawn out to burlesque proportions, while in Gulliver it is restrained though not refined. Where Rabelais delights in filth for comical effect, Swift's use of it is always disgusting and never suggestive. The general ideas for Gulliver's method of extinguishing the fire at the palace of Lilliput (25) and for the occupations of some of the professors at Lagado (26), were borrowed from similar situations in Rabelais, as I will show later; but the contrast in diction and tone is the contrast that would exist between a treatise on human physiology and a corresponding anecdote as told in the rear of any saloon.

Swift owes a more considerable debt to the style of his elder contemporary Thomas Brown, a pamphleteer of no mean ability, whose works have been shown to have been assimilated and extensively imitated by Swift (27). Brown in turn was steeped in the satiric humor of Lucian and Rabelais (28). His writings carry on the latter's note of obscenity, which appears in combination with sustained irony of the kind found in *Gulliver*. Brown's satire is less grotesque than that of

---

(23) See the study of Rabelais as a source in chapter 4, below. Also my article in *Mod. Lang. Notes*, November, 1922.

(24) This is pointed out later in connection with the study of the situations in which it is most marked. See especially chapters 5-7, below.

(25) *Lilliput*, chapter 5.

(26) *Laputa*, chapters 5-6.

(27) See the source study and references in notes 68-71 in chapter 4, below.

(28) Brown's second volume consists of "Letters from the Dead to the Living, together with Dialogues of the Dead, after the manner of Lucian." The influence of Rabelais is evident throughout Brown's works, and he is directly quoted in the following places: I, 86-88; II, 93-96; IV, 57-62. (Edition, 1760.)

Rabelais, and at the same time not so restrained nor so well proportioned as that of Swift. Rabelais writes with the queer turns of wit peculiar to the drunken man; Brown, with more coherence of thought and with much more consistent drollery, gives the effect of one who has taken a glass too much; but Swift is always sober. The danger is likely to be that Brown's influence be understated, rather than exaggerated. Just as in the Bickerstaff papers Swift continued Brown's joke at the expense of the astrologer Partridge (29), so in *Gulliver*, pages, satirizing physicians, soldiers, and lawyers, are all but verbal counterparts of similar passages in the works of Brown.

In general, the satiric treatment in *Gulliver* can be distinguished in three ways from the style of earlier *Voyages*. It is marked first of all by its pregnancy of thought, condensed to a degree that is frequently epigrammatic. Lucian pounds away at his historians, repeating endlessly that they are all liars, each time as though he were confiding a state secret, until the idea is all surface with no depth. Rabelais runs on and on with his cumulation of incident and synonym without knowing where to stop. The essence of his wit is good, but it could be extracted and bound up into a very thin volume. In *Gulliver* every paragraph is essential. The reader is surprised with satire within satire, with the ingenious wit which turns the subject over and over, always revealing something new. That which sets Swift above not only the other writers of *Philosophic Voyages*, but above all the other Queen Anne wits is the amazing number of his ideas per square inch.

A second distinction of *Gulliver* is the consistent pertinence of its prose style. Tom Brown crowds ideas into condensed space, but it was left for Swift to sort them out. In *Gulliver* there are no excursions into irrelevant fields, the main theme is never forgotten. The narratives of Cyrano are broken by the introduction of tiresome arguments about the nature of a vacuum and the constitution of the atom; and in most of the *Philosophic Voyages* incidents are introduced for their own sake alone. In *Gulliver*, the minutest detail, whether it be the measurements of pygmy life or a humorous incident, is essential. Not only is every idea essential, but the most insignificant details are stated with extreme accuracy. The size of the bed made for Gulliver by the pygmies, as well as his rations, are computed with the most scrupulous regard for the relative proportions assumed (30), in contrast to Rabelais' reckless method of shovelling hundreds of steaks and pies down the

---

(29) See chapter 4, below.
(30) See chapter 5, below.

throat of his giant, Gargantua (31). Minimum of digression and the lack of confusion found in *Gulliver's Travels* is the sort of achievement that comes but seldom, and then only with fasting and prayer.

Finally, the style of *Gulliver* is marked by an elevated tone, dignified and grave. Though Swift borrowed some of Rabelais' obscene ideas, he avoided the latter's scurilous language. This quality of classical restraint in diction is at once both an hindrance and a help., A certain gaiety and lightness of touch, in dealing with the comic, is lost. On the other hand the solemn treatment of trifles is a very effective device for ridiculing the petty actions of men, clothing them as it does with mock dignity. The net result is satire less spontaneous and comical than in some of the earlier *Voyages*, but infinitely more effective.

In conclusion, what are the achievements of Swift in satire in *Gulliver's Travels*, apart from the characteristics of style just considered? He must be credited with the originality of the idea which runs through the first two voyages, of first reducing and then magnifying the proportions of life to reveal its pettiness and its ugliness together. Lucian's *Voyage to Heaven* describes an insignificant world as it appears from a great height, but there is much more than this in *Gulliver* (32). Expanding a bare suggestion in Cyrano, Swift conceives of a relativity in human affairs, in accordance with which false sources of pride can be at once detected when they are viewed in true perspective. This satire of proportion becomes his acid test of true values. He discovers that dominion, rank, feminine beauty, etc., are of relative value, but there is no indication that courage, devotion, or intelligence would change its aspect in Lilliput or Brobdingnag (33). Gulliver's third Voyage is the most imitative, repeating for the most part borrowed ideas. By common consent of readers it is the least interesting of all (34). The satire in the fourth *Voyage* has been considered most distinctively Swiftian, though it is less original than the satire in the first two voyages. Contrary to the statements made by Sir Walter Scott, Temple Scott, John Churton Collins and others (35), the complete condemnation of the human race embodied in the contrast between the

---

(31) Rabelais, Book I, chapter 37.

(32) See my study of Lucian as a source, chapter 4, below. Also my article in *Mod. Lang. Notes*, June, 1922.

(33) See further chapter 8, below.

(34) See contemporary opinions of the third voyage quoted in chapter 4, note 24, below.

(35) All of whom depend upon the worthless thesis of Borkowsky in *Anglia*, XV. See Cyrano as a source in chapter 4, below.

Houyhnhnms and the Yahoos is not without precedent,—the
same satire, no less brutal, is in the second romance of Cyrano,
a work that was more carefully read by Swift than it has been
by his editors and critics since. There is, however, something
original about the satire in this *Voyage,* not its brutality, but
something else which a study of the fore-runners of *Gulliver*
has made very clear.

In all earlier *Voyages* when man was condemned in the presence of animals, the condemnation was of civilized man. The
fault was with his perverted training, his unnatural practices,
his abuse of intelligence, and his tyrannous institutions, the
state and the church. The philosophical position taken was
the plea for a return to nature, as described in the animal
kingdoms. All of this appears in Gulliver's fourth voyage
with the important difference that the lowest and filthiest lot
is reserved for the native Yahoo who is not a product of
European civilization at all, but man in a state of nature,
"cunning, malicious, libidinous, cowardly and insolent" (36).
Not that Swift takes refuge in civilization, the condemnation
of Gulliver is plain enough. But Gulliver is allowed by the
Houyhnhnms to be endowed with a spark of intelligence, by
so much above the Yahoos; the Governor of the Houyhnhnms
even fears that Gulliver may be contaminated by contact with
the Yahoos. No hope can be found for the race anywhere,
certainly not in letting it run wild according to the notions of
the individualist. The conclusion is complete pessimism. The
best thing that can be done is to subject the race to some rules
imposed from without, thereby curbing the mischief which it
fain would accomplish. If it be true, as a study by C. H.
Firth (37) has rendered probable, that in the Yahoos, Swift
represents especially the degenerate natives of Ireland, then
we are only more justified in concluding that the author of
Gulliver's fourth voyage was at heart an imperialist, though
indeed a very pessimistic one. He would no doubt modify the
doctrine of the "White Man's Burden" to make the white man
a part of a burden. At any rate Swift makes it very clear
that his indictment includes all mankind. The Abbé DesFontaines, who translated *Gulliver* into French, wrote to Swift
apologizing for his excision of the more objectionable passages,
which he said, with characteristic conceit, were inapplicable
to the French, though no doubt they were fair descriptions of
the English (38). To this Swift replied sharply, "The same

(36) *Gulliver,* 277.

(37) *The Political Significance of "Gulliver's Travels,"* C. H. Firth.
(*Proceedings of the British Academy,* IX, 1920.)

(38) DesFontaines to Swift, July 4, 1727. *Correspondence,* III, 397-8.

vices and follies reign everywhere; if I had written of England alone, or of this century alone, so far from meriting translation, my work would not deserve to be read" (39). The misanthropy increases steadily from the first voyage, where man appears as a strutting Lilliputian to the fourth, where he is a loathsome Yahoo. The pessismism extends, moreover, to all creatures. The peace-loving Brobdingnagians. when examined at close quarters, are ugly and disgusting (40) : the amiable Houyhnhnms, though virtuous and harmless, are at the same time ignorant, stupid, and innocent of any achievement of genius. The world through which Gulliver travels is a very bad world, and man is the worst creature on it.

---

(39) Swift to DesFontaines, July, 1727. *Correspondence*, III, 406-7.
(40) For the double picture of the Brobdingnagians, see chapter 8, below.

CHAPTER 4

The Literary Sources of *Gulliver's Travels*

(Wherein are contained many facts of interest to the Source-
Addict alone, which others may skip without loss.)

In the preceding chapters I have pointed out resemblances
and contrasts between *Gulliver* and various earlier works.
The question that suggests itself next is, which of these works
were actually known to Swift and to what extent did he borrow ideas and situations from them?
A host of individual parallels to incidents in *Gulliver* have
been pointed out in one place or another, by other critics,
whose contributions are referred to in the notes. These parallels will be discussed in full in their respective places, when
we come to study the voyages individually. The purpose of
this chapter is simply to present in as brief form as possible
the evidence for Swift's debt to his predecessors, and to summarize the nature and extent of their influence upon the composition of *Gulliver*. By means of the footnotes, the reader
can find the pages on which the situations are compared with
their sources in detail. A further limitation is imposed upon
this source-study. No attempt is made here, nor indeed anywhere in this book, to trace ideas in *Gulliver* to contemporary
affairs. Whatever Swift may have drawn from his experiences in public or private life, whatever political allegory there
may be in the satire [and there is a good deal (1)] is excluded
from this study, which is confined to the sources in literature.
The investigation of the sources of *Gulliver's Travels* is not
a new venture, though I am not convinced that the task would
be any harder were the field still virgin soil. Special credit
must be rendered, however, to Sir Walter Scott, whose statement of the sources, prefixed to his edition of *Gulliver*, 1814,
is remarkably free from error. The works of Philostratus,
Lucian, Cyrano, and Rabelais are mentioned by Scott in statements which are accurate, though not adequate. The voluminous contributions of subsequent critics have increased our
information and our confusion on the subject. A study by
Hönncher in *Anglia*, X, and another by Borkowsky in *Anglia*,
XV, are labored attempts to trace half a hundred miscellaneous

---

(1) See the monograph by C. H. Firth, "The Political Significance of
Gulliver's Travels," in *Proceedings of the British Academy*, IX. Read
before the Academy, Dec. 10, 1919.

passages in *Gulliver*, principally to the works of Godwin and
Cyrano, though other possible sources are not excluded where
they can be conscripted for the purpose of robbing Swift of
any claim to originality (2). These two contributions have
been of value in calling attention to Swift's debt to Cyrano,
but they are otherwise misleading and worthless (3). Their
very appearance of thoroughness has been disastrous in evok-
ing the misplaced confidence of later writers. The blunders of
Borkowsky, in particular, have been admitted to the Temple
Scott edition of *Gulliver*, 1899 (4), and to the otherwise excellent study of Swift by Churton Collins, 1893 (5). An excellent
article by Pietro Toldo, *Les voyages merveilleux de Cyrano de
Bergerac et de Swift et leur rapports avec l'oeuvre de Rabelais*,
1906 (7), contains much discerning criticism. Other minor
source-studies will be found listed together in the bibliography.
From their titles, the contributions of Max Poll, and Paul
Thierkopf would seem significant, but in point of fact they
contain nothing original of value, though they render service
in collating the opinions of others. In connection with each
source I note only the original discoverer, making no attempt
to give the later references.

Apart from the modification of previous opinion, it has been
my task to add to the list of sources the following works: the
Sequel to Lucian's *True History*, written by N. Perrot d'Ablan-
court (8); Lucian's *Voyage to Heaven, Dialogue between
Terpsion and Pluto*, and, *On Mourning for the Dead* (9);
Cyrano's second romance, *Histoire comique du soleil* (10);

(2) The misguided scholarship of Borkowsky is even less valuable
than it appears, for to a large extent his thesis is merely a restatement
of the parallel passages previously pointed out by Hönncher, *Anglia*, X.

(3) See the discussion of Borkowsky's errors, in section viii of this
chapter and notes.

(4) *Prose Works* of Swift, VIII, xxiii-iv. Dennis recognizes that
"Borkowsky's conclusions are weakened by his venomous delight in
taking away Swift's reputation for originality," but he follows the German critic in assuming that Swift used the *Histoire des Sévarambes*,
and *Jacques Sadeur*. See below, note 77.

(5) *Jonathan Swift*, by Churton Collins, edition 1902, pp. 204-5:
"There can be no doubt that in the *Voyage to the Houyhnhnms* he drew
on . . . Godwin's *Voyage of Domingo Gonzales*."

(7) In *Revue des Études Rabelaisiennes*, 1906-7, vol. 4, pp. 295-333,
continued in vol. 5, 24-44.

(8) *Modern Language Notes*, Nov. 1921, vol. 36, pp. 419-422.

(9) All three of these are discussed in another article of mine, *Mod.
Lang. Notes*, June, 1922.

(10) *Mod. Lang. Notes* (accepted but not yet published.) This
romance of Cyrano has been mentioned as a source for Laputa. (See
below, note 74.) My contribution has been to point out its far more
important influence on the satire in the *Voyage to the Houyhnhnms*.

George Berkeley's, *New Theory of Vision* (11) ; as well as several possible sources of importance which have not been noticed before (12).

I.

Philostratus, *Imagines*.

In 1814, Sir Walter Scott pointed out that the account in Philostratus of the capture of the sleeping Hercules by the pygmies was Swift's model for the first scene in Lilliput, where Gulliver is surrounded and attacked in a similar manner (13). Elsewhere, Scott describes Swift's personal copy of Philostratus, on the blank leaves of which Swift's opinions are scribbled in his own handwriting (14). Scott's statement has never been challenged, and it needs no modification.

II.

Lucian (125—*ca.* 185 A. D.)

Swift's familiarity with the works of Lucian, proved by his many borrowings from the satires of the latter, is verified by his purchase in 1711 of d'Ablancourt's "three little volumes of Lucian in French," as I have had occasion to point out in a recent study (15). It is practically certain that Swift also knew the *Dryden Lucian,* 1711, the first volume of which was completed in 1696 (16). The *Dryden Lucian,* of which Dryden

---

(11) George Berkeley, *A New Theory of Vision,* 1709. See analysis in chapter 6.

(12) See further, section IX of this chapter.

(13) *Works of Swift,* edition Sir Walter Scott, 1883, IX, 6-7. Scott's quotation from Philostratus is reprinted in chapter 5, below.

(14) *Ibid.,* I, 243:

> "Herodotus, Philostratus, and Aulus Gellius seem particularly to have engaged his attention, and he has written his opinion concerning each in the blank leaves of the volume."

In a footnote on the same page, Scott states that Swift's copy of Philostratus was found by Theophilus Swift, who wrote, "The passages marked are but few."

(15) *Prose Works,* II, 96. *Journal to Stella,* Letter xiii, Jan. 4, 1710-11. See reference in note 8.

(16) The four volume *Dryden Lucian* was published in 1711. In the dedication to volume I, we find the following:

> "The *Life* by Mr. Dryden and some of the dialogues were done in and before the year 1696."

Also at the close of the preface, volume II, the following:

> "I must advertise the Reader that the *Life of Lucian* was writ by Mr. Dryden near fifteen years ago . . . and if anyone doubt the Truth, he may convince himself by a View of the copy at the publishers."

himself wrote only the introduction, was the work of "several
eminent hands" according to the title-page; but the translator
of nearly one-half of the contents was Tom Brown, the writer
whose works Swift said he had "read entire" (17). In the
introduction, Dryden repeatedly states his preference for the
text of d'Ablancourt as the best of all of Lucian's translations (18). It is not at all unlikely that Swift's purchase of
the latter was suggested by reading Dryden's unstinted praise.

Swift's own contemporaries were quick to recognize the
influence of Lucian's *True History* in *Gulliver's Travels*.
Lucian's works were widely read in the eighteenth century,
while French literature was relatively neglected; hence the
popular association of *Gulliver* with the *True History*, and the
ignorance of the debt to d'Ablancourt and Cyrano. In Lyttleton's *Dialogues of the Dead*, No. 22, Lucian criticizes *Gulliver*
as an imitation of his own *True History* (19). In Fielding's
Amelia, the Unknown Author says of Swift, "There is one
whom I am convinced he studied above all others . . .
Lucian" (20).

In writing *Gulliver*, Swift seems to have had the *True History* in mind in his vehement satire on historians, "who have
the perpetual misfortune to be mistaken" (21). Furthermore,
Gulliver's reception in Lilliput, his discovery that the inhabitants are in imminent danger of attack by an enemy, his enlist-
ment and military service rendered, are very closely paralleled
in Lucian's initial experiences on the moon, and do not appear
elsewhere in the fore-runners of *Gulliver*, so far as I
know (22). Swift, must have had the *True History* in mind,
when he introduced into *Gulliver's Travels* the flying, dirigible
island of Laputa, whose inhabitants live in constant dread of
the sun (23). From the very first publication of *Gulliver*,
readers have condemned the story of the flying island, as the

---

(17) See note 70, and the quotation on page 64.

(18) Dryden's praise of d'Ablancourt may be found on the following
pages *Dryden Lucian*, I:14, 15, 38, 41, 48, 54, and 55.

(19) *Dialogues*, edition 1797, pp. 175-8.

(20) *Amelia*, Book VIII, chapter 5.

(21) *Gulliver*, 209 (*Laputa*, chapter viii). The passage quoted in my
study of Laputa, chapter 9, below, is a concise and forceful restatement
of the ideas that are repeatedly stated in Lucian's introductory essay,
How to Write History.

(22) See, further, the chapter on Lilliput, below.

(23) Pointed out by H. W. L. Hime, in his excellent little book,
Lucian, The Syrian Satirist, 1900. *Gulliver*, 169.

most uninspired part of the narrative (24); what they condemned is an obvious imitation of a situation in the *True History*. The imitation is evident even down to the detail of the relief felt by the traveller when he returns from the island to *terra firma* (25). Finally, Swift echoes the satire of the *True History* on the pedantic commentators of Homer, including the circumstance of Homer's surprising patience with them (26). The two points of satire in which Swift seems to follow the *True History*, namely the attack on historians and on commentators, are only incidental and occupy but a page or two, so that it may seem unreasonable to assume any direct influence. The significant point, however, is that both of these parallels appear in the account of Gulliver's visit with the departed spirits of Glubdubdrib, a situation which itself is unquestionably modelled on Lucian's *Dialogues of the Dead*. In general it may be said that the *True History* afforded numerous suggestions for *Gulliver*, but it must not be considered as the primary model for the narrative as a whole, nor a source for the more important aspects of the satire.

Swift owed a much more important debt to a sequel to the *True History*, written by N. Perrot d'Ablancourt (1606-1664), and included in the latter's translation into French of the works of Lucian, which was purchased by Swift in 1711. This I have discussed in full in a recent contribution to *Modern Language Notes* (27). D'Ablancourt continues the *True History*, adding visits to "L'île des animaux . . . quelle étoit environée de celle des géans, des magiciens, et des pygmées"; but the contribution to *Gulliver* is much more than the mere suggestion of the countries visited. The animal kingdom of ← d'Ablancourt is not limited to horses, it is true; in fact, the horse is but one of many species who live together. The parallel is rather in the contrast between the highly civilized

(24) Joint letter of Pope and Gay to Swift, Nov. 17, 1726. *Correspondence*, III, 360.
  "As to other critics they think the flying island is the least entertaining; and so great an opinion the town have of the impossibility of Gulliver's writing below himself, it is agreed that part was not writ by the same hand."
See also *Correspondence*, III, 368.
(25) Hime, *op. cit.*
  "On the fourth day about noon having a fair and gentle gale, we were let down upon the sea. As soon as we touched water you cannot imagine how greatly we rejoiced." (*Dryden Lucian*, III, 143.)
  "I was let down from the lowest gallery in the same manner as I had been taken up . . . I felt some little satisfaction in finding myself on firm ground." (*Gulliver*, 181.)
(26) Hime, *op. cit.*
(27) See my article, referred to in note 8.

animals, and the Yahoo type of human savages who are subject to the animals.   The animal king (like the Governor of
the Houyhnhnms) is very indignant when he learns from the
traveller of the gross injustice done to his domesticated
cousins in the antipodes.   Like Gulliver, the traveller becomes
convinced of the superior virtues of this animal commonwealth.

The island of the magicians bears no detailed resemblance
to the island of Glubdubdrib.   The island of the giants (which
adjoins that of the pygmies) is briefly described as a good
place for travellers to avoid.   The giants who fish for whales
and throw mountains about for exercise, are over five hundred
feet in height.

The race of pygmies is most important.   Unlike the little
savages who attack Hercules in the classical legend, but like
the Lilliputians, the pygmies of d'Ablancourt have a government, are ruled by a benevolent king, are skilled in waging
war and highly ingenious in the management of their domestic
affairs.   To be sure, the race is idealized, not ridiculed as it is
by Swift, but it is a source for the fiction, not the satire, that
we are seeking in d'Ablancourt.   There is also something of
Swift's careful proportions in the detailed account of pygmy
life.   The minute rations consumed, the diminutive utensils
used, are all in strict conformity to the scale of life.   In short,
no other account gives anything like such a parallel to Lilliput.
The points of agreement, moreover, are in details peculiar to
these two accounts alone, not a part of the pygmy tradition as
it was known through the classics or through the accounts of
travellers (28).

To the best of my knowledge, the influence of Lucian upon
Gulliver has been studied by others with respect to the *True
History* alone.   Recently I have pointed out a very important
source for the satire of Lilliput in Lucian's *Icaromennipus, or
a Voyage to Heaven,* in which civilization and man are ridiculed by a description of their petty appearance as it is viewed
from a great height (29).

To the foregoing should be added passages in Lucian's
Dialogue between Terpsion and Pluto, and the satire, *On
Mourning for the Dead,* where the hideousness of old age is
depicted in terms very suggestive of the Struldbruggs (30).
All of these works, are in the "three little volumes of Lucian

---

(28) See, further, the account of the pygmy tradition in chapter 5.

(29) *Dryden Lucian,* I, 304-326.   See my article referred to in note 9.
For the use of the same satiric idea in an imitation of *Lilliput,* see Voltaire's *Micromégas.*

(30) Discussed in the reference in note 8.   See also the study of the
Struldbruggs in chapter 9.

in French," by d'Ablancourt, and all but the sequel to the *True History* are contained in the *Dryden Lucian*. The total influence of the works of Lucian in *Gulliver's Travels* is thus quite considerable; the miscellaneous ideas borrowed by Swift are many. A careful comparison of the two authors, however, makes it clear that Swift loses none of his credit for originality. In the more significant aspects of his work, his satiric method and narrative art, Swift differs from Lucian in quality as he excells him in intellectual vigor.

III.

Rabelais [*ca.* 1490—*ca.* 1553] (31)

Ever since Lord Bathurst's playful threat, in 1730, to expose Swift's thefts from Rabelais, the Rabelaisian element in *Gulliver* has been noted and a debt assumed. The similarity in obscene incidents, and the obvious imitation of Rabelais in the description of the professors in the Academy of Lagado, have been taken as sufficient evidence of a direct literary debt. To these internal parallels previously noted by critics, I have nothing to add. A debt inferred wholly from parallel passages, however, must almost always remain subject to doubt (32). May not Swift have copied some one of the many imitators of Rabelais, instead of Rabelais himself? It is the purpose of this section to collect evidence from Swift's other writings to prove conclusively that Swift's mind was well stored with incidents out of Rabelais, whose works he must have known almost by heart, since he was able to quote him off-hand in his correspondence with verbal accuracy.

Not counting two general references to Rabelais as a prevaricator and a satirist (33), Swift four times quotes him

---

(31) This study of Rabelais is based upon the translation by Urquhart and Motteux, reprinted in three volumes of the collection, *Tudor Translations*, 1900. The same text is the one used in the commoner modern editions in English. I have not been able to ascertain whether Swift read Rabelais in French or in English. Urquhart's translation of the first three books was published in 1653; Motteux's translation of the fourth and fifth books followed in 1694. The high reputation and favorable reception accorded to this translation make it quite probable that we are following the text with which Swift himself was familiar.

(32) My own theory is that parallel passages alone, unless verbal duplicates, can seldom establish a direct literary debt; there is always the possibility of another intermediate work which may have been the one consulted. It is for this reason that I state, at what must seem unnecessary length, the evidence of Swift's familiarity with the works of Rabelais.

(33) *Prose Works*, X, 376, *Freeholder*, No. 31. Also, IX, 317, *Intelligencer*, No. III.

directly. In one of his contributions to the *Examiner* there is
the following:

> "I likewise remember the story of a giant in Rabelais, who used
> to feed upon windmills, but was unfortunately choked with a small
> lump of butter before a warm oven" (34).

Turning to Rabelais, we find,

> "For one Widenostrils, a huge giant . . . choaked himself with
> eating a huge lump of fresh butter at the mouth of a hot oven" (35).

In a letter to Bolingbroke Swift wrote,

> "The poor dead queen is used much like the giant Lougarou in
> Rabelais. Pantagruel took Lougarou by the heels and made him
> his weapon to kill twenty other giants, then flung him over a river
> into the town and killed two ducks and an old cat" (36).

The original in Rabelais is as follows:

> "He threw the body of Loupgarou, as hard as he could against the
> city, where falling like a frog upon his belly . . . he with the said
> fall killed a singed he-cat, a wet she-cat, a farting duck, and a
> brideled goose" (37).

That Swift employed another story of Rabelais in some writing now lost is proved by the statement of Bolingbroke in a
letter to Swift.

> "There never was a better application than yours of the story of
> Picrochole. The storks will never come and they must be porters
> all their lives" (38).

The allusion is to the following in Rabelais:

> "Picrochole . . . relating his misadventurous disasters, was fore-
> told by an old Lourpidon hag, that his Kingdome should be restored
> to him at the coming of the Cocklicranes . . . What is become of
> him since we cannot certainly tell, yet was I told that he is now a
> porter at Lyons, as testie and pettish in humour as ever he was
> before, and would be always with great lamentation enquiring at
> all strangers of the coming of the Cocklicranes, expecting assuredly
> . . . that at their coming he shall be re-established in his King-
> dom" (39).

Finally, and most important of all, Swift quotes directly
one of the Abstractors of Queen Whim's court, whose profes-

---

(34) *Ibid.*, IX, 119. *Examiner*, No. 20, Dec., 1710.

(35) Rabelais, Bk. IV, ch. xvii, page 104.

(36) *Correspondence*, II, 239, Sept. 14, 1714.

(37) Rabelais, Bk. II, ch. xxix, page 314. For Rabelais' two cats and
a duck, Swift has two ducks and a cat.

(38) *Correspondence*, III, 28 and note, March 17, 1718-19.

(39) Rabelais, Bk. I, ch. xlix, page 162.

sion is paralleled in the occupation of one of the professors of Lagado.

> "For as to your scheme of raising one-hundred-and-ten-thousand pounds, it is as vain as that of Rabelais, which was to squeeze out wind from the posteriors of a dead ass" (40).

Not only is this last a correct quotation from Rabelais, but it will be recognized as an accurate duplicate of the experiment performed by the physician whom Gulliver interviews in Lagado, except that the latter applies the bellows to a dog instead of to an ass.

It is of further interest to note that Swift's own contemporaries recognized the mantle of Rabelais upon his shoulders. Pope alluded to Swift's ability,

> "To laugh, and shake, in Rabelais' easy chair" (41).

In Lyttleton's *Dialogue*, already cited, Rabelais asks Lucian to judge between his works and *Gulliver's Travels*. Lucian says,

> "In comparison with you he (Swift) was decent and elegant, but whether there was not in your compositions more fire, and a more comic spirit, I will not determine."

A definite attempt to prove Swift's debt to Rabelais for incidents in *A Tale of A Tub,* was made by Voltaire (45), who elsewhere devotes an essay to a comparison of Swift and Rabelais as humorists, concluding,

> "Swift était moins savant que Rabelais, mais son esprit est plus fin et plus delie" (46).

In Fielding's *Amelia,* Booth says,

> "If Rabelais be Swift's master, he proves the truth of the common Greek proverb that the scholar is often superior to the master" (47).

Lord Bathurst, feigning anger with Swift, threatened to prove that the prose works "about which they made so much ado are but little improvement upon the humor" he had "stolen" from Rabelais. The work by Lyttleton, already cited twice (48), contains some interesting dialogue which bears upon our present attempt to determine the relation between Swift and Rabelais. Lucian insists upon making comparisons

---

(40) *Prose Works*, VII, 114. *An Answer to a Paper called, "A Memorial of the Poor Inhabitants of Ireland."*
(41) *Dunciad,* line 21.
(45) Voltaire, *Oeuvres Complètes*, 1879, 26:474.
(46) *Ibid.,* 26:491.
(47) See note 20.
(48) See note 19.

between *Gulliver* and the stories of Rabelais, very odious to
the latter, who finally retorts as follows:

> (Rabelais) "I would as soon undertake to measure the difference
> between the height and bulk of the giant Gargantua and his
> Brobdingnagian Majesty, as the difference in merit between my
> writings and Swift's. If anyone takes a fancy to like my book,
> let him freely enjoy the entertainment it gives him . . . If another
> person likes *Gulliver*, let him toast Dr. Swift. If a third likes
> neither of us, let him silently pass the bottle and be quiet."
>
> (Lucian) "But if he will not be quiet? A critick is an unquiet
> creature."
>
> (Rabelais) "Why then he will disturb himself, not me."

The nature and extent of the influence of Rabelais in
Gulliver need not detain us long, as they have been correctly
stated by previous critics (49). The Academy of Lagado is
largely modelled on the court of Queen Whim, Rabelais, Book
V, chapters XXI, and XXII, which Walter Scott reprinted in
the footnotes to Laputa, in his edition, 1814 (50). I submit
that the inherent probability of the debt, assumed by Scott,
has become a certainty in view of Swift's quotation of the
same passage from Rabelais in his correspondence. Dennis has
rightly noted (51) that the method employed by Gulliver to
extinguish the fire at the palace in Lilliput is modelled on the
obscene jest of Gargantua in causing a similar flood in the
streets of Paris. The parallel is first of all in the coarse
situation (a giant urinating shamelessly in the presence of a
crowd of pygmies) and second, in the devastation and wide-
spread terror produced in each case by the flood. Gargantua
causes much loss of life; Gulliver is banished from Lilliput to
prevent a recurrence of the flood (52). Swift also seems to
have a passage of Rabelais in mind when he makes Gulliver
comment on the shabby ancestors of the world's aristocracy,
whom he sees in Glubdubdrib (53). The satire in both is
identical; the idea being that popes and princes are in reality
bred from a long line of pick-pockets and gamesters.

So much for the definite borrowings from Rabelais. The
more general and important matter of Rabelais' influence on
Swift's style was discussed in the preceding chapter.

---

(49) See references in notes 13, 50, and 51.

(50) *Works of Swift*, edition Sir Walter Scott, XI, 215-217, note.

(51) *Gulliver*, 57, note. Parallel is in Rabelais, Bk. I, ch. xvii, page 70.
For analogues see also Bk. I, ch. xxxvi, page 126; and ch. xxxviii, page 132.

(52) These situations are compared in detail in chapter 5.

(53) *Gulliver*, 208. Rabelais, Bk. I, ch. 1. Before leaving Rabelais,
attention should be called to the fact that all but one of Swift's direct
quotations from Rabelais (notes 33-40) were made before 1720.
Gulliver's Travels was published in 1726.

IV.

Cyrano de Bergerac [1620-1655] (54)

Swift's actual borrowings of incident and idea from the *Fantastic Voyages* of Cyrano are more extensive and more numerous than from any other source. The evidence for this debt is wholly internal; nowhere does Swift mention Cyrano or his works. It is therefore necessary in this place only to summarize the nature of the influence and refer the reader to the discussion of the parallels.

In his *History of Prose Fiction*, 1814 (55), Dunlop gives an excellent synopsis of Cyrano's *Histoire comique de, la lune* (56), which he ably proves must have been the model for the adventures of Gulliver in Brobdingnag. Borkowsky has collected a score or more of additional, minor parallels which he finds scattered through the four voyages of Gulliver. In the case of some of these the resemblance is very close, as for example in the traveller's surprise on discovering that the native "bêtes-hommes" are in all respects like human beings. Cyrano says,

> "Quand je les pus discerner de près, je connus qu'ils avoient la taille et la figure comme nous' (57).

And Gulliver's comment on seeing the Yahoos at close range,

> "My horror and astonishment are not to be described when I observed in this abominable animal a perfect human figure" (58).

---

(54) There is no complete edition of the works of Cyrano. The best edition of his two *Fantastic Voyages*, and the one upon which this study is based is the following:

> "Nouvelle édition revue et publiée avec des notes et une notice historique." Paris, 1858. P. L. Jacob (Paul Lacroix) 1 vol. in-8, 380 pp.

(55) Edition of Henry Wilson, 1911, II, 527-535.

(56) The *Fantastic Voyages* of Cyrano were published posthumously in 1657; the exact dates of composition cannot be determined. In so much as the earlier work, *Histoire de la lune*, shows unmistakable dependence upon Godwin's *Voyage of Gonzales* (Cyrano meets Gonzales in the moon) we can assume a date posterior to 1648, in which year appeared the first French translation of Godwin's story, by Jean Baudouin.

(57) *De la Lune*, 116. The first to call attention to Cyrano's influence on Swift was Charles Palissot (de Montenoy) in *Memoires pour servir à l'histoire de la littérature française*. Paris, 1771. In the article devoted to Cyrano, Palissot says,

> "Ce qu'il y a de plus remarquable c'est qu'il a fourni a M.de Fontenelle, au Dr. Swift . . . plusieurs idées dignes d'avoir été mises en oeuvre par ces hommes célébres."

(58) *Gulliver*, 238 (*Houyhnhnms*, chapter 2).

It would be impossible to condense or summarize the miscellaneous parallels; most of them will be given in my study of
the individual voyages, later. Suffice it to say that in *Brobdingnag* especially the type of detail that appears in both
works leaves no doubt about the influence upon Swift.

Several distinct and considerable contributions to the substance of *Gulliver* can be noted. In the first place, the nature
and the sequence of the adventures in Brobdingnag are based
on this romance of Cyrano, as Dunlop first remarked, and as I
show fully in chapter seven.

In the second place, the *Histoire de la lune* anticipates the
idea of the relativity of our physical world, implied in the contrast between Lilliput and Brobdingnag. Cyrano does not
embody the satire found in *Gulliver*, but he asserts the philosophic concept of an infinite series of worlds with no absolute
scale as the norm. Gulliver says,

> "Undoubtedly philosophers are in the right when they tell us that
> nothing is great or little otherwise than by comparison. It might
> have pleased fortune to have let the Lilliputians find some nation
> where the people were as diminutive with respect to them as they
> were to me. And who knows but that even this prodigious race of
> mortals might be equally overmatched in some distant part of the
> world whereof we have yet no discovery" (59).

And in Cyrano,

> "Il me reste à prouver qu'il y a des Mondes infinis dans un Monde
> infini. Représentez-vous donc l'univers comme un animal; que les
> étoiles, qui sont des Mondes, sont dans ce grand animal, comme
> d'autres grands animaux, qui servent réciproquement de mondes à
> d'autres peuples, tels que nous . . . et que nous, à notre tour,
> sommes aussi des Mondes à l'égard de certains animaux encore
> plus petits . . . Car, dites-moi, je vous prie, est-il malaisé à croire
> qu'un pou prenne votre corps pour un Monde, et que, quand
> quelqu'un d'eux voyage depuis l'une de vos oreilles jusqu'à l'autre,
> ses compagnons disent qu'il a voyagé aux deux bouts de la Terre,
> ou qu'il a couru de l'un à l'autre Pôle" (60)?

The influence in *Gulliver* of Cyrano's second romance, *Histoire comique du soleil* has been consistently either ignored or
misrepresented from Dunlop down to the most recent writer
on the subject. After doing so well with the lunar romance,
Dunlop dismisses its companion piece with this misleading and
incorrect remark:

> "As Cyrano's journey to the moon is the origin of Swift's Brob-
> dingnag, so the *Histoire des États du Soleil* seems to have suggested
> the plan of the voyage to Laputa" (61).

---

(59) *Gulliver*, 89. (*Brobdingnag*, chapter 1).
(60) *De la Lune*, 163-4.
(61) *Op. cit.*, II, 535.

Since Dunlop wrote these words, it has become clear that the resemblance to Laputa is less marked than in several other *Philosophic Voyages* which ridicule the vanity of academic learning, as I will show later in chapter nine. In his ostensibly exhaustive source study of *Gulliver*, Borkowsky hardly mentions the *Histoire du soleil*, and when he does it is only to extract another minor parallel from its context. Dennis follows Borkowsky in ignoring the influence of the second romance, while Churton Collins follows Dunlop in connecting it with Laputa alone.

The *Histoire du Soleil* did not furnish Swift with so many miscellaneous ideas as did the lunar narrative, but what it did do, which has been completely overlooked, was to serve as the model for the withering satire that is heaped on Gulliver by the Houyhnhnms. Cyrano is tried by a tribunal of animals (birds not horses) and is found guilty of the unspeakable sin of being a human monster (62). Cyrano, however, does not like Gulliver escape with mere banishment; he is sentenced to be devoured by insects (63). As in the case of Gulliver, the charges against him are, perverted intelligence, cruelty, and impudence in setting himself above his fellow creatures. As Cyrano appears in the court-room, a spectator faints, overcome by the horror of gazing upon a man (64). Seizing upon the only means of escape, Cyrano pleads that he is not at all what they have mistaken him for, a base human being, but is in reality a perfectly respectable monkey (65). One bird attempts to defend the traveller, but its evidence is ruled out on the ground that the character of the witness has been debased through association with mankind (66). The advocate, appointed by the fair-minded judge to defend Cyrano, rises to say,

> "Il est vrai, Messieurs, qu'ému de pitié, j'avois entrepris la cause de cette malheureuse bête; mais, sur le point de la plaider, il m'est venu un remords de conscience, et comme une voix secrète qui m'a défendu d'accomplir une action si détestable. Ainsi, Messieurs, je vous déclare, et à toute la Cour, que, pour faire le salut de mon âme, je ne veux contribuer en façon quelconque à la durée d'un monstre tel que l'Homme" (67).

---

(62) Du Soleil, 286-293.

(63) *Ibid.*, 290.

(64) *Ibid.*, 290-1.

(65) *Ibid.*, 279. Cyrano joins his accusers in the denunciation of man, and offers to submit to death gladly, if they can prove that he is not a monkey.

(66) *Ibid.*, 289-290. "Ma Pie se présenta pour plaider à sa place; mais il lui fut impossible d'avoir audience, à cause qu'ayant été nourrie parmi les hommes, et peut-être infectée de leur morale, il étoit à craindre qu'elle n'apportât à ma cause un esprit prévenu."

(67) *Ibid.*

When we remember that nowhere else in the *Philosophic Voyages* before *Gulliver* is there such scathing satire directed at the human race, the significance of the *Histoire Comique du Soleil* as a source for Gulliver's fourth voyage becomes apparent.

V.

Tom Brown [1663-1704]

The influence of Cyrano upon Swift is apparent only in *Gulliver's Travels;* but in the case of Tom Brown, as in the case of Rabelais, the influence was a much wider one, affecting the work of Swift at many points. Obviously, it would be beyond the scope of this book to investigate this larger literary debt. I will mention only the points that concern *Gulliver's Travels.*

In 1917, Elbert N. S. Thompson called attention for the first time to the influence of Brown upon Swift (68). He showed that the Bickerstaff papers were but a continuation of Brown's joke at the expense of the astrologer, Partridge, which he had published serially in 1700 as burlesque predictions. Thompson also noted unmistakable borrowings from Brown's *Amusements Serious and Comical,* in the occupations of some of the members of the Academy of Lagado, though in this connexion, as I will show later in chapter nine, Thompson overlooked some of his strongest evidence. It is possible, I believe, to go much further and point out close imitation of Brown in the coarse poems of Swift, especially those dealing cynically with marriage, and also in Swift's collections of satiric epigrams and witty sayings (69). For our present purposes, however, enough has been done already to prove that Swift was deeply influenced by the satiric style of his witty contemporary, who is forgotten today, only because he was excelled by his disciples, Swift and Addison. For evidence of Swift's familiarity with the works of Brown, Thompson cites Swift's own remark in the *Introduction to Polite Conversation,*

> "(I) read Mr. Thomas Brown entire, and had the honor to be his intimate friend, who was universally admitted to be the greatest genius of his age" (70).

---

(68) *Mod. Lang. Notes,* 1917. Vol. 32, pp. 90-94. The edition of the works of Tom Brown employed in this study is the ninth edition, 1760. 4 vol. in-12.

(69) Compare Swift's *Thoughts Moral and Diverting,* with Brown's *Laconics,* IV, 100-118. Also Swift's poems: *Strephon and Cloe, The Ladies' Dressing Room,* and *The Progress of Marriage,* with Brown's obscene poems, notably the one found in I, 58.

(70) *Prose Works,* XI, 221.

In 1918, Edward Bliss Reed added to the works of Brown mentioned above, the latter's translation, 1702, of the *Circe* of Giovanni Battista Gelli (71), consisting of ten dialogues between Ulysses and the beasts, of which I have given some account in the preceding chapter, and of which more in chapter ten, below. The remarks of the horse (Dialogue VII), in which the superiority of that animal to man is set forth, must certainly have suggested passages in the conversations of Gulliver with the Governor of the Houyhnhnms.

Brown's influence in *Gulliver* may be summed up as follows: several hints for Lagado, including its division into departments of experimental science and speculative learning; the method used by the Laputan tailor to measure Gulliver for a suit of clothes by means of a quadrant; the indictment of a man as an intemperate animal, in contrast with the gentler disposition of the horse. For Brown's influence upon the style of *Gulliver*, see above, chapter three.

VI.

Berkeley, *Theory of Vision*, [1709].

The skeptical view of man's greatness, the rejection of any stable unit of measurement, implied in the Lilliputian and Brobdingnagian views of man, is based upon Berkeley's *Theory of Vision*. As this work touches *Gulliver* in but one well-defined place, its significance will be treated once and for all in our examination of the philosophy of the first two voyages, in chapter six, below. There the reader will find the evidence for Swift's familiarity with the works of Berkeley, and a full discussion of the abstract concept which seems to have been suggested by the latter's *Theory of Vision*.

VII.

To the list of certain sources should be added the description of a storm in Samuel Sturmy's *Mariner's Magazine*, 1679, which Churton Collins has shown was copied verbatim by Swift in the description of the storm on the way to Brobdingnag (72). I have reprinted the parallels at the close of chapter seven, below, footnote 97. The obvious reason for this particularly verbal theft, so unlike Swift's general prac-

---

(71) Reed's contribution to *Mod. Lang. Notes*, 1918, Vol. 33:57-8.

(72) *Gulliver*, 86. The descriptions are printed in parallel columns in Churton Collins, *op. cit.*, 206-7, and in the footnotes to chapter 7 of this book.

tice, was that he desired to heighten the realism of the narrative by accuracy of nautical language, which he could not hope to counterfeit with any measure of success.

VIII.

Several works have been claimed as sources for *Gulliver* without sufficient evidence. The statement by Churton Collins that "several strokes for the Yahoos were borrowed from the *Travels* of Sir Thomas Herbert" (73), is not substantiated by him, nor is it confirmed by a reading of Herbert's *Travels* (74). Careful study of the romances of Cyrano has also made it very doubtful whether Swift ever saw the *Voyage of Domingo Gonzales,* by Godwin (75), since the points of resemblance to *Gulliver* appear to better advantage in the *Histoires comiques* (76). Borkowsky's labored attempt to prove that Swift used the *Histoire des Sévarambes,* and the *Voyage of Jacques Sadeur,* rests upon a very few parallels which are far

---

(73) *Some Years Travels into Africa and Asia, by Tho. Herbert,* 1638. It is a dull book of fictitious travel, closing with the discovery of America in 1170 by Madoc Ap Owen Gwyneth.

(74) *Op. cit.,* 205. This statement by Churton Collins is, for him, an unusual illustration of the worst kind of scholarship. All because Swift's personal copy of Herbert's *Travels* has been found, it is inferred that the work must have influenced *Gulliver's Travels.* As a matter of fact, the savages described by Herbert bear no resemblance to the Yahoos that cannot be duplicated in a dozen or more similar works which Swift never saw. It happens in this case that we have Swift's opinion of the book in question, scribbled in his own handwriting on the fly-leaf, and the opinion does not indicate that Swift caught much inspiration from the reading:

> "If this book were stripped of its impertinence, conceitedness, and tedious digression, it would be almost worth reading, and would then be two-thirds smaller than it is." (*Notes and Queries,* Ser. I, vol. vi, page 271, March 20, 1852. Signed: W. Sneyd, Owner of the Copy.)

(75) Godwin's story is reprinted in *Anglia,* X, 428 ff. and also in the *Harleian Miscellany,* 1811, VIII, pp. 344 ff.

(76) *Op. cit.,* 205. "There can be no doubt . . . that in the *Voyage to the Houyhnhnms* he drew . . . on Godwin's *Voyage of Domingo Gonzales."* The same position is maintained by Hönncher, *Anglia,* X. Dennis, *op. cit.,* rightly notes that Swift's use of *Gonzales* is questionable (*Gulliver,* xxi, note). Max Poll takes one step nearer to the truth, than any, by saying that it is quite improbable, *op. cit.*

from convincing (77) ; while his effort to prove indebtedness to More's *Utopia* is all but a parody of scholarship (78).

IX.

Three other works, however, must be substituted for the above as possible sources. Their marked resemblance to *Gulliver* is discussed elsewhere in this book; here I shall state the information which leads me to class them as possible sources, in the hope that some one else may supply the information necessary to change the doubt into a certainty.

(a) Holberg's, *Klimius*.

A synopsis of the contents of *Klimius* is given in chapter one above. Sir Walter Scott suggested (79) that this work may have been founded upon *Gulliver*, but this is by no means certain. The date of composition of *Klimius* is unknown and

---

(77) *Anglia*, XV. In the *Histoire des séverambes*, Borkowsky unearths two sentences, which he is convinced are copied in *Gulliver*. For one, the Sevarambi are said to write aslant the page, as do also the Lilliputians and English ladies (*Sevarambes*, p. 469; *Gulliver*, 58-9). Also, it appears that the Sevarambi calculate the year by the revolutions of the sun and moon, as do likewise the Houyhnhnms (*Sévarambes*, 315-6; *Gulliver*, 284). According to this, Campanella's *Civitas Solis* would have to be a source for something, for we find there,

> "They measure months by the course of the moon . . . They divide the seasons according to the revolution of the sun." (Morley's *Ideal Commonwealths*, 1896, page 261.)

Borkowsky asserts *Sadeur* to have served as a model for *Gulliver*, because Sadeur finds that the Australians have difficulty in comprehending the European diseases described by the traveller, a difficulty shared, however, not only by the Houyhnhnms but by nearly every ideal race in the *Philosophic Voyages*. (*Sadeur*, 339-340; *Gulliver*, 264.)

(78) Borkowsky begins by noting that Gulliver mentions More as one of the companions of Brutus with whom he converses in Glubdubdrib (*Gulliver*, 205). Then he finds, among the laws of Lilliput that "the disbelief of a divine providence renders a man uncapable of holding any public station." (*Gulliver*, 61) a law, which it develops, holds sway in Utopia as well. Second, he lights upon the statement that politicians are the parasites of society (*Gulliver*, 140) the one statement, before all others, which Borkowsky would have been sure to find not only in More's *Utopia*, but in almost any account of an idealized society. On these grounds Borkowsky argues seriously that Swift borrowed directly from More.

(79) Edition of Sir Walter Scott, XI, 5, note.

> "Though I do not know the precise date of the first edition, I have no doubt that it is posterior to Swift's work and has been founded upon it."

This is the only mention of *Klimius* in connection with *Gulliver* that has ever been made.

seems likely to remain unknown. Holberg states in his autobiography that the work remained in manuscript for several
years before publication. He says,

> "I endeavored to suppress this work which I had composed several
> years before, although I was incessantly importuned to publish
> it" (80).

No dates are given, however, in connection with this statement. Later, under date of 1732, he mentions a review of his
work in the Hamburg *Gazette* (81), before which date, therefore, the manuscript had not only been published but translated. The date of the first edition in Danish cannot be far
from the time of the publication of *Gulliver* in 1726. There
is at least a possibility that the Danish story may have suggested to Swift some of the situations in *Gulliver* which
resemble it so closely.

(b) Hall's *Mundus*

A synopsis of this work may be found in the preceding
chapter, but for the striking parallel to *Gulliver* see especially
chapter nine. The *Mundus Alter et Idem* was written in Latin
by Joseph Hall about 1610. The only known attempt at translation is one made by Swift's friend, Dr. William King, sometime before his death in 1711. It is a translation of the first six
chapters only; less than one-third of the entire work. For
several years Swift and King were associated on rather inti-
mate terms. Swift succeeded King as editor of the *Examiner*,
and later secured employment for him as gazetteer, on giving
his pledge to the effect that King would remain sober (82).
There is at least the possibility that Swift saw King's partial
translation of the *Mundus;* or on the other hand Swift may
have interested King in it himself. This sort of reasoning is
wholly gratuitous and proves nothing; we have no real reason
for believing that Swift ever saw the satire of Hall. It is,
however, at least suggestive to note that the only existing
English translation of the *Mundus* was made by a friend and
associate of Swift, sometime before 1711.

(c) *Wasobiyoe*

Finally, mention must be made of a very interesting
Japanese work entitled, *Wasobiyoe*, published in Japan, 1774,

---

(80) *Memoirs of Lewis Holberg, written by himself in Latin, and now
first translated into English*, London, 1927, page 70.

(81) *Ibid.*, 179.

(82) *Correspondence*, I, 315-6, and 316, note. Letter of Swift to King,
Jan. 8, 1711-12. See also *Correspondence*, I, 319 and 339, note.

King's fragment of the *Mundus* is in Morley's *Ideal Commonwealths*,
pp. 267-284.

in four small volumes. The book contains a number of *Fantastic Voyages*, at least two of which resemble parts of *Gulliver* quite as closely as do any of the known sources. These analogues of Brobdingnag and Struldbruggland are analyzed in chapters seven and ten below.

The *Imaginary Voyages* of Wasobiyoe include visits to the Lands of Shams, Antiquaries, Paradoxes, Perennial Life, and the Land of Giants. My information about the work is based upon a translation of the two voyages last named (Perennial Life and Giant Land) by Basil Hall Chamberlain, 1879 (83). Chamberlain entitles his translation *A Japanese Gulliver*, and notes the parallels to the accounts of the Struldbruggs and of Brobdingnag. The Japanese tale agrees with the general idea of Swift to the effect that the Brobdingnagians differ from ordinary man in physical bulk alone, an idea not stressed in other giant stories. Wasobiyoe says on leaving the country,

> "It would seem as if this foolish country were superior to the rest in nothing but size; tenanted as it is by such emptyheaded folk. It is nothing more than a great overgrown asparagus of a country."

A striking and verbally exact parallel occurs in the circumstances of the travellers' entrance into giant land, their reception by the giants, and the initial adventures, for which see further chapter seven. It is only right to state, however, that the incidents are of a sort which might naturally occur in any story of a human traveller among giants; and as I shall show later, the same general type of adventures are found in the *Arabian Nights* story of Hassân al Bassri (84).

The other parallel is in the account of the immortals visited by Wasobiyoe; a people who, like the Struldbruggs, desire death above all else. Further than this, Wasobiyoe, like Gulliver, is finally converted to the native notions concerning the hatefulness of old age (85). These ideas are not so common to fiction as giant stories are; and the unusual agreement with ideas in *Gulliver's Travels*, if a coincidence, is a very remarkable one. Wasobiyoe's journeys to the Lands of Shams, Antiquaries, and Paradoxes, have not been translated; their very titles, however, suggest possible parallels to the ridicule of learning in Laputa. It is to be regretted that the Japanese text has been unobtainable, even from the Imperial Library,

---

(83) *Journal of the Asiatic Society of Japan*, 1879, VII.

(84) Mardrus, *Les mille nuits et une nuit*, X, 36. Noted by Pietro Toldo, *op. cit.*

(85) See the study of the tradition of the immortals in literature in chapter 9, below.

otherwise the study would have been pushed beyond the partial translation by Chamberlain.

What has this Japanese story, published in 1774, got to do with the sources of *Gulliver's Travels?*

A contributor to the *Saturday Review*, 1886 (86), made a brief study of the two works, suggesting a possible influence of *Gulliver* in the Japanese work. He rightly noted that the Struldbruggs are said to live near Japan; that in both works the traveller stops at Nangasac; and that both of the travellers speak Dutch. Using then as arguments the fact that Dutch traders are known to have kept up trade with Japan (after that country had been closed to the Western world in 1637) using the port of Deshima, near Nangasac; and the further argument of the later date of the Japanese work; the writer of the article in question concluded that *Gulliver* was carried to Japan by Dutchmen, and served as a model for the anonymous Japanese author, if indeed there were any connexion at all between the two works.

So far the reasoning is good. When all the facts are taken into consideration, however, the probability is rather of an influence the other way. To begin with, the date of the earliest known edition of *Wasobiyoe*, 1774, means little or nothing. The story may have circulated long before, in forms now lost. At any rate I have the word of a prominent Japanese scholar that the story goes back to the writings of a Chinese philosopher who lived two thousand years ago (87). Then, also, the fact that Japan deliberately shut herself off from European influences for a long period of years, would make it more likely that the Dutch traders would bring back a Japanese tale to Europe, than that a Japanese author should copy the work of an Englishman. All of this, however, is but pernicious conjecture. There is something much more tangible and significant to guide us in the problem. In the account of the Struldbruggs, Swift (or rather Gulliver) makes the following statement:

> "There is indeed a perpetual commerce between this kingdom (Struldbrugg) and Japan, and it is very probable that the Japanese authors may have given some account of the Struldbruggs . . . I hope the Dutch upon this notice will be curious and able enough to supply my defects" (88).

---

(86) *Saturday Review*, vol. 62, 392 ff., Sept. 18, 1886.

(87) I have this information by correspondence from Professor Yoshi Kuno, of the Department of Oriental Literature, University of California.

It is certainly possible that Swift may have got hold somehow
of the story of Wasobiyoe, perhaps from the Dutch traders
themselves, while he was secretary to Sir William Temple. I
do not assert that *Wasobiyoe* is a source for *Gulliver's Travels,*
but before the possibility is dismissed, some satisfactory
interpretation must be made of the passage quoted above.

---

(88) *Gulliver,* 224. Surely the possible significance of this passage is
not lessened by the untrustworthy claim to entire originality which
Gulliver made in the preceding paragraph:

"I thought this account of the Struldbruggs might be some entertainment to the reader, because it seems to be a little out of the
common way; at least I do not remember to have met the like in
any book of travels that hath come to my hands."

Part II

The Travels of Lemuel Gulliver

1

Lilliput

"Tiny race, and nation void of brain."

(Addison's *Machinae Gesticulantes*, 1699.)

"The *Travels* of Capt. Gulliver have been so much the amusement of both sexes for some years past, that I need not acquaint the reader, either with the character of the author, or of his book. However, I cannot forbear giving my opinion of that performance, and I shall endeavor to do it with all possible candour and conciseness.

Criticism, altho' so much decryed by the unlearned, and so injudiciously managed by some writers, is an art of infinite advantage; because it directs the judgments of those who otherwise might be misled, both to disrelish compositions which merit our esteem and to approve of those which are only worthy of our contempt . . .

I hope and expect, that all future commentators will copy the example I have given them in this *Critical Essay:* and that, hereafter, they will be at least as studious to shew their own learning, as to illustrate their author.

I am pretty well assured . . . that the highest honour to the critic, and the surest test of his genius, is to demonstrate the truth and existence of those things, which the whole world beside determine to be false and fictitious."

("Critical Remarks On *Gulliver's Travels*." By John
Arbuthnot, Jan. 26, 1734-5.)

CHAPTER 5

Lilliput, and Other Pygmy Commonwealths in Literature.

The reader of the third and last part of this book will discover one fact that is safe from all dispute; namely, that the
Voyage to Lilliput was by far the most popular part of
Gulliver's Travels. Considered as a romantic tale alone, apart
from any satiric meaning, the story of Lilliput appealed tre-
mendously to the imagination of its readers everywhere;
"From the highest to the lowest it was universally read, from
the cabinet council to the nursery" (1). It will be our business
in this chapter to make plain the reasons for this extraordinary
popularity by a close study of Swift's narrative art. Before
this is attempted, however, it is first necessary to review the
literary uses of pygmy commonwealths before *Gulliver*.

Certain limits to the consideration of the fore-runners of
Lilliput can be set up at once. It is not our concern here to
examine the authenticity of the reports of actual pygmy races;
they existed in literature, and that is enough. Furthermore,
that problem has already been thoroughly investigated (2).
Neither are we concerned here with "little folk" in general.
It might conceivably be shown that traditions of folk-lore
represented fairies comparable to the Lilliputians in size or in
disposition, but such will not be our task. Lilliput will be
treated as a part of a tradition of flesh and blood pygmies, a
race that for two thousand years had been repeatedly "discovered" inhabiting some part of the earth's surface, a race that

---

(1) Joint letter of Pope and Gay to Swift, Nov. 17, 1726. *Correspondence*, III, 359.

(2) *Essay Concerning the Pygmies of the Ancients*, by Edward Tyson,
M.D., 1699. The title page also states, "Wherein it will appear that they
were all either Apes or Monkeys, and not Men as formerly pretended."
(Reprinted in Bibliothèque de Carabas, 1894, with an introduction by
Bertram Windle, from which edition my quotations are taken.) See also
Pygmies, by M.de Quatrefages translated by Frederick Starr, 1895. Both
Tyson and Quatrefages deal primarily with the historical and biological
problems of pygmy existence, not with fiction. Tyson discusses and re-
futes, chapter by chapter, the *Opusculum de Pygmaeis* of Gaspard
Bartholinus (1585-1629), a book written to prove the authenticity of
the pygmy myth. The classical accounts are also discussed in the chapter "Certain Varieties of Man," in John Ferriar's *Illustrations of Sterne*,
1812, vol. I, pp. 69-82. The literary accounts of pygmy commonwealths
discussed in this chapter are not mentioned by these authors, have never
been collected, and have never been connected with *Gulliver's Travels*.

had progressed in culture from the little, long-haired cave-men of Ctesias, who rode on goats, to the dainty, high-heeled courtiers of Lilliput.

I.

(a) The "Ancient Pygmaean Empire."

Not alone Swift but every one of his predecessors, fortunate enough to be educated in the classics, was familiar with the pygmy myth recorded by more than a dozen of the writers of antiquity: poets, historians, and travellers. Books might be written, and indeed have been written, about the classical pygmies. For us, however, the importance of those accounts is not so much due to the fact that Homer and Aristotle and Juvenal mentioned pygmies, as to the circumstance that the myth, originated by them, was current and popular in and before Swift's time. We will not, therefore, pause long over the classical allusions, which have been collated with great care by others, but will devote our attention for the most part to the elaboration and modification of the pygmy tradition by writers of *Imaginary Voyages*.

The elements of the classical myth that became matters of common report may be summed up as follows: A savage race of pygmies, about one cubit high, located variously from northern Africa to India, lives in caves, and wages a defensive warfare continually against the cranes, by whom it is finally exterminated. Of the various accounts I will cite only those most frequently quoted by later writers, and those which we can prove that Swift himself read. Homer's allusion to the war between the pygmies and the cranes was by far the most influential source, though it is not copied in Lilliput.

> "With shouts the Trojans, rushing from afar,
> Proclaim their motions, and provoke the war;
> So, when inclement winters vex the plain
> With piercing frosts, or thick-descending rain,
> To warmer seas the cranes embodied fly,
> With noise, and order, thro' the midway sky;
> To pygmy nations wounds and death they bring,
> And all the war descends upon the wing" (3).

Aristotle is a little more specific, but does not tell us much.

> "The cranes . . . travel from Scythia to the marshes in the higher parts of Egypt, from which the Nile originates. This is the place where the Pygmies dwell; and this is no fable, for there is really, as it is said, a race of dwarfs, both men and horses, which lead the life of troglodites" (4).

---

(3) Iliad, Bk. III, lines 4-10. (Quoted in Pope's translation.)
(4) Aristotle, The History of Animals, Bk. VIII, chapter xiv, par. 2. (Translation by Cresswell (1897), p. 209.)

In *A Tale of a Tub* (5) Swift refers specifically to the account of the pygmies given by Ctesias in his *History of India*, quoting a detail recorded by that writer alone.

> "In the middle of India there are black men, they are called pygmies, using the same language as the other Indians; they are very little, the tallest of them being but two cubits, and most of them but a cubit and a half high. They have very long hair, reaching down to their knees and lower; and a beard larger than any man's. After their beards are grown long they wear no cloaths, but the hair of their head falls behind a great deal below their hams; and that of their beards before comes down to their feet . . . They have a penis so long, that it reaches to the ancle, and the thickness is proportionable. They are flat-nosed and ill-favored. Their sheep are like lambs, and their oxen and asses scarce as big as rams. They are good archers" (6).

Herodotus, one of Swift's favorite authors (7), alludes to a diminutive race in Lybia (west of Egypt) that was identified with the pygmies by his readers.

> "While they (the Nasamonians) were gathering, some diminutive men, less than men of middle stature, came up and having seized them carried them away; and that the Nasamonians did not at all understand their language, nor those who carried them off the language of the Masamonians" (8).

The only classical account to which Swift was indebted is Philostratus' story of the capture of the sleeping Hercules by the pygmies, which I have proved (9) was the source for the corresponding scene in Lilliput.

> "The pygmies . . . having found Hercules napping in Lybia, mustered up their forces against him. One phalanx assaulted his left hand; but against his right hand, that being the stronger, two phalanxes were appointed. The archers and slingers besieged his feet, admiring the hugeness of his thighs; but against his head, as the arsenal, they raised batteries, the King himself taking his post there. They set fire to his hair, put reaping hooks in his eyes; and, that he might not breathe, clapped doors to his mouth and nostrils;

---

(5) *Prose Works*, I, 104. A Tale of A Tub, section vii:
"The happy genius of our age and country was prophetically held forth by that ancient typical description of the Indian pygmies, whose stature did not exceed above two feet; *sed quorum pudenda crassa, et ad talos usque pertigentia*."

(6) Tyson, *op. cit.*, 21-24.

(7) Sir Walter Scott wrote, concerning Swift's library:
"Herodotus, Philostratus, and Aulus Gellius seem particularly to have engaged his attention, as he has written his opinion concerning each of them in the blank leaves of the volume." (*Works of Swift*, I, 243.)

(8) Herodotus, *Euterpe*, *cap.* 32. Translation by Cary (1898), p. 107.

(9) See, above, chapter 4.

but all the execution they could do was only to awake him, which, when done, deriding their folly, he gathered them all up, into his lion's skin and carried them to Euristhenes . . . " (10).

The parallel to Lilliput is quite close. Gulliver falls asleep, like Hercules, not knowing where he is. On awaking, he is attacked by forty men armed with bows and arrows, the leader of whom marches up his leg and body to attack his head. One of the pygmies breaks out into vocal admiration of the Man-Mountain's hugeness, shouting, *Hekinah degul.* "In an instant I felt above an hundred arrows discharged on my left hand, which pricked me like so many needles; and besides they shot another flight into the air . . . whereof many I suppose fell on my body (though I felt them not) and some on my face which I immediately covered with my left hand . . . They discharged another volley larger than the first, and some of them attempted with spears to stick me in the sides, but . . . I had on a buff jerkin which they could not pierce" (11). Then the Lilliputians erect a battery near to Gulliver's head, from which the "principal person" delivers the ultimatum to the invader. The parallel to Philostratus is very close, but Swift's debt to the latter must not be over-estimated. Swift copied the incident of the **gigantic visitor** being surrounded while asleep, the attack with bows and arrows, and the invulnerability of the giant; but the pygmies of Philostratus cannot be identified with the Lilliputians.

The quotations made from Ctesias and Philostratus represent the most extended account of pygmies given by any of the ancient writers, from which it will be seen at once that the classical stories of the pygmies were all of the most fragmentary nature, affording no detailed description of a pygmy civilization. More important anticipations of Lilliput are the elaborations of the classical tradition of pygmies in the works of writers nearer to Swift's time.

(b) Revivals of the Classical Tradition of Pygmies, and its Popularity in Swift's Time.

We shall see a little later in this chapter that certain features of the classical tradition, and particularly the Homeric fiction of the crane-warfare, reappeared frequently in the accounts of pygmy commonwealths reported by travellers, real and imaginary. There, however, the classical debt is incidental. In this place I wish to call attention to two independent literary productions, which represent, exclusively, a revival of the classical myth.

---

(10) Tyson, *op. cit.*, 80-81. Philostratus', *Imagines.*
(11) *Lilliput*, 20-21.

Among Addison's Latin poems, published in 1699 and included in all complete editions of his works, appeared a mock heroic poem, *Praelium Inter Pygmaeos et Grues Commissum* (12). For several reasons this poem is important for our study. In the first place, as it was written by Addison in 1699, Swift must surely have read it before he wrote the *Voyage to Lilliput*. Then, too, the artistic versification of the pygmy myth at that time makes it certain that the notion of a pygmy people was familiar to the educated readers of *Gulliver's Travels*. Addison's ironical description of the haughty pygmy chieftain suggests the emperor of Lilliput, who is "taller by the breadth of my nail than any of his court; which alone is enough to strike an awe into the beholders" (13). Lord Macaulay felt sure that the passage in Addison's poem about the twenty-inch chieftain of imperial mien suggested the above to Swift, but I do not believe that this can be affirmed with any certainty (14). The poem is interesting for its own sake because of the novel turn given to the pygmy myth at the close. Driven from their homes by the cranes, the pygmies have taken to the woods, where their "frisking forms" may be seen "amid the moonlight glade," and "Fairy-people is the name they love." So far as I know, Addison is the only writer to associate the pygmies with the fairies of folk-lore (15). The extract that follows is taken from Beattie's translation (16) of Addison's poem.

(12) *Musae Anglicanae*, 1699, vol. II.

(13) *Lilliput*, 29.

(14) Macaulay, *Life of Addison*. *Works*, ed. 1860, V, 331-2.

"Our favorite piece (speaking of Addison's Latin poems) is the 'Battle of the Pygmies and the Cranes' . . . Swift boasted that he was never known to steal a hint, and he certainly owed as little to his predecessors as any modern writer. Yet we cannot help suspecting that he borrowed, perhaps unconsciously, one of the happiest touches in his 'Voyage to Lilliput' from Addison's verses."

Macaulay quotes the following lines as the ones copied by Swift:

"Jamque acies inter medias sese arduus infert
Pygmeadum ductor, qui majestate verendus
Incessuque gravis reliquos supereminet omnes
Mole gigantea, mediamque assurgit in ulnam."

(See Waller's ed. of *Gulliver*, p. 18n. Also a note by Max Poll in the *Bulletin of the University of Cincinnati*, 1909, No. 24, page 8.)

(15) The same identification is implied by Addison in another of his Latin poems of the same date, *Machinae Gesticulantes*, for the discussion of which see below, chapter 6, p. 108. This poem has never been mentioned in connection with *Gulliver's Travels*.

(16) *Poetical Works of James Beattie*. *Aldine Poets*, 1864, vol. 10, pp. 76-83.

"The Battle of the Pygmies and the Cranes"

"The pigmy-people, and the feather'd train,
Mingling in mortal combat on the plain,
I sing. Ye Muses, favour my designs,
Lead on my squadrons, and arrange the lines;
The flashing swords and fluttering wings display,
The long bills nibbling in the bloody fray;
Cranes darting with disdain on tiny foes,
Conflicting birds and men, and war's unnumber'd woes.

. . .
  Where India reddens to the early dawn,
Winds a deep vale from vulgar eyes withdrawn;
Bosom'd in groves the lowly region lies,
And rocky mountains round the border rise.
Here, till the doom of fate its fall decreed,
The empire flourish'd of the pigmy breed;
. . .

. . . . Roused by war's alarms,
Forth rush'd the madden'd mannikin to arms;
Fierce to the field of death the hero flies
The faint crane fluttering flaps the ground, and dies;
And by the victor borne, (o'erwhelming load)
With bloody bill loose-dangling marks the road.
And oft the wily dwarf in ambush lay,
And often made the callow young his prey;
With slaughter'd victims heap'd his board, and smil'd
T'avenge the parent's trespass on the child.
Oft, where his feather'd foe had rear'd her nest,
And laid her eggs and household gods to rest,
Burning for blood, in terrible array,
The eighteen-inch militia burst their way;
All went to wreck; the infant foeman fell,
When scarce his chirping bill had broke the shell.

. . .
  High in the midst the chieftain-dwarf was seen,
Of giant stature, and imperial mien;
Full twenty inches tall he strode along,
And view'd with lofty eye the wondering throng;
And while with many a scar his visage frown'd
Bared his broad bosom, rough with many a wound
Of beaks and claws, disclosing to their sight
The glorious meed of high heroic might.

. . .
  Encompass'd round with heaps of slaughter'd foes,
All grim in blood the pigmy champion glows,
And on th'assailing host impetuous springs,
Careless of nibbling bills, and flapping wings.
And midst the tumult, wheresoe'er he turns,
The battle with redoubled fury burns.
From every side th'avenging cranes amain
Throng, to o'erwhelm this terror of the plain.
When suddenly (for such the will of Jove)
A fowl enormous, sousing from above
The gallant chieftain clutch'd, and, soaring high,
(Sad chance of battle) bore him up the sky.

The cranes pursue, and clustering in a ring,
Chatter triumphant round the captive king.
But ah, what pangs each pigmy bosom wrung,
When, now to cranes a prey, on talons hung,
High in the clouds they saw their hapless lord,
His wriggling form still lessening as he soar'd.

. . .

But now at length the pigmy legions yield,
And wing'd with terror fly the fatal field.
They raise a weak and melancholy wail,
All in distraction scattering o'er the vale.
Prone on their routed rear the cranes descend;
Their bills bite furious, and their talons rend;
With unrelenting ire they urge the chase,
Sworn to exterminate the hated race.
T'was thus the pigmy name, once great in war,
For spoils of conquer'd cranes renown'd afar,
Perish'd . . .

. . .

And now with lofty chiefs of ancient time
The pigmy heroes roam th'Elysian clime.
Or, if belief to matron-tales be due,
Full oft, in the belated shepherd's view
Their frisking forms, in gentle green array'd,
Gambol secure amid the moonlight glade.
Secure, for no alarming cranes molest,
And all their woes in long oblivion rest.
Down the deep dale, and narrow winding way,
They foot it featly, ranged in ringlets gay.
'Tis joy and frolic all, where'er they rove,
And Fairy-people is the name they love" (17).

From the autobiographical *Memoirs of Goldoni* we read of an
Italian puppet-show (Bambocciata) by P. J. Martelli, entitled,
The Sneezing of Hercules, written sometime before 1727 (the
date of Martelli's death) and hence probably anterior to
Gulliver's Travels; but as a recent critic has shown (18),
there is no reason to suppose that this Italian burlesque had
found its way into Swift's hands. From the brief account of
it given by Goldoni, it is plain that the *Sneezing of Hercules*
is nothing more than a dramatization of the incident already
quoted from Philostratus.

"The imagination of the author sent Hercules into the country of
the pygmies. Those poor little creatures, frightened at the aspect

---

(17) The lines quoted represent about one-half of the entire poem.
(18) *Memoirs of Goldoni,* translation by John Black, 1814, I, 105-6.
Originally published in 1787. Goldoni states that he staged the puppet
show himself for the entertainment of Count Lantieri; his account of it
may therefore be regarded as first hand. The parallel to *Lilliput* was
first noted by C. Forbes in *Notes & Queries,* May 28, 1853, Ser. I, vol. vii,
p. 523. It was claimed as a source for *Gulliver* by David Asher in *Anglia,*
VII, *Anzeiger,* p. 93 ff. Asher was refuted by Max Poll, *op. cit.,* pp. 6-8.

of an animated mountain with arms and legs, ran and concealed
themselves in holes. One day as Hercules had stretched himself out
in the open field, and was sleeping tranquilly, the timid inhabitants
rushed out of their retreats and, armed with prickles and rushes,
mounted on the monstrous man and covered him from head to foot,
like flies when they fall on a piece of rotten meat. Hercules waked
and felt something in his nose, which made him sneeze, on which
his enemies tumbled down in all directions. This ends the piece . . .
The thoughts and sentiments are all proportionate to the size of the
personages. The verses even are short, and everything indicates
pygmies."

The above suggests Lilliput at several points. Gulliver says,

"The young natives had the curiosity to see how I looked when I
was asleep . . . One of them . . . put the sharp end of his half-
pike a good way up into my left nostril, which tickled my nose like
a straw and made me sneeze violently" (19).

Hercules is spoken of as an "animated mountain," and Gulliver
is named "The Man-Mountain" by the Lilliputians. The statement of Goldoni that "the verses were shòrt" suggests a parallel to the Lilliputian Odes (of two-stress, three-syllable lines)
which were in fashion in England in the years immediately
following the publication of *Gulliver's Travels* (20).

The classical tradition of pygmies, with its scattered and
fragmentary records of a savage race of grotesque dwarfs,
offers no instance of an elaborate pygmy commonwealth comparable to Lilliput; and it would receive no more than passing
mention in this study, were it not for the evidence of its popularity with Swift's contemporaries. Pygmies were not only
a matter of interest and curiosity but a point of scholarly controversy, in the years before the publication of the *Voyage to
Lilliput*. As previously in regard to witches, and as today in
regard to mediums, the minds of the people were divided into
the credulous and the incredulous, not a few educated people
believing the ancient writers without any misgivings. To
combat this superstition, a man of science, Edward Tyson,
Master of Arts and Doctor of Medicine, Cambridge, wrote an
exhaustive *Essay Concerning the Pygmies of the Ancients*,
1699, in which the classical allusions to pygmies are assembled,
collated, translated, and exposed as fictitious. Among the false
witnesses whom he examines are the following: Homer,

(19) *Lilliput*, 25-6.

(20) The vogue of the Lilliputian Ode, produced in large numbers between 1727 and 1733, is discussed in Part III below. The best known
one is probably the one by Pope, which may be found in any complete
edition of his works, but which is also included in various editions of Gay
and Swift, entitled, "To Quinbus Flestrin, The Man-Mountain. An Ode,
by Titty-Tit, Esq. Poet-Laureate to his Majesty of Lilliput."

Strabo, Athenaeus, Aelian, Pomponius Mela, Pliny, Juvenal,
Aristotle, Ctesias, Philostratus, Adrian Spigelius, Herodotus,
and others. This essay, over one hundred pages in length,
represents a great deal of laborious research, inspired wholly
by the writer's ambition to undermine the popular faith in
pygmies. Addison's poem, already cited in this chapter, seems
to have added fuel to Tyson's wrathful fire. In discussing the
alleged warfare between the pygmies and the cranes, he writes,

> "This may well enough, in a poet's phancy, be magnified, and repre-
> sented as a dreadful war; and no doubt of it, were one a *Spectator*
> of it, 'twould be diverting enough."

In his preface, Tyson states that his purpose is to prove the
pygmies to be "Only a creature of the brain, produced by a
warm and wanton imagination, and that they never had any
existence or habitation" (21). It is not unlikely that Swift
read the essay himself.

In 1724 a distinguished French scholar, the Abbé Banier,
an authority on the classics and author of a three-volume study
of the relation between history and mythology, replied to Tyson
in a contribution to the *Académie des Belles Lettres* (22).
Banier stated that he was refuting Tyson, who had asserted
that pygmies, along with nymphs and gnomes, were fabulous.
In defence of the pygmies he pointed out that all, except
Strabo, of the ancient writers, who mentioned pygmies seem
to have believed firmly in their existence. Later writers, and
many travellers have confirmed their statements. Admitting
that the accounts were inconsistent and frequently embroidered
by the writer's imagination, Banier insisted that the fact of
the ancient pygmy race is not improbable, and certainly has
not been disproved; that the assertions of Aristotle and his
fellows are to be preferred to the conjectures of a modern
physician, *etc., etc.* Banier keeps his temper as Tyson does
not, and handles the classical sources in a much more intelligent
manner. For us it matters not whether Tyson or Banier was
right; certainly I will not attempt to decide the point for the
reader. Our interest in the controversy consists in the light
which it throws on the contemporary popularity of the pygmy
superstition. This much, at least, is clear. So far from invent-

---

(21) Tyson, *op. cit.*, p. 4.

(22) *Memoires des inscriptions de l'académie des belles lettres*, 1729, V,
101 ff. Under date of Feb. 1, 1724. Banier also discusses the pygmies
of the ancients in the notes to his translation of Ovid's *Metamorphoses*,
1732, I, 333-338. In both places he refers to a work which I have not
seen, entitled, *Mythologo Graecorum de Pygmaeis*, by a German, Hermann
Wonderart, Leipsic, 1714.

ing the Lilliputians merely on a suggestion inspired by turning over the pages of his Philostratus, Swift was taking advantage, no doubt consciously, of a very definite contemporary curiosity and a wide-spread credulity in pygmies. It is for this reason, among others, that the *Voyage to Lilliput* was universally read, from the cabinet council to the nursery.

(c) Pygmy Commonwealths Discovered by Imaginary Travellers.

Brief mention of pygmy races was made by many travellers, real and imaginary, from the early Middle Ages down to the eighteenth century (23). The index to almost every large collection of *Voyages*, such as those of Purchas or Hakluyt, gives many references to pygmy races. This section is no such index, but rather a study of the relatively few commonwealths of pygmies which are sufficiently characterized to make them fore-runners of Lilliput. These accounts have never before been collected or mentioned in connexion with *Gulliver*. They are of independent origin, bearing no historical relation to one another, and will therefore be taken up in the only remaining logical sequence, that of chronology.

In the fictitious *Travels* of Mandeville, 1371, there is an account of pygmies detailed enough and yet not too long to merit quotation in full.

"That river goeth through the land of Pigmies, where that the folk be of little stature, and be but 3 spans long, and they be right fair and gentle, after their size, both the men and women. And they marry when they be but half a year of age and get children. And they live not but 6 year or 7 at the most; and he that liveth 8 year, men hold him there right passing old. These men be workers of gold, silver, cotton, silk, and of all such things, the best of any other that be in the world. And they have often times war with the birds of that country, that they take and eat. This little folk neither labour in vines nor in lands, but they have great men among them of our stature that till the land and labour amongst the vines for them. And of those men of our stature have they as great scorn and wonder as we would have among us of giants if they were amongst us. There is a good city, among others, where there is dwelling great plenty of those little folk, and it is a great city and a fair. And there be great men that dwell amongst them, but when they get any children, they be as little as the pigmies. And therefore they be, all for the most part, all pigmies; for the nature of the land is such. The great Chan makes keep this city full well, for it is his. And albeit that the pigmies be little, yet they be full reasonable, according to their age, and know enough both of good and of evil" (24).

Mandeville's pygmies are more than three times as tall as the Lilliputians, and yet as short as any of the others that we shall study presently. One sentence is of special interest: "And of those men of our stature have they as great scorn and wonder as we would have among us of giants if they were amongst us." The normal human stature is here employed as a mean, and a purely relative mean, between the extremes of pygmy and giant life. This is an exact parallel to the relative scale set up by Swift in the first two voyages of Gulliver, according to which the Lilliputians have as much "scorn and wonder" of Gulliver as he would have of the Brobdingnagians, if he were among them. This idea is peculiar to Mandeville and Swift.

Of miscellaneous mention of pygmy peoples by real travellers in the sixteenth and seventeenth centuries one typical illustration will suffice. In *Purchas His Pilgrimes*, 1625, in a description of a voyage to Greenland we read the following:

"The pigmies represent the most perfect shape of man, that they are hairy to the uttermost joints of the fingers, and that the males have beards downe to the knees. But although they have the shape of men yet they have little sense or understanding, nor distinct speech . . . They are unreasonable creatures and live in perpetual darkness . . . Some say they have warre with the cranes."

I quote the above to illustrate the confusion of mythology with fact that is characteristic of the pygmies reported by travellers. The beards that reach to the knees, and the cranes, suggest Ctesias and Homer rather than Greenland. According to other accounts, the pygmies turned out to be a remnant of the Jewish race living in caves on a mountain in Palestine. In almost all cases of real voyages the pygmies reported were said to be over three feet tall. It is only in the professedly fictitious accounts that we find the road leading toward Lilliput.

---

(24) *Adventures and Travels of Sir John Mandeville, KT*. Edited by Arthur Layard, 1895, p. 259 ff. It would seem that Mandeville's pygmies are related in a suspicious manner to those described by Friar Beatus Odoricus, 1330.

"And thence I went into a certaine river called Thalay, which where it is most narrow is 7 miles broad . . . and it runneth through the midst of the land of Pygmaei, whose chief city is called Cakam . . . These pygmaeans are three of my spans high, and they make larger and better cloth of cotton and silke than any other nation under the sun." (*Hakluyt's Voyages*, Ed. 1904, Glasgow, IV, 427-8.

The earliest version of Mandeville is dated 1371.

In the sequel to his translation of Lucian's *True History*,
written about 1648, d'Ablancourt describes a pygmy commonwealth with more circumstantial detail than is to be found
elsewhere before *Gulliver*. As this sequel is one of the sources
for *Gulliver*, and as the pygmy story there told is unusually
ingenious, I will quote it in full, in my own translation.

"We left this island and approached that of the pygmies . . . a
very small island, not more than four or five leagues long, in contrast to that of the giants, which is more than five or six hundred.
Yet though these two islands were very near each other, the inhabitants managed to live in friendly accord under the authority of
the poets, who governed each by laws which were entirely acceptable. We were very much astonished, on arriving, to see that the
tallest men of this country were not more than one cubit tall, on
which account they have been given the name, PYGMIES. We
thought at first that they were rabbits, all the more so because we
saw them gathered together as in a warren; but on approaching
we saw distinctly that they were men. They were returning from
a war against the cranes, having won a great victory; each one
carried two o three heads of the enemy, which were borne on their
shoulders in the manner of crowbars, the pygmies holding them by
the beaks. They had taken out of the nests, after the battle, forty
or fifty thousand eggs, which their wives carried in baskets to eke
out their sustenance. It is an admirable thing to see with what
valor they face their enemies, which are as giants in their sight,
and who could with one blow of the beak break their skulls, were not
they protected by helmets made out of the shells of nuts. But
nature has given them a great deal of cunning to make up for their
weakness; and it said that they run under the cranes in battle and
break their legs, which are very slender. They were frightened at
our approach, but when they had seen our certificates, and learned
that we had passed across the Empire of Fables without creating
any disorder, they came up to us with great rejoicing, and jumped
up to our waists like little dogs, who wish to caress their masters.
The most eminent among them were mounted on rams and on goats,
who knelt like camels for their masters to mount on their backs. We
accompanied them to their huts which are dug in the earth like bur-
rows (25) but they went very slowly, and did not make but fourteen
leagues in fifteen days, a pace which was quite annoying to us.
You will say, perhaps, that I misrepresent to make them journey so
far, having given only four or five leagues as the length of the
island; but it is because their island is composed entirely of valleys
and hills, so that in reality it has two or three times the extension
that it appears to have. It was said that nature so formed the surface of the island expressly for the convenience of the inhabitants,
who lodge themselves in holes. Besides, because of this the island
holds many more people than it could otherwise.

The day after their arrival, the booty was divided, and the ceremony was accompanied by the music of reeds, which they have in
place of trumpets, and the sound of which resembles the rattling of

(25) According to Philostratus the pygmies were troglodytes. (*Vita
Appollon. Tyranoei*, lib. 3, cap. 14.) See also Aristotle, *Hist. Animal.*, *loc.
cit.* Both are quoted by Tyson, *op. cit.*, 32, 40-1.

must bring to ground by means of a millet seed shot through a straw. The field where they exercise is more than two hundred inches long; because they measure by inches as we do by fathoms. drums. After this they shot at a bird, as is their custom in a public celebration. This bird is a fly, caught in a spider's web, which they As others have remarked before me, the pygmies do not live more than eight years; and the women conceive at the age of five. As soon as their children are born, they hide them in holes, as rabbits do their young, to keep them from the cranes, who eat them at one gulp as though they were little turnips.

These little men are very ingenious; and in the evening for our amusement they gave us a puppet-show (Marionnette) which pleases them as much as a comedy does us. They are very sober, deeming it a great excess if one eat the leg of a lark at a meal, because ordinarily they eat only two or three flies on a spit, or maybe a little more, according to the size of the family. Their spits are made from the bristles of an hedgehog, but the larger ones, on which they roast the larks, are made from the quills of a porcupine. They drink out of little glasses made out of pits of cherries, and their beverage consists of two or three drops of dew, which they gather in the spring and conserve in the eggs of ostriches, which serve as hogsheads; and because they are very fond of their liquor they keep it in place of casks of malmsey. Their plates are the shells of carp, the most beautiful of which are gilded, and their dishes are little chalices of acorns. It is from these acorns that the little dwarf trees grow, for all their forests are low thickets, which nature has made expressly for them, so that they will not break their necks in trying to climb to the top. Here also we saw the vineyards which they love, because they believe the vines creep just to be accommodating to their weakness. The pygmies are very well proportioned in respect to their small stature, and they made fun of our height, because of the danger that would follow upon a fall from so great an altitude to the ground."

In the above account we may note a number of points suggestive of Lilliput. In the first place, there is the contrast between pygmies and giants. The pygmy island is four or five leagues long, and the inhabitants feed on flies; the island of the giants is five or six hundred leagues long, and its inhabitants (as is stated later in the story) feed on whales. The juxtaposition of these two races, so disproportionate in size, is the only analogue, I know of, to Gulliver's first two voyages, which are unquestionably bracketed together by Swift (26). Though d'Ablancourt's pygmies are by no means a civilized race, neither as they merely wild savages. Like the Lilliputians, they are highly ingenious in the management of their affairs. Intelligence, thrift, and technique, mark every action. They fight with unerring strategy, and carry home enormous heads of cranes by taking advantage of the laws of leverage.

(26) Passages in the second voyage make it clear that Swift is developing a single idea in the joint descriptions of Lilliput and Brobdingnag, as I explain below in chapter 6. See *Brobdingnag*, 89, 94, 109, and 110.

Like Swift, d'Ablancourt makes an effort to authenticate his story. Seeing that the reader must be struck with the inconsistency of the statement that they travelled fourteen leagues across an island four leagues long (as though that were the only improbable element in the story) he explains the apparent contradiction in a thoroughly scientific manner. The trifling nature of the amusements and sports of the pygmies is in keeping with their insignificant size, so that the traveller feels himself to be in a country where not only the bodies but also the minds of the inhabitants are Lilliputian. Here is really a pygmy world, where men's interests are as small as themselves. Furthermore, in no other account before *Gulliver* do we find the illusion of a miniature world worked out with any such attempt at consistency. The size of the normal ration is stated, it "being a great excess if one eat the leg of a lark at a meal," while in Lilliput the normal ration is "smaller than the wing of a lark" (27). And so we might go on illustrating from other details of pygmy life as told by d'Ablancourt (28), but the total effect is after all the really important parallel to Lilliput. Where earlier accounts always gave the reader the impression that the pygmies were abnormalities, d'Ablancourt attempts the reverse. The pygmy scale is the true norm in this island. The trees themselves are diminutive; and the vines creep to accommodate the little folk. The only monstrosity on the landscape is the human traveller, whose grotesque height is the object of ridicule by the pygmies, who point out that he is ill-formed to sustain a possible fall. The author makes the traveller, not the pygmy, the real curiosity. I scarely need to remark that in this reversal of the point of view d'Ablancourt's pygmies anticipate the Lilliputians.

The accounts of pygmy life so far discussed are all of a fragmentary character, covering in the original a few pages at most. There is one pygmy story, and only one, comparable to the *Voyage to Lilliput* in length. In 1675 there was published in London a book devoted exclusively to a voyage to a land of pygmies, entitled, *Gerania, A New Discovery of a Little People, anciently discoursed of, called Pygmies, with a lively description of their stature, habit, manners, buildings, knowledge, and government, being very delightful and profitable. By Joshua*

---

(27) *Lilliput*, 22. And on page 59, "(I observed) a cook pulling a lark, which was not so large as a common fly."

(28) D'Ablancourt states that "nature has made the dwarf trees grow . . . expressly for them . . . The vines creep to be accommodating." So in Lilliput, "As the common size of the natives is somewhat under six inches high, so there is an exact proportion in . . . plants and trees . . . The tallest trees are about seven foot high . . . the other vegetables are in proportion." *Lilliput*, 58.

Barnes, of Emmanuel College, Cambridge. It is a small duodecimo volume of about one hundred and fifty pages, twice as long as the *Voyage to Lilliput.* As the work is little known and very difficult to obtain, I will give an abstract of its contents.

The frontispiece shows a pygmy mounted on a goat in the act of hurling a spear at a descending crane.

In the preface, the author complains that, "Most men will admit nothing that is not obvious and only reckon credible what is visible . . . The fact of pygmy life has been established by unimpeachable authority of ancient authors of pregnant ingenuity, solid judgment, and authentic esteem . . . Why should it be thought improbable that nature should somewhere produce men of a smaller character than ourselves, considering those capital letters (giants I mean) have been known to exceed us on the other side." The author further tries to verify the existence of pygmies by referenc to the Tom Thumbs, which his readers have seen displayed at fairs. The preface ends with, "My intended discourse, if not altogether true, yet is not altogether vain, nor perhaps deficient in what may exhilirate a witty fancy, or inform a bad moralist."

On the seventh of November, the ship in which the writer was sailing on the Ganges, veered to the larboard and was driven by a cold, dry north wind into a great lake on the uttermost borders of India. There the ship moved very slowly as though the crew had cast anchor in the Dead Sea, making only three leagues toward land in twenty-eight hours. As they neared the shore, they were alarmed by a curious rustling of the leaves. On landing they were met by a few "microscopic" persons, who gesticulated wildly, but uttered no sound. It turned out that they had no mouths and consequently no voices. Their chief aliment was the smell of posies. (This description is obviously copied from the *True History.*) Their thirst was quenched by a nourishing juice, which they sucked through a small pipe into tiny oral orifices. On their heads they wore green boughs, "whose leaves seemed more vocal than their bearers, by attempting to whisper." Twenty men remained in the ship to guard the provisions, while the writer with thirty-five companions went ashore, and inland toward the mountains, directed by signs from the pygmies. On the way they met, what seemed to be children, but were in reality smaller pygmy people, driving an herd of kids. "The little imps beholding our gigantic size, ran away shrieking." One of the travellers, a poet named Eucompsus, addressed an oration to the company, to which the pygmies listened with fear and trembling. Eucompsus concluded as follows: "They must be men, not fairies or devils. I have often heard of pygmies . . . that they ride on goats. Then let us view them; their manner of government, their buildings, customs and labours, which will prove no doubt the most delectable adventure that all our travels did yet present us with." An unreasonable fellow of the company, called Pandeison (a Romanist) objected to being led to hell by a whimsical poet, and warned the rest that, "The kids and goats are the damned, which the devils are driving to a place of torment."

The first province of Gerania to be visited was Gadazolia, where lived the fairest, largest, and most stately of all the pygmies. The travellers arrived at a beautiful palace made out of well-carved

wood, called Geranophonon, "which contrary to the nature of all
other, dies when it is in the earth, but when it is felled down it
becomes more veget than before." As they approached the gate,
they were met by nine young "dandy-prat gallants, about two feet
and a half high, attired in party-coloured silk . . . Each wore a
small chain of silver, whereon a rich sword about a foot long
was hung, every one bestriding a lusty ram." The travellers replied, to their inquiries, that they had come to increase their knowledge by observing the customs of the pygmies. The travellers
passed through the castle gates, which were opened by silken cords
pulled by twenty pygmies. The visitors were ushered into the
presence of the pygmy king, an ancient little man, gorgeously
arrayed in a long robe of flowered satin. When they sat down to
dinner, a native priest came in and asked the Divine Blessing in
English. During the meal the poet Eucompsus entertained the company by reciting English poetry. After dinner the travellers were
put to sleep with poppies.

This ends the adventures in Gerania. The remaining one-third
of the book is devoted to an exposition of the pygmy civilization by
the priest Dramesco, who, fortunately for the travellers, speaks
English. Dramesco's speech is in substance as follows:

Though the pygmies are short-lived, nevertheless many of them
speak fifty-four languages, and all are well-skilled in science. The
climate of Gerania is so excellent, that lack of time is compensated
by vigilant aptitude to industry. The pygmies sleep only one hour
in twenty-four. This is made possible by the drinking of the juice
of the berry, Anthypuum, which refreshes the body better than
sleep. All of the pygmies are either gardeners, husbandmen, miners,
or militia: the last named are sent to the sea-side to break the eggs
of the young cranes and to kill the old ones. Every pygmy is contented and happy, because the desire of riches is unnatural to him,
and the ways of deceiving unknown. There are no taxes; the government being supported by voluntary contributions. (As he approaches his per-oration, Dramesco waxes eloquent in the praise
of his native land): "Our monarchial government is the most
natural and the best; all arts and sciences are cherished by the
king, who fears nothing but vice and flattery . . . We are all
naturally healthful, all honest and generous, all affable and religious. We are utterly unacquainted with prostitution, partly because the nature of our women is so modest, and partly because
they abhor to gain anything unlawfully . . . How silent, cleanly,
industrious, and loving our wives are; how devout, sober and grave,
our matrons; how loving, ingenious, and chaste, our virgins."

After Dramesco's lecture series is over, the travellers declared
their determination to leave before he should enter upon another
wearisome discourse. Bidding their hosts good-bye, they set out
on their return voyage, at which point the narrative comes abruptly
to an end.

It is hard to find any method or any central motive in the
Gerania. Certainly the work is not a satire; and it is equally
hard to see its merit as a straight narrative. The rams on
which the pygmies ride, and the cranes whom they fight, are
derived from the classical accounts of the pygmies. Most distinctly out of keeping with the ordinary representation of

pygmies is the fantastic, poetic, atmosphere of the story: the vocal branches, which the natives wear on their heads, the undying wood, the turbans of linen covered with cloth of gold, and the robes of flowered satin. All of these suggest the creation of a heat-oppressed brain. As a story of a pygmy commonwealth, the *Gerania* is very bad. There is very little to suggest pygmies at all, beyond the statement that the inhabitants are small. The laws and customs, the ceremonies and the industries, bear no essential relation to the size of the inhabitants, as they do in Lilliput, and they might as easily be applied to a race of giants. As a fore-runner of the *Voyage to Lilliput*, the *Gerania* is important because it is a *Philosophic Voyage* concerned exclusively with a journey to a land of pygmies, where the adventures are followed by a detailed description of the native life, for didactic purposes. Although it is true that the pygmies of Gerania are idealized, where in Lilliput they are ridiculed, nevertheless the two accounts have this in common, that they both employ the medium of a pygmy society for an extended commentary on life, with elaboration unequalled in any other fore-runner of Lilliput.

One pygmy commonwealth remains to be considered. In 1696 there was published at Lyons a small volume entitled *Furetiriana* (29), consisting chiefly of the witty sayings of Antoine Furetière. In it is a spurious letter purporting to have been written by a missionary in Madagascar, which describes, among other things, a race of pygmies called the Taribots. The extract that follows is given in my own translation.

"Lettre envoiée de Sancace en l'île de Madagascar a Monsieur l'Abbé de . . . par Monsieur l'Abbé de . . . sur von voiage."
. . . .
"The Taribots are not, however, less surprising; they are little savage men, inhabitants of the tops of mountains. They have their bodies covered very often with thick hair, long like that of a goat; but they have none on the face or hands. Their feet are very much like ours, excepting the soles, which are equipped with scales as heavy as the hoofs of a horse. The largest of these little dwarfs is not eighteen inches high (30) . . . Their commonest occupation is the hunt, by which they are fed. The seeds of the fir-cone serve them for nourishment; their drink is water in which they crush strawberries and red currants, which they have in abundance in

(29) First edition, Lyons, 1696. The extract that follows is translated from the Paris edition, 1702, pp. 43-53. The *Furetiriana* contains also a letter supposed to be written by a traveller in Siam.

(30) The English cubit is eighteen inches, so that the Taribots are about as tall as the pygmies of d'Ablancourt and Mandeville.

the woods and mountains. They have continual warfare with the great magots (monkeys) with blue tails . . . These queer little people are as bold as lions. They raise little animals of the shape of the weasels in France, who hunt the mountain rats, and who catch more than our hunters do with their dogs and their harriers. These rats are as good as rabbits, and have besides a more delicate flavor. These dwarfs talk and converse together like other men; they have their laws, a kind of religion, and they divert themselves. That which is most common is a kind of farce. Out of the trunks of trees they hollow theatres where they play their comedies, which consist of pleasantries and grotesque postures. One thing which is quite remarkable is that all, who go to the spectacle, go armed with a whistle made out of a reed to hiss the actors when they do not play their rôles well, and when they begin to say lascivious words or to take indecent postures. But it is never permissible to whistle *mal-apropos*. When this is done, all the others make the offender go upon the stage himself, and if he acts better, he replaces the one at whom he hissed as professional actor. But if he acts worse, he is made to leave the assembly in shame, and is prohibited from ever entering again . . .

They have a kind of 'Sacrificers' who are consecrated for the cult of their religion. The rest, who do not belong to this priesthood, never pray to their gods; they say that this should be left to those who are thoroughly devout, because they do it more reverently. When misfortune falls upon them, they take their troubles to the Tonibras (which is what they call the Sacrificer) who must perform his duty well or lose his life. They keep the Tonibras out of all public affairs, to the end that he may better perform his duties. It is for fear lest a woman be an obstacle to this, that they do not permit him to approach one . . . They have no houses on the mountains other than the trunks of large fir-trees, which they adroitly hollow out . . . "

A recent writer is of the opinion that the above "must have been known to Swift" (31), but he gives no reason for the statement. To me it seems there is little in the account of Lilliput to suggest any debt to the *Furetiriana*. Like the pygmies of d'Ablancourt, the Taribots have their own theatres, while in addition they have religion, and in this respect they are unique among the fore-runners of the Lilliputians. The interesting point about the Taribots is the fact that in the account of their priests there is very clearly an allusion, and a satiric one, to the enforced celibacy, and formalism of the Catholic clergy. Here then for the first time a custom of Europe is projected into the pygmy commonwealth. We have to do here, not merely with a regional curiosity but with an allegory of European practices: the author intends the reader

(31) Footnote of Henry Wilson in his edition of Dunlop, *op. cit.*, II, 535-6n.

to think, not of Madagascar but of France. Besides the reflection upon the impractical seclusion of the clergy from public life, there is a criticism of the "piety by proxy," which fanned the flames of the Reformation, in the statement, "The rest who do not belong to this priesthood, never pray to their gods; they say that this should be left to those who are thoroughly devout, because they do it more reverently." The account of the Taribots is the only instance, before Lilliput, of the allegorical representation of human practices under the disguise of a pygmy society: it is the only fore-runner of Lilliput, of which we can say that it was written to vex as well as to divert the world.

II.

Lilliput.

In the foregoing section resemblances have been pointed out between earlier accounts of pygmy commonwealths, and the *Voyage to Lilliput;* we will now turn to a closer study of the latter to see especially in what respects it differs from its fore-runners, and what are its own merits and defects as a story.

The chief distinction of the *Voyage to Lilliput* is that the picture of pygmy life there given is a consistent and a convincing one. Lilliput is in every respect a pygmy world. "It is not the size of the people only that is diminutive; their country, seas, ships, and towns, are all in exact proportion; their theological and political principles, their passions, manners, customs, and all the parts of their conduct, betray a levity and littleness perfectly suitable." In this attempt to portray a pygmy commonwealth in which everything is petty, Swift was anticipated by d'Ablancourt alone; and there the narrative is so short, and the detail so scant, that no real parallel to Lilliput is to be found.

So thoroughly consistent is the representation of Lilliputian life, that the reader soon ceases to wonder at the smallness of the Lilliputians, and begins to feel their astonishment and awe of the gigantic, six-foot, Gulliver, for it is the latter alone who is out of proportion to the environment. This illusion is created not merely by the reiteration of the discrepancy in size, as in the statements that six hundred beds were required to make one bed for Gulliver, and that fifteen hundred of the largest horses were employed to draw him to the capitol. If statements of this sort were all we had, the outstanding impression might still be the smallness of the abnormal pygmies. Swift's more subtle art is seen in the wholesale and persistent adoption of the pygmy point of view with regard to dimensions. For example, Gulliver's snuff-box is not called by name, but is described as "a huge silver chest, with a cover of the small metal"; his comb is "a sort of engine from the back of which were extended twenty long poles resembling the palisadoes before your Majesty's court."

The claim has been made for Swift that, not only is there "an air of truth apparent through the whole" sufficient to satisfy the uncritical reader, but that the measurements applied to Lilliput are calculated with mathematical accuracy in all cases. That this claim is not altogether true is due to the fact that, like most critical opinions, it has been pushed too far. As a matter of fact, there is more truth in the assertion than the careless reader would ever guess. What is necessary is not a general statement to the effect that the proportions are accurate; that is to be found in every introduction to *Gulliver;* but rather a definite analysis with a few illustrations to show how Swift went to work to build up his toy world of Lilliput.

The key to Swift's basis for computation is found in the earliest mention of the Lilliputians, where we read that they are "not six inches high" (62). As the average man may well be described as "not six feet high," we may conjecture that the world of Lilliput is constructed on the scale of one inch to our foot (63). By applying this scale to the measurements in the story, it will be found to be exactly right. Conversely, when Gulliver gets to Brobdingnag, he finds himself in a country constructed on the scale of one foot to our inch. Gulliver says of the first Brobdingnagian whom he meets, "He . . . took about ten yards at every stride as near as I could guess" (64). Ten yards would be thirty times twelve inches, and as the average human stride is thirty inches, we have in Brobdingnag a race twelve times as large as man, just as the Lilliputians are twelve times as small.

In stating the volume of solids Swift conforms to the scale above stated with an accuracy that leaves no question about his conscious use of it. The volume of a solid in Lilliput should be 1/12.12.12., or 1/1728 of our corresponding measure. In

---

(62) *Lilliput*, 20. Further on Swift states the scale in so many words. "His Majesty's mathematicians having taken the height of my body by the help of a quadrant, and finding it to exceed theirs in the proportion of twelve to one . . . " *loc. cit.*, 45.

(63) See the study by De Morgan in *Notes & Queries*, Aug. 14, 1858. Ser. II, vol. vi, 123-6.

(64) *Brobdingnag*, 88.

the articles of agreement drawn up by the Lilliputians it is
stipulated that,

> "The Man-Mountain shall have a daily allowance of meat and drink
> sufficient for the support of 1728 of our subjects" (67).

The same accuracy is observed with regard to liquid measure.

> "They slung up . . . one of their largest hogsheads . . . I drank
> it off at a draught . . . for it did not hold half a pint" (68).

Gulliver's 1/2 pint, or 1/16 gallon would be 1728/16, or 108
Lilliputian gallons, the capacity of the ordinary large hogshead (69). Nor has Swift forgotten the scale in describing
the bed improvised for Gulliver.

> "Six hundred beds of the common measure were . . . worked up in
> my house; an hundred and fifty of their beds sewn together made
> up the length and breadth, and these were four double, which, how-
> ever, kept me but indifferently from the hardness of the floor, that
> was of smooth stone" (70).

If xy be taken to represent the area of a bed large enough for
a Lilliputian to sleep on, then Gulliver's bed should be
12x.12y., or 144xy,, in area. A minimum of 144 beds would
thus have to be sewn together; that 150 were used is due to
the fact that the edges had to be turned in when they were
sewn together. Gulliver rightly complains of the thinness of
the mattress provided for him, which is four Lilliputian mat-
tresses deep instead of twelve. As a result he sleep on a stone

---

(67) *Lilliput*, 44-5, where we also read the following:

> "The reader may please to observe, that . . . the Emperor stipu-
> lates to allow me a quantity of meat and drink sufficient for the
> support of 1728 (1724) Lilliputians. Some time after, asking a
> friend at court how they came to fix on that determinate num-
> ber; he told me that his Majesty's mathematicians, having taken
> the height of my body . . . and finding it to exceed theirs in the
> proportion of twelve to one, they concluded from the similarity of
> their bodies, that mine must contain at least 1728 (1724) of theirs."

G. R. Dennis, the editor of our text, prints 1728, and gives the following
footnote:

> "The number is correctly given in the first and second editions, but
> all later issues have misprinted it 1724." (*Gulliver*, 45n.)

Against this statement is the fact that the so-called "AA" issue of the
first edition, 1726, which I have seen, gives the number as 1724. The
second volume of this issue is labelled "Second Edition," so that it does
not in all probability represent the best text. Dennis bases his text on
the "A" issue, which I have not seen.

(68) *Ibid.*, 22.

(69) According to our own common measure a hogshead is a large
cask with a capacity of from 100 to 140 wine gallons.

(70) *Lilliput*, 31.

floor on a mattress one-third the thickness to which he was
accustomed.

Professor De Morgan has taken no little pains to undermine
Swift's reputation for mathematical precision, by pointing out
several "inconsistencies" in the *Voyage to Lilliput*. He asserts
that it would be impossible for Gulliver to drag fifty Blefuscan
men-of-war behind him through the water (71). Professor
De Morgan states the difficulty as follows: "Could a man up
to his neck in water drag a boat which would hold seventeen
men not closely packed?" I feel sure that many sailors are
capable of doing this same feat with a life-boat whose capacity
is much more than seventeen passengers, but perhaps it will
be better on the whole to let the objection stand (72). If we
want to hunt for inconsistencies, we might find another in the
conflicting statements about the shape of the earth, which is
variously described by the Lilliputians as flat and as
spherical (73). What do these minor exceptions prove, however, if they do not emphasize the rule that in most particulars
Swift was scrupulously careful to preserve consistency?

So much then for Swift's achievements in the fabrication of
a pygmy world. Of the eight chapters in the *Voyage to Lilliput*
nearly one-half are devoted to an account of native learning,
laws, and customs, which concern the satire rather than the
narrative and will be discussed in the next chapter. In one
respect the adventures of Gulliver in Lilliput differ markedly
from earlier stories of a traveller among pygmies. In the
earlier accounts, already discussed in this chapter, the traveller acted as a spectator only. In Laputa and in Houyhnhnmland, Gulliver is likewise a spectator and little more, but in
Lilliput and Brobdingnag he plays a more active rôle. Indeed,
one of the chief sources of amusement in the story is the
effect produced among the pygmies by the performances of the
Man-Mountain, such as his part in extinguishing the fire at
the palace of Lilliput, his supposed amour with a court lady,
and his victory over the Blefuscan fleet (74).

The ideas for these adventures were suggested to Swift, not
by other pygmy stories, but by the burlesque adventures of —
the giants of Rabelais, Gargantua and Pantagruel. In some
particulars the parallel is so close that Swift's dependence up-

(71) *Ibid.*, 52.

(72) Swift would have kept within the range of possibility were it not
for the statement that Gulliver drew the ships after him "with great
ease."

(73) *Lilliput*, 43 and 59.

(74) *Ibid.*, 56-7, 66-7, 51-3, respectively.

on Rabelais is a certainty (75). This is particularly true of
the obscene performances of Gulliver. He puts out the fire
at the palace by voiding in torrents the supply of urine occasioned by drinking plentifully of a most delicious wine. The
terror produced by this performance is so great that Gulliver
is banished for this reason, among others, lest he "might at
another time raise an inundation by the same means to drown
the whole palace" (76). Similarly, on the occasion of Gulliver's first relief of natural necessity, the pygmies "immediately opened to the right and left . . . to avoid the torrent
which fell with such noise and violence" (78). The prototype
for this in Rabelais is as follows:

> "How Gargantua Paid his Beverage to the Parisians," (Book I,
> chapter 17).

> "Et tant molestement le poursuyvirent, qu'il feut contrainct soy
> reposer suz les tours de l'église nostre Dame. Auquel lieu estant,
> et voyant tant de gens à l'entour de soy, dist clerement: 'Je croy que
> ces marroufles voulent que je leurs paye icy ma bien venue et mon
> proficiat? C'est raison. Je leur voys donner le vin, mais ce ne
> sera que par rys.' Lors, en soubriant, destacha sa belle braguette,
> et, tirant so mentule en l'air, les compissa si aigrement qu'il en
> noya deux cens soixante mille quatre cens dix et huyt, sans les
> femmes et petiz enfants. Quelque nombre d'iceulx evada ce pisse-
> fort a legereté des pieds" (79).

This type of obscene incident is found frequently in Rabelais.

> "Je men voys doncques (dit il) pisser mon malheur. Lors pissa si
> copieusement, que l'urine trancha le chemin aux pelerins."
> "Soubdain print envie à Pantagruel de pisser . . . et pissa parmy
> leur camp si bien et copieusement qu'il les noya tous; et y eut
> deluge particulier dix lieues à la rond" (80).

From the character of Swift's quotations from Rabelais, cited
in a previous chapter (81), it is evident that his use of filth,
and particularly its manifestation in the *Voyage to Lilliput,*
was modelled on Rabelais.

The warfare carried on between Gulliver and the pygmies
is also distinctly reminiscent of Rabelais; both in respect to
the feeble effect of the shots upon the giants, and in respect

---

(75) See discussion of Swift's borrowings in chapter 4, above.

(76) *Lilliput*, 72. "Articles of Impeachment against Quinbus Flestrin."

(78) *Lilliput*, 24. Swift's obscene passages are disgusting rather than
suggestive, with one exception. I will not quote, but merely refer the
reader to *Lilliput*, 42.

(79) *Oeuvres de Rabelais*, 1858. (Bibliothèque Elzévirienne, vols. 114,
115.) The quotations are from I, 154; and from chapter 38, I, 117.

(80) *Ibid.*, Bk. II, chapter 28. Vol. I, 308.

(81) See chapter 4, above.

to the latter's fear for his eyes as the only points of vulner-
ability. In describing the fight Gulliver says,

> "In an instant I felt above an hundred arrows . . . which pricked
> me like so many needles . . . Some of them had the impudence to
> shoot their arrows at me, whereof one very narrowly missed my
> left eye" (82).

And again later,

> "The enemy discharged several thousand arrows, many of which
> stuck in my hands and face . . . My greatest apprehension was
> for mine eyes, which I would have infallibly lost, if I had not
> suddenly thought of an expedient" (83).

Rabelais sends Gargantua into several fights which resemble
those in Lilliput, the closest parallel being the following:

> "A ruffian gunner . . . let fly and hit him (the giant Gargantua)
> with that shot most furiously on the right temple of the head, yet
> did him no more hurt than if he had cast a prune or a kernel of a
> winegrape at him . . . Those within ran to the towers from
> whence they shot at him above nine-thousand-and-five-and-twenty
> falcon shot and harquebusades, aiming all at his head, and so thick
> did they shoot at him that he cried out, 'Ponocrates, my friend,
> these flies here are like to put out my eyes" (84).

In general, the way in which Gulliver manipulates the
pygmies, letting them dance on his hand, march between his
legs, and manoever on his handkerchief (85), resembles the
pranks of the Rabelaisian giants. Gargantua all but devours
six pilgrims who have fallen accidentally into his salad (86);
and Pantagruel covers a whole army with his tongue to protect them from a shower of rain (87). Then, too, in the feeding

---

(82) *Lilliput*, 21 and 30.
(83) *Ibid.*, 52.
(84) Rabelais, Bk. I, chapter 36.
(85) *Lilliput*, 38, 42, and 40-1, respectively.
(86) Rabelais, Bk. I, chapter 38.
(87) Ibid., Bk. II, chapter 27. For the sake of completeness, and for
no other reason, I will quote here Rabelais' story of the pygmies created
by Pantagruel, a good example of the disgusting sort of thing that
Rabelais intends to be amusing.

> "Ce voyant, Pantagruel en voulut autant faire; mais du pet qu'il
> fist la terre trembla neuf lieues à la ronde, duquel avec l'air cor-
> rumpu engendra plus de cinquante et troys mille petitz hommes
> nains et contrefaictz, et d'une vesne qu'il fist engendra autant de
> petites femmes acropies, comme vous en voyez en plusieurs lieux
> . . . 'Et quoy,' dist Panurge, 'voz petz sont-ilz tant fructueux?
> Par Dieu, voicy de belles savates d'hommes et de belles vesses de
> femmes; il les fault marier ensemble, ilz engendreront des mouches
> bovines.' So did Pantagruel, and called them pygmies. Those he
> sent to live in an island thereby, where, since that time, they are
> increased mightily; but the cranes make war against them con-
> tinually, against which they do most courageously defend them-
> selves . . . for these little ends of men and dandy-prats are
> commonly very testy and choleric." (Rabelais, Bk. II, chapter 27.)

and clothing of Gulliver, Swift is repeating ideas of Rabelais, although the procedure is vastly different.   Two hundred seamstresses are employed to make Gulliver's shirts (88); three hundred tailors to make his clothes; three hundred cooks to dress his vituals; and one hundred and twenty waiters to pass the dishes of meat, barrels of wine, and the fowl of which Gulliver could take up twenty or thirty at the end of his knife. Orders are given to prepare for the Man-Mountain a daily supply of "six beeves, forty sheep, and other victuals . . . together with a proportionable quantity of bread, and wine, and other liquors (89).   The capacity of Pantagruel is even greater.

> "At every one of his meals he supped up the milk of four thousand six hundred cows; and to make him a skillet there were set to work all the braziers of Anjou, Normandy, and Lorrain" (90).

The food prepared for Gargantua's supper includes,

> "Sixteen oxen, three heifers, two-and-thirty calves . . . three hundred barrow pigs souced in sweet wine, eleven score partridges . . . For venison . . . only eleven wild boars . . . and eighteen fallow deer . . . " (91).

and a great deal more that would take too long to quote. Rabelais devotes a whole chapter (92) to the task of clothing Gargantua, a task which requires eleven hundred and five ells and a third of white broadcloth for his breeches alone.   There is not, of course, any correspondence between these figures and those in *Gulliver*, but it is obvious enough, to any one who will compare the two narratives, that in feeding and clothing Gulliver, as well as in the obscene and ludicrous character of Gulliver's antics in Lilliput, Swift is following the lines of grotesque humor devised by his master, Rabelais.

---

(88) *Lilliput*, 64-5.
(89) *Ibid.*, 32.
(90) Rabelais, Bk. II, chapter 4.
(91) *Ibid.*, Bk. I, chapter 37.
(92) *Ibid.*, Bk. I, chapter 4.

CHAPTER 6

The Philosophy of the *Voyage to Lilliput*.

The romantic and fictional elements in *Lilliput* are related
to the literature of pygmy peoples, which, as shown in the
preceding chapter, took diverse forms in the writings of Swift's
predecessors, from Homer to Addison in poetry, and from
Ctesias to Antoine Furetière in books of travel. The didactic
content of the *Voyage to Lilliput* can not claim so rich an
ancestry. In satiric method it conforms to the Utopian setting
of the *Philosophic Voyages* in one chapter only (93) ; in its
broader philosophic premise it is even more unique. From
this latter point of view, our study of the literary relations
of the *Voyage to Lilliput* will of necessity be brief, for its
relatives are few.

In respect to one fundamental idea the *Voyages to Lilliput*
and *Brobdingnag* must be considered together (94), and that
idea is the relativity of human life and of its values. It is
clear that Swift intends mankind to be viewed in three different aspects. The first representative of the race is Gulliver
himself, a typical human being, in no way extraordinary, who
learns many things, in the course of his travels, to the shame
and humiliation of his race. Certain lessons learned by Gulliver in Lilliput are intended likewise to instruct the reader,
among which may be counted the idea that a false accuser
should, in accordance with absolute justice, be treated with
the same severity usually shown in our courts to a guilty

---

(93) *Lilliput*, chapter 6, where the Lilliputians are no longer the representatives of man, but a utopian race. See further below, page 111.

(94) Swift has made the joint theme of the first two voyages very
clear. Gulliver compares his status in Brobdingnag with his earlier
position in Lilliput.

"In this terrible agitation of mind I could not forbear thinking of
Lilliput, whose inhabitants looked upon me as the greatest prodigy
that ever appeared in the world . . . I reflected what a mortification it must prove to me to appear as inconsiderable in this nation,
as one Lilliputian would be among us." (*Brob.*, 89. See also 94,
and note 98, below.)

than open theft; that good morals as well as great ability are
desirable in the discharge of public responsibility; and that
our puritanic notion that a father should tyrannize over his
children like a Hebrew patriarch, is all wrong, inasmuch as
a child is not born by his own choice nor is birth into this
miserable world such a blessing that he is under obligation to
his parents for any favor (95). In the exposition of these
precepts, Swift is instructing Gulliver, and through Gulliver,
his readers. Here Gulliver is man. So also in the incident of
Gulliver's discharge of the necessities of nature (96), a circumstance unnecessarily expanded for the loathsome effect,
Swift is certainly reminding the reader of the disgusting
necessities of his own life, an early attack on human vanity
later intensified by the description of the filthy Yahoo. In all
these passages, Gulliver is the allegorical representative of
man, as truly as Christian is in *Pilgrim's Progress*.

In the second place Swift represents the human race in the
life and actions of the Lilliputians, a race of pygmies six
inches tall. The Lilliputians mimic mankind (97), strutting
about with exaggerated and absurd pride of rank, being
governed in a childish manner by a Hanoverian sovereign
who distributes ribbons and trains his courtiers to jump over a
stick. Swift implies that man is in effect a Lilliputian; not
only is the physical disparity no real distinction, but the mental
and moral aspect of human civilization is as absurd and as
petty as that of Lilliput. Finally in the persons of the Brobdingnagians, Swift pictures mankind grotesquely magnified,
so as to bring out into the light of day the coarse and unpleasant features of the human body, which is viewed by Gulliver
offender; that a breach of trust is a more serious moral sin

---

(95) See, above, note 93. Swift makes it clear enough that these
particular customs of the Lilliputians do not represent the pratices of
his "own dear country," as do the wars of the Big-Endians and the
Little-Endians, *etc.*

> "There are some laws and customs in this empire very peculiar;
> and if they were not so directly contrary to those of my own dear
> country, I should be tempted to say a little in their justification."
> (*Lilliput*, 59.)

(96) *Lilliput*, 28.

(97) See Swift's own statement of this satiric concept, in the words of
the King of Brobdingnag, quoted below, page 105.

at close range (98). Of this, more in a later chapter. To the
parts played by Gulliver and by the Lilliputians respectively
in the satire of the first voyage, I will return later. First of
all it is necessary to discuss the underlying theory of relativity,
by which man is seen not only as a well-proportioned being of
respectable deportment, but as a strutting puppet and a disgusting overgrowth as well.

The search in literature for a fore-runner of this satiric
concept with the implications regarding human values given it
by Swift, has been carried through without reward. As far
as the purely physical side of the picture is concerned, however, we find an interesting discussion of the relativity of all
magnitude in Berkeley's *Theory of Vision,* published in
1709 (99). Swift was a close friend of the philosopher, and
an admirer of his writings. Repeated allusions in his letters
and other prose writings prove that Swift was associated with
Berkeley for many years (100), visited with him, dined with
him (101), recommended him for a position of responsi-

---

(98) *Brob.,* 94. After describing the nauseous appearance of the
nurse's breast, whose "nipple was about half the bigness of my head,
and the hue both of that and the dug so varied with spots, pimples, and
freckles," Gulliver says,

> "This made me reflect upon the fair skins of our English ladies,
> who appear so beautiful to us, only because they are of our own
> size, and their defects not to be seen but through a magnifying
> glass, where we find by experiment that the smoothest and whitest
> skins look rough and coarse and ill-coloured. I remember when I
> was at Lilliput the complexion of those diminutive people appeared
> to me the fairest in the world, and talking upon this subject with
> a person of learning there, who was an intimate friend of mine, he
> said that my face appeared much fairer and smoother when he
> looked on me from the ground, than it did upon a nearer view . . .
> which he confessed was at first a very shocking sight. He said he
> could discover great holes in my skin, that the stumps of my beard
> were ten times stronger than the bristles of a boar, and my com-
> plexion made up of several colours altogether disagreeable; al-
> though I must beg leave to say for myself, that I am as fair as
> most of my sex . . . and very little sunburnt by my travels. On
> the other hand, discoursing of the ladies in that Emperor's court,
> he used to tell me one had freckles, another too wide a mouth, a
> third too large a nose, nothing of which I was able to distinguish."

(99) *An Essay Towards a New Theory of Vision,* George Berkeley,
Bishop of Cloyne, 1709.

(100) *Correspondence,* I, 212-3, and notes. Also *Prose Works,* I,
xxxvi-vii.

(101) *Correspondence,* II, 16n. *Prose Works,* II, 459.

bility (102), and praised his philosophical works on at least two occasions (103).   Certainly Swift must have read the *Theory of Vision,* which if it did not suggest the sceptical view of man's greatness reflected in the satirical picture in *Gulliver* of man as a creature of six inches, six feet, or seventy-two feet, is at least such a significant anticipation in contemporary philosophy that we cannot afford to pass it by.

Gulliver himself points us to the "philosophers" whose theories have been confirmed by his own strange experience.   He says,

> "Undoubtedly philosophers are in the right when they tell us, that nothing is great or little otherwise than by comparison" (104).

This is what Berkeley had told the world in his *New Theory of Vision* seventeen years before the publication of *Gulliver's Travels.*   Gulliver's opinion of the Lilliputians is the result of his greater range of vision, just as in Brobdingnag his impressions are the reverse because he sees parts instead of the whole.   Similarly Gulliver's personal effects, his watch and hat, etc., are not recognized as such by the Lilliputians whose, "sight is much more acute than ours" (105).   On this point Berkeley says,

> "The judgments we make of greatness do, in like manner as those of distance, depend on the disposition of the eye; also on the figure, number, and situation of objects, and other circumstances that have been observed to attend great or small tangible magnitudes. Thus, for instance, the very same quantity of visible extension, which in the figure of a tower doth suggest the idea of great magnitude shall in the figure of a man suggest the idea of much smaller

---

(102) *Correspondence,* III, 212-3. *Prose Works,* I, xxxvi-vii; II, 457-458, and especially II, 456, from which I quote the following:

> "I went to court today on purpose to present Mr. Berkeley . . . to Lord Berkeley of Stratton.   That Mr. Berkeley is a very ingenious man and great philosopher, and I have mentioned him to all the ministers, and given them some of his writings; and I will favor him as much as I can.   This I think I am bound to do, in honour and conscience, to use all my little credit toward helping forward men of worth in the world."   (*Journal to Stella,* Letter LXIII, Apr. 7, 1713.)

(103) *Correspondence,* III, 262.   Swift to the Earl of Oxford, Aug. 14, 1725,

> "I am glad your Lordship is pleased to countenance the Dean of Derry, Dr. Berkeley.   He is a true philosopher and an excellent scholar."

(See also quotation in note 102, above.)

(104) *Brob.,* 89.

(105) *Lilliput,* 37.   Also 58, "Nature hath adapted the eyes of the Lilliputians to all objects proper for their view; they see with great exactness, but at no great distance."

magnitude. That this is owing to the experience we have had of
the usual bigness of a tower and man, no one, I suppose need be
told" (106).

The ideas we form about magnitude are, then "owing to the
experience of usual bigness," not to any objective standard.

The question of whether man is six feet or six inches tall is
likewise anticipated by Berkeley a little further on in the
Theory of Vision as follows:

> "Inches, feet, etc. are settled, stated lengths, whereby we measure
> objects and estimate their magnitude. We say, for example, an
> object appears to be six inches or six foot long. Now that this
> cannot be meant of visible inches etc. is evident, because a visible
> inch is itself no constant, determinate magnitude" (107).

There is, therefore, nothing essentially constant about our
units of measurement. Gulliver himself does not grow or
diminish in tangible magnitude; he is something less than
six of our feet, whether he is in Lilliput or Brobdingnag. His
visual magnitude, however, depends wholly on the attitude
from which he is viewed, and ranges from a huge man-mountain to an insignificant *relplum scalcath* or *lusus naturae*.
Similarly the human race itself assumes corresponding magni-
tudes in Lilliput and Brobdingnag, but in inverse order (109).
The judgments that man bases on his vision are ridiculed both
ways, and nothing is (of fixed magnitude) but what is not.
Berkeley proceeds further to summarize the matter as follows:

> "It is manifest, that as we do not perceive the magnitude of ob-
> jects immediately by sight, so neither do we perceive them by the
> meditation of anything which has a necessary connexion with them.
> Those ideas that now suggest unto us the various magnitudes of
> external objects . . . might possibly have suggested no such thing:
> or they might have signified them, in a direct contrary manner; so
> that the very same ideas, on the perception whereof we judge an
> object to be small might as well have served to make us conclude
> it great. Those ideas being in their own nature equally fitted to
> bring into our minds the idea of small, or great, or no size at all
> of outward objects" (110).

---

(106) Berkeley, *op. cit.*, section LVII.

(107) *Ibid.*, section LXI.

(109) That is to say, Swift makes his point clear by causing the
Brobdingnagians to speak of Gulliver as he intends the reader to think
of the Lilliputians; and by causing the Lilliputians to regard the Man-
Mountain in the same light that the latter visualizes the Brobdingnagians. The reciprocal scale of one-to-twelve makes this possible.

(110) Berkeley, *op. cit.*, LXIV. From this point on Berkeley proceeds
to illustrate by reference to the moon. Who, he says, can define the visual
magnitude of the moon? Nobody, because it varies according to the
moon's position, being thrice as large on the horizen as it is overhead,
while in misty weather it is larger still. Perhaps we see all objects
through a perpetual mist. (Sections LXII-LXXIX.) Berkeley's theory
has never before been mentioned in connexion with *Gulliver*.

In this last section, Berkeley is referring to the doctrine of "innate ideas" promulgated by Locke, and not to the fallacy of vision discussed in the earlier quotations. His attack is a double one, aimed at both visual impressions and innate ideas. The same position is maintained by Swift in the first two voyages of Gulliver. The fallacy of vision is exposed in the differing conclusions reached by the Lilliputians and Brobdingnagians respecting the size of Gulliver,—a size which remains constant. The delusion of innate ideas is made clear in Gulliver's discovery that mankind is not the six-foot race he had always supposed it to be, for his experiences with two manifestations of the race are, "equally fitted to bring into our minds the idea of small, or great." Swift was well acquainted with Berkeley and his writings—that we know. Whether *Gulliver's Travels* reflects the theories of Berkeley or Swift's independent ideas would be difficult to determine. The resemblance to the *Theory of Vision* is so marked, that it seems logical to assume that among the philosophers, who Gulliver says are undoubtedly in the right, is to be numbered Swift's personal friend, Berkeley.

Besides raising the philosophical problem of objective magnitude, the first two voyages suggest the scientific possibility of a series of civilizations of differing size, not yet discovered. The reader is interested, much as he might be in a treatise on ant life, wherein he reads that the ants have a civilization of their own and are subject to like passion as are we. As a book of travel *Gulliver* appeals especially to that credulity which the most scientific reader is apt to accord to the accounts of the explorer. Gulliver says,

> "It might have pleased fortune to have let the Lilliputians find some nation, where the people were as diminutive with respect to them, as they were to me. And who knows but that even this prodigious race of mortals might be equally overmatched in some distant part of the world, whereof we have yet no discovery" (111).

This passage is in the *Voyage to Brobdingnag*, the story of which is largely based on Cyrano de Bergerac's *Histoire de la Lune*. In this romance of Cyrano occurs a statement of a theory which was probably the source for the above quotation and an inspiration for the grotesque contrast between Lilliput and Brobdingnag. Cyrano suggests that there is an infinite series of worlds within our own world; that as we are insignificant objects compared to the globe on which we live (which may itself be animate) so we in turn have the appearance of immense planets in the sight of yet smaller beings. "When a

---

(111) *Brob.*, 89.

flea travels from one of a man's ears to the other, do not his
companions say that he has compassed the globe and passed
from one pole to the other?" (112)   The flea, furthermore,
mistakes the hair of a man's head for the forests of his native
land.   Something of the same sort is suggested in *Gulliver*.
Forty Lilliputians advance slowly up the left leg of the Man-
mountain (113).   In Brobdingnag Gulliver has desperate bat-
tles with the native flies (114), and escapes by a miracle from
a rat whose tail alone measures five feet eleven inches (115).
What Cyrano and Swift have in common is the idea that the
scale of life which man is accustomed to regard as normal is
only one of a series.   Just as a human body is a planet in the
eyes of a flea, so too "it might please fortune to have the
Lilliputians find a race as diminutive with respect to them as
they are with respect to Gulliver."   Swift's philosophy of the
relativity of human life is anticipated by Berkeley and by
Cyrano, only in respect to physical magnitude.   Gulliver's discovery that intellectual and moral values are similarly decep-
tive and unstable, is the most original and distinctive
achievement of his four voyages.

II.

While the common theme of Lilliput and Brobdingnag is a
skeptical rejection of accepted values, the special burden of
the satire in *Lilliput* is the pettiness of human life and the
inconsequential character of human politics.   The full force
of the allegory is perhaps missed by the reader, as it was not
comprehended by Gulliver himself, until the second voyage,
where Gulliver assumes the proportions of a Lilliputian and
resembles in every way the puny creatures he had laughed at
in his first voyage.   The text for Lilliput is expounded by the
King of Brobdingnag as follows:

> "He could not forbear taking me up in his right hand and stroking
> me gently with the other, after a hearty fit of laughing, asked
> me, whether I were a Whig or a Tory.   Then turning to his first
> prime minister . . . he observed how contemptible a thing was
> human grandeur, which could be mimicked by such diminutive
> insects as I. 'And yet' said he 'I dare engage, these creatures have
> their titles and distinctions of honour, they contrive little nests
> and burrows, that they call houses and cities; they make a figure
> in dress and equipage; they love, they fight, they dispute, they

(112) *Histoire de la lune*, 163-4.   The passage is quoted in full in
chapter 4, above.

(113) *Lilliput*, 20.

(114) *Brob.*, 111-112.

(115) *Ibid.*, 95.

cheat, they betray.' And thus he continued on, while my colour
came and went several times, with indignation to hear our noble
country, the mistress of arts and arms, the scourge of France, the
arbitress of Europe, the seat of virtue, piety, honour and truth,
the pride and envy of the world, so contemptuously treated.

But . . . upon mature thoughts, I began to doubt whether I
were injured or no . . . If I had then beheld a company of English
lords and ladies in their finery . . . strutting and bowing and
prating, to say the truth, I should have been strongly tempted to
laugh as much at them as the King and his grandees did at me . . .
I really began to imagine myself dwindled many degrees below
my usual size" (116).

Imitators of Swift caught up this idea readily, and Lilliput
became a favorite convention in the hands of grub street
satirists (117) ; but no one, as far as I know, ever attempted
to imitate the Brobdingnagian picture of the human race.
Evidently the idea of man's insignificance was, to the eighteenth century, more acceptable than that of man's ugliness
as seen by microscopic eyes.   And yet there seems to be
no parallel in contemporary philosophy to the method used by
Swift, that of a diminutive race, mimicking the civilization of
man.   The relative popularity of the satire in the first voyage
may be attributed, first to the ingenuity with which it is
developed, but also to the fact that philosophical trends in
both theology and science had caused man to dwindle many
degrees below his former size.   Ever since Calvin had promulgated his pessimistic dogma, his definition of man as a miserable, ineffectual worm, helpless and insignificant in all that he
attempts, had influenced the thought of many besides his own
followers.   Similarly the Copernican revolution in astronomy
had dethroned man from his high place in the universe and
in his own esteem, causing him to shrink rapidly and boast
cautiously.

Not to follow wandering fires too long, let us fix our attention upon the particular form of the satire in *Lilliput*.   No
earlier account of pygmy life embodies the same satiric method,
so that pygmies will not appear in the fore-runners to be
examined.   The *Philosophic Voyages* before *Gulliver*, ridiculing as they frequently do the folly and the emptiness of human
pride, do not stress its pettiness.   Indeed, in only one case, is
there any use made of a reduced scale of life to expose the
gratuitous nature of human vanity.   In the first chapter of
The Journey of Nicholas Klimius to the World Underground,
the traveller finds himself in a subterranean universe with a

(116) *Ibid.*, 109.
(117) See below, Part III.

"smaller sun, smaller planets, smaller stars, all in due proportion, connexion and systematic arrangement" (118). Klimius
himself, as he hovers in the air, is mistaken for a moon. The
only satiric use made of this reduced scale, is in this first chapter, in which Klimius is filled with exaggerated pride on discovering that he is himself of no less importance than a
celestial body, and further, on the discovery that he is the
center of attraction for smaller satellites.

> "I became now fully sensible that I was not only suspended and
> dangling in the celestial air, but that the perpendicular line, in
> which I had hitherto descended, was now changed into a circle.
> At this discovery I must acknowledge that my hair stood on end,
> fearing as I did, that I must be metamorphosed into a planet or a
> satellite, to be twirled round in perpetual motion until the world's
> end. When I considered, however, a little within myself, that my
> reputation and honour were in no wise likely to be tarnished
> through such a circumstance, and that a celestial globe, was, at
> any time, able to outlustre and eclipse a poor hungry *Studiosus
> Philosophiae*, my spirits again revived . . . I just then remem-
> bered that I had a biscuit in my pocket . . . on taking the first
> mouthful I quickly perceived that all earthly food was become
> entirely nauseous; I therefore cast it from me as useless incum-
> brance. How great was my amazement on this occasion, when I
> discovered that the biscuit not only hung dangling in the air, but
> —O wonderful to relate—began to describe around me a planetary
> orbit . . . I was now elated on beholding myself exalted, not
> only to a self-subsistent planet, but to such a one even as would
> always be attended by a moon; and therefore ought to be ranked
> among stars of the first magnitude . . . I was so immoderately
> inflated by this good fortune, that had I then met with all the
> burgomasters and all the senators of Bergen, I would merely have
> vouchsafed them a single glance, in order to have looked down
> upon them as insignificant atoms" (119).

Before he has travelled very far in the underworld, Klimius
discovers that his self-satisfaction is ill-founded. Similarly
Gulliver, intoxicated with his prominence in Lilliput where he
felt himself to be "a match for the greatest armies they could
bring against him" (120), discovers later the fallacy of his
supposed grandeur and begins "to imagine himself dwindled
many degrees."

Ridicule of mankind was no doubt familiar to Swift through
the mimicry of the puppets in the *Punch and Judy* shows.
Accustomed though we are to regard these puppet shows as

---

(118) Holberg, *op. cit.*, page 7. See synopsis in chapter I, above.

(119) *Ibid.*, 8-10.

(120) *Lilliput*, 21. See also *Brob.*, 89, where Gulliver thinks wistfully
of the country "where I was able to draw an Imperial fleet in my hand,
and perform those other actions which will be recorded forever in the
chronicles of that empire."

burlesque amusements only, it is not unlikely that an element
of satire entered into the performances. Certainly the opportunity was present to ridicule the serious actions of men, and
to represent in parody the persons of statesmen, in the figures
of the tiny puppets. At all events, it is a point of supreme
interest to note that Addison attributed to the puppets this
significance in one of his Latin poems, published in 1699,
Machinae Gesticulantes, a poem, which Swift certainly must
have read as he must have read its companion piece, the
Praelium inter Pygmaeos et Grues Commissum (121). The
following extracts from a translation of the poem will speak
for themselves; but I would call attention to the fact that
Addison had conformed the puppets, on the one hand to the
Lilliputians as, "A tiny race, and nation void of brain," as
well as further on where he says,

> "Our pomps, our cares contracted to a span,
> The little mimics play gigantic man."

and especially in the description of Homuncio, proud of his
"huge, two-handed sway." On the other hand, Addison twice
alludes to the puppets as pygmies, who have escaped the "airy
terrors of the hostile cranes." Whatever particular philosophy
may have suggested the ridicule of mankind found in the
Voyage to Lilliput, it was the *Machinae Gesticulantes* of Addison that first combined the pygmy legend with a Lilliputian
parody of the human race.

The Puppet Show, translated, 1788, from Addison's

Machinae Gesticulantes, 1699.

"The wondrous pageants of an humble train,
A tiny race, and nation void of brain,
I sing . . .
'Mid scanty scenes, like us they sport or jar,
In narrow passes forms th'embattled war;
Our pomps, our cares contracted to a span,
The little mimics play gigantic man.

But o'er the rest see Punchinello rise,
Of hoarser accent, and tremendous size.
. . .
Proud of his bulk, and 'huge two-handed sway,'
He reigns, the tyrant of the puppet-play.
Gibes his poor wooden slaves in wanton fit,
'And shakes the clumsy bench-with 'antic wit.'
. . .
And oft with glittering paste and tinsel gay,
In marshalled order trip the ladies bright,

---

(121) Both published in *Musae Anglicanae*, 1699, II. See chapter 5.

And lordlings sparkle on the vulgar sight,
While the small people, joining in the press,
Revive the dream of pygmy happiness:
As if the warlike dwarves, relaxed from toils,
In knightly glories rich, and feathered spoils,
Had quenched in gentle ease, and soothing strains,
The airy terrors of the hostile cranes.

So when the stars their middle station keep,
The sportive fairies o'er the greensward sweep;
. . .

But sudden clouds the happy scene o'ercast,
Wars, horrid wars resound their dreadful blast.
Their hasty arms the wooden warriors seize,
And desperate combat interrupts their ease.
So short our pleasures: thus our bliss withstood.
So dashed with care is every mortal good" (122).
. . .

While the Lilliputians take themselves very seriously, Gulliver is amused by their activities. He sees that their pomp is ridiculous and their statesmanship, childish. The reason for this difference of opinion is to be found in the quality of vision. Their own conduct seems, to the pygmies, imposing and dignified; viewed, however, in its true perspective from a sufficient altitude, life in Lilliput loses its importance and becomes extremely provincial. If a giant from Brobdingnag should come across Lilliput, it is questionable whether he would even notice the existence of the beautiful city of Milendo, while the emperor's cavalry, the pride of the land, would resemble a troop of ants, if indeed they were noticed at all. From this point of view, Swift's theory of relativity amounts to this: that man's egotism is the result of his failure to see human life as a whole, in its proper relation to the universe. Unable to see over the heads of his fellows, man has been foolish enough to accept the homage reflected in their eyes. The real aspect of civilization would appear at once in all its absurdity to any one who could look down upon it as Gulliver looks down on Lilliput. For the source of the satiric theory we must turn once more to the works of Lucian, which have been shown already to have influenced the composition of *Gulliver's Travels* at a number of points (123). In his satire entitled *Icaromenippus, or A Voyage to Heaven* (124), Lucian represents Menippus as recently returned from a flight above the clouds.

---

(122) John Ferriar, *Illustrations of Sterne, with Other Essays*, 1812, I, 147-159.

(123) See, above, chapter 4.

(124) *Dryden Lucian*, 1711, I, 312 ff.

A friend asking him to describe the appearance of the world
from that altitude, Menippus replies in part as follows:

"Fancy you see a small spot, not by so much as being as the moon,
so that . . . one would wonder where were all those mighty mountains, those vast seas . . . But more intently directing my eyes,
I could discern all the transactions of human life, some sailing,
some fighting, some plowing, some quarrelling . . . To behold the
actions of private persons is very odd and ridiculous . . . not to
mention others breaking their neighbors houses, lying with their
wives, going to law, exacting usury; all which put together make a
most ridiculous farce . . . Above all I could not but heartily laugh
at those that contest the bounds of their countries, one taking pride
in living in Licyon, another that he was master of a thousand acres
in Acarnania. When all Greece appeared to me at that height not
a span over, and Attica the least part of that too. I began to
think what it was that men of estate value themselves upon when
he that had the most acres had no more than one of Epicurus'
atoms . . . But the merriest of all was to see the wealthy men
strut and look big with their rings, plate, etc., when the whole
Pangaeum was no bigger than a millet-seed.

(Friend)—But the cities and the men in them, how do they
appear?

(Men.)—I suppose you have seen a nest of Pismires, some
crowding together at home, some going abroad, others returning,
others loading out ordure . . . I believe too, since they compose a
small republic, they may have architects, physicians, magistrates,
philosophers amongst them, and other necessary members of
society. Just like these animals do great cities appear . . . "

What Swift borrowed from the above satire of Lucian is,
after all, but one idea, but it is an idea which underlies the
conception of *Gulliver's Voyage to Lilliput;* the voyage which,
when all its sources and fore-runners have been taken into
account, remains the most original and the most successful part
of Swift's most famous work.

III.

The particular objects of the satire in the *Voyage to Lilliput*
need not detain us long, for they concern the political allegory
and not the literary relations of *Gulliver's Travels.* Where
the latter voyages satirize human institutions, learning, and
instincts in the abstract, the *Voyage to Lilliput* alone is primarily an allegory of court life in England. It would therefore
be confusing rather than illuminating to trace parallels in
literature for incidents that are copied from contemporary
affairs. The occasional and even personal nature of the satire
in *Lilliput* has been recognized by critics for a long time (125);

---

(125) The political allegory in *Gulliver* is fully discussed in the interesting paper by Firth, *op. cit.* The editions of Taylor and Dennis repeat
in the notes the most significant allusions to contemporary affairs.

it is discussed fully in a recent study by C. H. Firth in the *Proceedings of the British Academy*, 1921. In the first place, it has been noted that Gulliver's adventures in Lilliput are all connected with the court. He does not live with a farmer, as in Brobdingnag, nor visit with the professors, as in Laputa. Unmistakable allusions to conditions in England during the reign of George I, have been pointed out by the recent editors of *Gulliver* and are familiar to its readers. Lilliput is England, its enemy Blefuscu is France; they are even separated by a channel (126). The colored threads given as prizes to the courtiers who leap over the stick held out by the emperor represent the ribbons of the Garter, Bath, and Thistle as Swift himself explains in one of his poems (127), Flimnap is Sir Robert Walpole, the "hobbling prince" (128) is the Prince of Wales, later George II, and so on. The Big-Endians and Little Endians (129) are no doubt the Roman Catholics and Protestants, as the wearers of high and low heels are High and Low Churchmen respectively.

The political allegory holds good for all but a part of chapter VI, which represents a distinct point of view. The satire of Gulliver's first voyage is not consistent, inasmuch as in this chapter Swift abandons the allegorical method, otherwise observed throughout, and resorts to the description of customs which are contrasted with those of the traveller's native land.

---

(126) *Lilliput*, 51. Swift has reversed the situation, making France an island, and England part of the mainland. Later, in various imitations of *Gulliver*, Blefuscu represented Ireland, but Lilliput was always England. See note 18, above.

(127) *Ibid.*, 39-40. I quote the following poem of Swift, written in 1725, from W. E. Browning's edition of Swift's *Poems*, I, 203, (Bohn Library, 1910):

> "Verses On the Revival of the Order of the Bath,
> During Walpole's Administration"

> "Quoth King Robin, our ribbons I see are too few
> Of St. Andrew's the green, and St. George's the blue.
> I must find out another of colour more gay,
> That will teach all my subjects with pride to obey.
> · · ·
> And he who'll leap over a stick for the King
> Is qualified best for a dog in a string."

The ribbons awarded in Lilliput are green, blue, and red.

(128) *Lilliput*, 49.

(129) *Ibid.*, 49-50.

In this chapter Lilliput is not England, but is Lilliput, a foreign country in which the traveller observes strange and excellent customs. The chapter is obviously an addition, inserted after Swift had worked out the general scheme for the *Voyage to Lilliput* (132). Its inclusion is an artistic fault, an inexcusable mistake. Apparently Swift allowed himself to be misled by the impatience of the satirist, to the confusion of the narrator's art. The ingenious illusion created with the greatest care, is all but destroyed by this diversion between the acts. That the inconsistent character of chapter VI has not been more frequently noted is itself a tribute to the success with which the earlier chapters have dispelled the reader's suspicion of any inconsistency.

In this chapter the Lilliputians are credited with rather common Utopian customs: a party, wrongfully accused of any crime, is recompensed for his loss of time four-fold and receives a decoration from the emperor. Lack of good faith in trustees is considered worse than theft; and rewards for the law-abiding, of greater importance than punishment for law-breakers. Public officers are required to be morally upright as well as professionally capable. As in More's *Utopia*, "the disbelief of a Divine Providence renders a man uncapable of holding any public station" (133). Another belief attributed to the Lilliputians was probably suggested by a passage in Cyrano. Gulliver says,

> "They will never allow, that a child is under any obligation to his father for begetting him, or to his mother for bringing him into the world, which, considering the miseries of human life, was neither a benefit in itself, nor intended so by his parents, whose thoughts

---

(132) This is made clear by Firth, *op. cit.* In Lilliput, chapter 4, page 47, Gulliver says,

> "I shall not anticipate the reader with further descriptions of this kind, because I reserve them for a greater work . . . containing a general description of this empire . . . with a particular account of . . . laws, learning, and religion . . . their peculiar manners and customs . . . "

At the opening of chapter 6, Swift indicates that he is departing from the scheme of the "greater work" and is inserting some of the reserved ideas into the *Voyage to Lilliput*.

> "Although I intend to leave the description of this empire to a particular treatise, yet in the meantime I am content to gratify the curious reader with some general ideas" (p. 58).

(133) *Lilliput*, 61. See More's *Utopia*, Everyman ed. page 102. Also chapter 4, note 78, above.

in their love-encounters were otherwise employed . . . Their opinion is, that parents are the last of all others to be trusted with the education of their own children" (134).

In Cyrano we find,

"Ainsi peut-être vous n'êtes non plus redevable à votre père de la vie qu'il vous a donnée, que vous la seriez au Pirate qui vous auroit mis à la chaîne, parce qu'il vous nourriroit. Et je veux même qu'il vous eût engendré Prince, qu'il vous eût engendré Roi: un présent perd son mérite, lorsqu'il est fait sans le choix de celui qui le reçoit . . . Votre père consulta-t-il votre volonté, lorsqu'il embrassa votre mère? Vous demanda-t-il si vous trouviez bon de voir ce siècle-là, ou d'en attendre un autre? Si vous vous contenteriez d'être fils d'un sot, ou si vous auriez l'ambition de sortir d'un brave homme? Hélas! vous, que l'affaire concernoit tout seul, vous étiez le seul dont on ne prenoit point l'avis" (135)!

In *Klimius* the normal order of things is inverted, and parents obey their children, a procedure which Holberg implies to be fully as logical as the reverse practice which prevails among men. In the state, *Quamboja*, Klimius sees old men grey with age playing at hopscotch in the street. "The boys, as they passed, would oft reproach these old people, and would not infrequently lash them home to their children." The native law on subordination reads,—"Old man and old women shall be dutiful and obedient to their children."

The account of the education of children and their lack of filial obligations ends the section which Swift seems to have inserted at a later date. From that point on to the end of the sixth chapter the narrative is a part of Gulliver's original adventures in Lilliput.

Though appreciation is not the chief concern of this study, a final word regarding the satire of the *Voyage to Lilliput* may not be out of place. Swift delivers a well-aimed blow at human vanity, at false sources of pride, at man's exaggerated conception of his own importance, and the blow is remarkably effective. The attack is successful, above all, because it is carried through in good honour; the feeble note of bitterness is absent, and in its place there is the deadly note of genial ridicule, deadly because it wins admiration and persuades the reader. The distinctive charm of Gulliver's first voyage is the equality between the story and the satire, the harmony between theme and adventure. The absurdity of human pomp is unfolded

---

(134) *Ibid.*

(135) *Histoire de la lune*, 156-7. Quoted by Hönncher, *Anglia*, X, 142, who was the first to notice the parallel.

with perfect naturalness and propriety by the strutting pygmies. The author does not have to suspend the narrative to deliver a wearisome invective. In the adventures related, story and philosophy are equally important, mutually appropriate, and evenly balanced. Swift's literary art is supreme in *Lilliput*, holding his indignation in check and preventing that unpleasant exaggeration of satire, which, in the fourth voyage, mars the narrative. In the *Voyage to Lilliput* more than in any of the others, the reader is betrayed into joining with Swift in laughing at his own,

"Tiny race, and nation void of brain."

The Travels of Lemuel Gulliver

II

Brobdingnag

"I reflected what a mortification it must prove to me to appear as inconsiderable in this nation as one single Lilliputian would be among us."

(Brobdingnag, chapter 1.)

CHAPTER 7

Brobdingnag—The Land of Giants

In the preceding chapters I have tried to show that the Lilliputians were, to some extent, an outgrowth of a very definite and ancient pygmy myth. The preliminary sketch of the *Travels*, included in the *Memoirs of Martinus Scribblerus*, 1714, stated,

> "That in his first voyage he was carried by a prosperous storm to a discovery of the ancient Pygmean empire" (1).

Many classical writers had testified to the existence of the pygmies; imaginary travellers had repeatedly reported their discovery of the race; and scholars were actually debating the fact of pygmy life during Swift's lifetime. Unfortunately for the popularity of the second *Voyage*, there was no so unified and definite credulity about giants. Nearly every locality had its giant mythology, but no authoritative tradition about giants held sway over the minds of the public. As a result, we find that the inhabitants of Brobdingnag resemble the giants of various, independent stories, to each of which they must be compared in turn. Lest the reader remain in doubt as to the result of this study, I will state here, that the only thesis that I hope to prove is the negative one, that the giants in *Gulliver's Travels* do not represent any single, local tradition.

I.

Giants of Mythology and Folk-lore.

The Brobdingnagians bear no special resemblance to the giants of classical mythology. The *Memoirs of Martinus* advertise the second voyage as follows:

> "In his second (voyage) he was happily shipwrecked on the land of the giants, the most humane people in the world" (2).

Neither in this statement nor in the account of the Brobdingnagians is there any attempt to recall the classical giants. The Titans, for example, were by no means humane, but were fierce, barbarous brutes. The Homeric story of Ulysses among

---

(1) *Pope's Works*. Elwin and Courthope, 1886, X, 337-8. *Memoirs of Martinus Scriblerus*, chapter xiii.

(2) *Ibid.*

the Cyclops, one of the most ancient of all *Imaginary Voyages,*
affords a good illustration of the classical giant. Polyphemus
is a cannibalistic, untamed cave-dweller of prodigious size and
strength, but of negligible mentality. In a *Philosophic Voyage*
the Cyclops would have been useless. In the first place they
had no civilization for the traveller to study; and in the
second place they made short work of their visitors. To be like the
Brobdingnagians a race of giants must be humane and
friendly, otherwise no exchange of ideas is possible. The classical giant is fundamentally unapprochable (3).

The humorous giants of Germanic mythology, on the other
hand, do share some of the qualities of the Brobdingnagians.
They are hospitable, fraternal, and gifted with a sense of
humor which expresses itself in practical jokes. The familiar
adventures of Thor in the court of Utgard-Loki illustrate well
the character of the northern giant; he is, on the whole, well-
disposed toward his guests, while even his most bloody deeds
are done in jest rather than in malevolence. The story of
Thor and Loki, as given in the *Prose Edda* covers more than
thirty pages; what follows is quoted from the excellent
synopsis by Kaufmann.

> "At dawn, Thor left the house and found an enormous man asleep
> and snoring mightily. When the man awoke, he gave his name
> as Skrymir . . . Then Thor perceived that they had used the
> glove for shelter for the night, and that he had taken refuge in
> the thumb. Skrymir offered to travel with them, and took food
> for them all in a bundle on his back. In the evening they rested
> under a great oak. The giant soon fell asleep, and as Thor could
> not undo the straps of his wallet, he had to go fasting. In his
> anger at this he struck Skrymir with his hammer on the forehead.
> The giant awoke, asking whether an oak leaf had fallen on his
> head. Twice again Thor's hammer struck him, but he did not
> feel it . . .
>
> Thor, with his companions, then visited Utgard-Loki, a giant
> dwelling far away at the edge of the earth. Loki showed his skill
> in eating . . . Thor in drinking. Thrice he raised the drinking-
> horn to his lips and found at the end that the liquor was only a
> little lower. Then a cat came running in. Thor put his hand
> under her body, but was able only to raise one of her feet from
> the ground. Finally, Thor wished to wrestle. Utgard-Loki gave
> him as his antagonist an old woman, . . . and Thor was easily
> thrown by her. In the end it appeared that Utgard-Loki was no
> other than Skrymir, who had thus continued to make game of
> Thor" (4).

---

(3) For a study of the classical myths of giants, see the dissertation
by Heinrich Spindler, *Der Gigantenmythus in seiner älteren Uberlie-
ferung.* Leipsic, 1888.

(4) Friederich Kaufmann, *Northern Mythology.* Translated by M.
S. Smith, 62-3.

In this Eddic myth, as in the *Voyage to Brobdingnag,* the giants are kind to the traveller, laugh at his conceit, and enjoy the predicaments into which he falls. The mighty Thor, beaten by an old woman, and Gulliver (the mighty hero of the Blefuscan war) abused by the baby, dwarf, and monkey in Brobdingnag, are not dissimilar examples of the indulgent, grotesque, but always fraternal spirit of the Germanic giant (5).

Several years ago a contributor to *Modern Language Notes,* A. C. L. Brown, pointed out resemblances between Gulliver's adventures in Brobdingnag and an Irish folk-tale entitled, "The King of the Lepracane's Journey to Emania, and How the Death of Fergus Mac Leide, King of Ulidia was Brought About" (6). Brown stated it as his opinion that no influence of the Irish tale upon Swift can be asserted, for although Swift lived for many years in Ireland there is no evidence of interest on his part in Irish folk-lore. To my mind the parallel is not less interesting on that account. The synopsis that follows will give the reader an idea of the resemblance to *Brobdingnag,* but it must fail utterly to do justice to the charm of the complete story.

> Iubhdan, King of the Luchra, brags, at a feast, of the peerless might of his warriors. The poet Esirt says, "'I wot of a province that is in Ireland, and one man of them would lift captives from all four battalions that here ye muster of the Luchra.'" Esirt is arrested for the insolent speech, but is released so that he may produce proof for his assertion.
>
> When Esirt comes to Emania, the gate-keeper "beheld there a tiny man, extraordinarily comely and of a most gallant carriage, in respect of whom the close-cropped grass of the green was so long that it reached to his knee, aye to the thick of his thigh." The gate-keeper reports the wonder to King Fergus. "All inquired whether he (Esirt) were less than Aedh: this Aedh being Ulster's poet and a dwarf that could stand on full-sized men's hands; but the gate-keeper said, 'Upon Aedh's palm, he, by my word, would have room enough.' Whereupon the guests, with pealing laughter, desired to see him . . . Then all, both men and women, had free access to him, but Esirt cried, 'Huge men that ye are, let not your infected breaths so closely play upon me, but suffer yon small man, that is the least of you to approach me; who, little though he be, would yet in the land where I live be accounted of great stature.' Into the great house, therefore, and he standing upon his palm, the poet Aedh bore him off."

---

(5) The giant lore of the English race follows the Germanic rather than the classical tradition. The resemblance between Swift's giants and the giants of contemporary folk-lore is pointed out, below, 122-3.

(6) *Mod. Lang. Notes,* XIX, 45-6. Another Irish tale relates the story of a dwarf who stands on the hands of his giant hosts. See, *More Celtic Fairy Tales,* by Joseph Jacobs. Compare also, Alfred Nutt, *Voyage of Bran,* I, 201n.

Esirt is brought into the assembly, then in the enjoyment of a feast, and refuses the food offered to him. " 'By our word,' quoth Fergus, 'Seeing thou are a flippant and a mocking fellow, it were but right to drop thee into a beaker, where at all points round about thee thou shouldst impartially quaff the liquor.' At which hearing, the cupbearer closed his hand on Esirt and popped him into the goblet, in which upon the surface of the liquor that it contained he floated round, and 'Ye poets of Ulster,' he vociferated, 'Much desirable knowledge and instruction there is which . . . ye sorely need to have of me, yet ye suffer me to be drowned.' "

Esirt asks for a giant to return with him to confront King Iubhdan. " 'I will e'en go with thee,' . . . said Aedh, that used to lie in the good warriors' bosoms, yet by Esirt's side was a giant; for this latter could stand upon Aedh's palm." A magic horse carries them across the waters. On their return, the people of the Luchra cry, " 'Esirt approaches and a giant bears him company.' " Esirt replies, " 'No giant is he, but Ulster's poet . . . and the king's dwarf. In the land whence he comes he is the least, so that in their great men's bosoms he lies down and . . . stands on the flat of their hands. For all which he is yet such that before him ye would do well to be careful of yourselves.' 'Alack man,' they cried to Esirt, 'Thy giant is huge indeed.' "

Iubhdan is interested but not wholly convinced. He, together with his queen, Bebo, mount the magic horse and set out for Emania. "They gained the inside of the palace and found there the great cauldron having in it the remnant of the people's porridge. Iubhdan drew near, but might by no means reach it from the ground. 'Get thee upon thy horse,' said Bebo, 'And from the horse upon the cauldron's brim.' This he did but, the porridge being too far down and his arm too short, could not reach the shank of the silver ladle that was in the cauldron; whereupon he, making a downward effort, his foot slipped, and up to his very navel he fell into the cauldron . . . In which plight when they saw him the people sent up a mighty roar of laughter . . . 'My conscience,' said the King, . . . 'What art thou at all mannikin, and out of what region come?' "

"Said Iubhdan, 'But if it may please thee to show me some favour, suffer me no longer to be among yonder loons, for the great men's breaths do all infect me.' "

On his return to Emania, Aedh tells of his adventures among the little Luchra. " 'Bebo's women . . . their bodies are pure white, and their locks reach to their ankles . . . Seventeen pretty girls lay in my bosom . . . The King's strong man, Glombar . . . stern doer of mighty deeds: he could fell a thistle at a sweep' " (7).

In Emania, as in Brobdingnag, a giant's dwarf is introduced as a means of emphasizing the diminutive size of the traveller. Gulliver says,

"Nothing angered and mortified me so much as the Queen's dwarf, who being of the lowest stature that was ever in that country (for

---

(7) Taken from *Silva Gadelica*, II, 269-285, Standish H. O'Grady, 1892.

I verily think he was not full thirty feet high) became insolent at
seeing a creature so much beneath him, that he would always
affect to swagger and look big as he passed by me . . . and he
seldom failed of a smart word or two upon my littleness" (8).

In a larger sense, Gulliver himself is a mean between the Lilliputians and the Brobdingnagians. His experience in passing
from the one country to the other is much like that of Aedh.
To each, the ladies of the smaller race appear fair and beautiful (9) ; and there is a suggestion of Lilliput in the "stern
doer of doughty deeds" who could fell a thistle at a sweep.
Both are of the size to stand upon the hands of the giants.
Furthermore, in the humiliation of Iubhdan, we have a parallel
to the *reductio ad absurdum* of human pride in Brobdingnag,
where Gulliver's patriotic boasts are received with amusement
by the giants, and his self-respect lowered into a bowl of
cream (10).   In both narratives there is the scene at the
giants' feast, at which the visitor and the dwarf are present.
Esirt is dropped into a beaker where he nearly drowns.   When
Gulliver falls head over heels into the bowl, he says, "If I had
not been a good swimmer, it might have gone very hard with
me."   At another time he is thrust into a marrow bone where
he makes a very ridiculous figure, to the amusement of the
malicious dwarf (11).   Another parallel is to be noted in the
common disgust felt by both travellers at the offensive odors
that oppress them whenever they are in too close proximity to
the persons of the giants (12).   On the whole, it is rather
curious that two stories of independent origin should have so
many points of similarity.

The popular tradition of giants in English folk-lore, as it
was known to the contemporaries of Swift, is best represented
by the cycle of *Jack and the Giants,* or, as it is otherwise
known, *Jack, The Giant Killer.*   The stories appeared in print,
at least as early as 1711, at which time they circulated in chap-

---

(8) *Brob.*, 100. See also the following, p. 106.

"They would not allow me to be a dwarf, because my littleness was
beyond all degrees of comparison; for the queen's favorite dwarf,
the smallest ever known in that kingdom, was near thirty foot
high."

(9) *Brob.*, 94.

(10) *Ibid.*, 110.

(11) *Ibid.*, 111.

(12) *Ibid.*, 120-1.

books (13). John Ashton, who has collected and edited these early eighteenth century versions, gives the following account of the common features of this most popular of folk epics.

> "All agree in their story. Jack was the son of a wealthy farmer near Land's End, in Cornwall, and he was . . . extremely subtle. The country at that time seems to have been under the terrorism of a race of giants, and Jack's mission was their destruction. For the greater part, as we shall see, they were a simple and foolish race, very ferocious, but with no brains, and they fell an easy prey to the astute Jack . . . Alas for the blindness of these huge dunderheads. Two strong cords had been left most imprudently in Jack's room, in which he made running nooses, and, as the giants were unlocking the gates, he threw the ropes over their heads and strangled them, cut off their heads, and delivered them captives."

In Flintshire, Jack falls into the hands of a very terrible giant who betrays his plans by talking in his sleep. So Jack resorts to the stratagem of placing a billet of wood in his bed and standing up in the corner of the room all night. The giant hacks the wood to pieces, sure that he has disposed of Jack, and is, of course, "utterly astounded at seeing Jack alive and well in the morning." Jack turns the tables as follows:

> "Crafty Jack, however, made the foolish giant destroy himself as follows: Soon after, the giant went to breakfast on a great bowl of hasty pudding, giving Jack but little quantity; who, being loath to let him know he could not eat with him, got a leather bag, putting it artfully under his coat, into which he put his pudding, telling the giant he would show him a trick. So taking a large knife he ripped open the bag which the giant thought to be his belly, and out came the hasty pudding; which the Welsh giant seeing, cried out, 'Cot's plut, hur can do that hurself;' and taking up the knife he ripped open his belly from top to bottom, and out dropped his tripes and trullibubs, so that he immediately fell down dead."

---

(13) John Ashton, *Chapbooks of the Eighteenth Century*, 1882, pp. 185-192, where is reprinted the title page and illustrations of, *The Second Part of Jack and the Giants . . . Newcastle, 1711.*

See also especially pages 200-220, where Ashton reprints, *The Famous History of Tom Thumb, 1700*, which contains parallels to the adventures of Gulliver in Brobdingnag. Tom is abnormally small among people of normal stature, not really giants. This is of course the same situation that Swift attempts to create in Brobdingnag, by skillfully proportioning the many features of Brobdingnagian life. Tom falls into a pudding bowl where he is, "lost and almost drowned." A raven carries him away "just like a grain of corn." A cook sticks a fork into Tom's breeches and bears him to the king. Tom is nearly killed by a farmer's cat, but finally manages to run her through with his sword, much as Gulliver rids himself of the rat in Brobdingnag. In the end Tom loses royal favor on account of his lustful attempt to violate the person of the queen. These burlesque stories of Tom Thumb may have served as models for Gulliver's ludicrous adventures in Brobdingnag.

Frequently Jack triumphs by magic means, employing at various times an invisible coat, a cap that would furnish him with knowledge, a miraculously sharp sword, and shoes of incredible swiftness. The implication in these cases is none the less that the giant is the victim of his own stupidity. Supernatural aids to cunning, as well as strategy of the more ordinary kind, are incomprehensible to him. He reckons on physical strength alone, and consequently reckons without his more versatile antagonist. In the chapbooks, Jack's opponents are repeatedly described as "big stupid lubbers," and "overgrown simpletons." The larger the giant, the blunter is his mind, and the harder his fall.

Our principal concern in this study will be with giant races in *Imaginary Voyages*. For the purpose of studying the typical giant of fiction, however, such stories as those of *Jack and the Giants* are of greater significance. If there be any universal characteristics of giants, they will appear in the oral traditions of the people. Swift may not have copied Cyrano, Godwin, or Lucian. Certainly he would not expect his readers to have their works in mind. Conversely, neither Swift nor his readers, nor any of us who remember our childhood, could be ignorant of the exploits of Jack among the giants.

2. Real Giants, and Notions about Them.

The Brobdingnagians do not correspond to any race of giants that existed, or was supposed to exist, in the eighteenth century; they are too prodigious to be classed with the giant peoples reported in books of actual travel. Some of Swift's contemporaries did believe in the existence of pygmies, and one old gentleman is said to have gone to his map to search for Lilliput. We are not told about any man old or credulous enough to look for Brobdingnag. The Lilliputians and the Brobdingnagians are equally removed from the normal human proportions, and yet the latter have seemed to the readers of *Gulliver* further from real life than the former. The reason is a natural though not a sound one. No human being over twelve feet high ever has been seen, while stunted babies and dwarfs under twelve inches are not unknown. Travellers did indeed report giant races, but the latter were seldom credited with more than ten feet in height. The seventy feet of the Brobdingnagians brand them as thoroughly grotesque and wholly fictitious, not to be connected with human monstrosities.

Though it is true that no one of Swift's contemporaries anticipated the discovery of a Brobdingnagian race, some of them did, nevertheless, believe in the former greatness of the human body. Eight years before the publication of *Gulliver's Travels*, M. Nicholas Henrion presented to the *Académie Royale des Inscriptions et Belles Lettres* a dissertation entitled *Un eschelle chronologique de la différence des tailles humaines depuis la création du monde jusqu'à Jesus Christ*. To Adam, Henrion assigned the height of 123 ft. 9 in., and to Eve, 118 ft. 9 3/4 in. Noah, he made 20 feet less than Adam; Abraham, he reduced to between 27 and 28 feet; Moses to 13 feet; Hercules, to 10; and Alexander to 6. For all the computations of this learned and wholly serious study the writer produced copious evidence. Swift seems to have been aware of the theory, for the book which Gulliver finds in the chamber of Glumdalclitch is said to cover "the usual topics of moralists" among which he reads the following:

> "Nature was degenerating in these latter, declining ages of the world, and could now produce only small, abortive births, in comparison to those in ancient times. It is very reasonable to think, not only that the species of men were originally much larger, but that there must have been giants in former ages; which, as it is asserted by history and tradition, so it has been confirmed by huge bones and skulls, casually dug up in several parts of the kingdom, far exceeding the common dwindled race of men in our days."

To those of its early readers who held this theory, the fiction of *Brobdingnag* must have been doubly interesting. Gulliver pretends to have discovered, in some uncorrupted current of this world, a remnant of human greatness. To those who believed that man had once been Brobdingnagian, the second voyage of Gulliver would have seemed more real than it does to us who are so sure that we know better.

3. Giant Races in *Imaginary Voyages*.

While we may look to folk-lore and to biological theories for the characteristics of the giant of fiction, it is in the fully developed *Imaginary Voyages* that we find genuine parallels to Brobdingnag. To constitute a parallel of importance, the account must treat of truly monstrous beings, not of so-called giants of eight or nine feet, and it must concern itself, not with a solitary giant, but with a race of giants visited by a traveller. Several *Imaginary Voyages* have been considered already. The stories of Ulysses and Polyphemus and of Esirt and Aedh might have been treated in this section of the chapter, were it not for the fact that they illustrate to better advantage where they are.

(a) Lucian's *True History*

Lucian discovers a race of giants on the moon.

> "The men from the waist upwards were as big as the Colossus of
> Rhodes, and their horses as large as a good merchantman; I pur-
> posely omit to set down their vast numbers, because they may
> seem incredible."

When fighting, these giants ride upon,

> "Prodigious beasts, furnished with wings, and resemble our ants,
> only they are infinitely bigger, for one of the largest takes at
> least two acres of ground."

Lucian's giants are briefly characterized as barbarous and grotesque monsters, unlike, not only the Brobdingnagians, but also
unlike the civilized giants placed upon the moon by Godwin
and Cyrano (14).

(b) Godwin's *Voyage of Gonzales to the Moon*

The size of the moon-men is a very important element in
Bishop Godwin's romance. On his arrival on the moon, Gonzales is immediately impressed by the extraordinary dimensions of all lunar objects.

> "For I observed, first . . . all things there were ten, twenty, yea
> thirty times larger than ours" (15).

The first house entered by the traveller is described as follows:

> "There was no door about the house less than thirty feet high, and
> twelve broad; the rooms were forty or fifty feet in height, and
> answerable in proportion; neither could they be much less, the
> master thereof being full twenty-eight high, and I suppose his body
> would weigh twenty-five or thirty of ours" (16).

---

(14) See below, pp. 125-9. The giants in d'Ablancourt's sequel to the
True History, are as grotesque as those of Lucian.

> "We avoided the island of the giants, although we were consumed
> with curiosity to see them, of whom we had heard many marvels.
> We were told how the giants step across rivers as we might, across
> a small stream; how they fish for whales, using for a line, a ship's
> cable, and the anchor for a fish-hook. We also heard about their
> custom of playing ball with mountains, which they throw about
> for exercise, which is the reason why one frequently finds a moun-
> tain standing up all by itself in the center of a wide plan, where it
> has been left by the giants in their play."
> (Translated from *Voyages Imaginaires*, XIII, 104.)

(15) Reprint of the *Voyage of Gonzales*, Anglia, X, 422 ff.

(16) *Ibid.*, 443.

Later, Gonzales discovers that this man of twenty-eight feet
is in reality one of the smallest of the Lunarians. He meets
another, "Much taller than the former, being the principal
man in all those parts, though there is one supreme monarch
amongst them, much greater of stature than he (17)." Here
Godwin introduces an idea that is quite original. It seems
that on the moon, merit, ability, and general intelligence, are
in direct proportion to height. No one of the inhabitants by
taking thought can add one cubit unto his stature, but each
extra cubit carries its own increased capacity for thought.

> "This is generally noted, that, the taller the people are of stature,
> the more excellent are their endowments of mind . . . for their
> stature is very different; great numbers not much exceeding ours
> . . . These they account base, unworthy creatures, but one degree
> above brute beasts, and employ in mean and servile offices, calling
> them bastards, counterfeits, or changelings. Those whom they
> account true Lunars, or moon-men, exceed ours generally thirty
> times in quantity of body" (18).

Gonzales is questioned by the King of the giants, much as
Gulliver is in Brobdingnag. Like Gulliver, too, the traveller
is in danger of maltreatment, not by the normal giants, but
by the dwarfs, though there is only one in Brobdingnag. The
two stories agree in assigning to the stunted natives a meaner
spirit than is accorded to those who have attained their normal
growth.

> "He . . . inquired diverse things by signs, which I answered in
> the same manner to the best of my skill; . . . He delivered me to
> a bodyguard of a hundred of his giants . . . strictly charging
> them, that I should want nothing fit for me; that they should
> suffer none of the dwarf-lunars, or little moon-men, to come near
> me" (19).

Godwin's giants are highly sophisticated persons, and quite
friendly hosts; two respects in which they differ from the
giants of Lucian and d'Ablancourt, and resemble the inhabitants of Brobdingnag.

(c) Cyrano's *Histoire de la lune*

The real prototype for the story of Gulliver's second voyage,
and the undoubted source of suggestion to Swift, is the *His-*

---

(17) *Ibid.*
(18) The employment of the "human counterfeits" by Godwin suggests the parallel condition of servitude in which Gulliver discovers the
Yahoos. In both stories the traveller finds that in the new world, men
of his own type are kept in ignoble slavery.
(19) *Ibid.*, 444. So also the Governor of the Houyhnhnms is anxious
lest the traveller be corrupted by contact with the native specimens of
his own race.

toire comique de la lune of Cyrano de Bergerac, the romance
which furnished more hints for *Gulliver's Travels* than did
any other single work. What follows is not a synopsis of the
story; that has been given already in the first chapter. It
is rather a statement of the parallels that appear in the two
works (20).

As far as the mere fact of a gigantic race is concerned,
the Selenites of Cyrano are altogether unequal to the Brobdingnagians, being eighteen feet high instead of seventy-two.
This lack of agreement in the size of the giants does not
affect the essential parallel between the two stories, which
consists in the constant emphasis placed upon the difference
in size between the traveller and his hosts. Throughout their
narratives, both Swift and Cyrano use the relative greatness
of the giants as a means for humiliating the traveller (21).
On his arrival in the moon, Cyrano is at once made the subject
of a learned discussion, the purpose of which is to determine
his species.

> "Lorsque ce peuple me vit si petit . . . ils ne purent croire que je
> fusse un homme . . . Ils consultoient ensemble ce que je pouvois
> être" (22).

The moon-philosophers conclude, at last, that the tiny traveller
must be a monstrosity, the issue of a debased stock, lacking
the strength imparted by nature to creatures which she wishes
to preserve (23). Precisely the same discussion takes place
in Brobdingnag.

> "His Majesty sent for three great scholars . . . These gentlemen,
> after they had awhile examined my shape with much nicety, were
> of different opinions concerning me. They all agreed that I could
> not be produced according to the regular laws of nature, because
> I was not framed with a capacity of preserving my life . . . One
> of these virtuosi seemed to think that I might be an embryo, or
> abortive birth" (24).

---

(20) For critical opinions on the debt of Swift to Cyrano, see, above,
chapter 4.

(21) Neither, however, makes size the absolute measure of perfection,
as does Godwin. Nevertheless, all three authors agree in th implication
that there is a direct proportion between the traveller's diminutive size
and his depravity.

(22) *Histoire comique*, 117.

(23) *Ibid.*, 142.

(24) *Brob.*, 105-6.

The idea that the traveller could not have been produced according to the regular laws of nature is again emphasized by Cyrano in a later passage as follows:

> "Alléguant que cela seroit bien ridicule de croire qu'un animal tout nu, que la Nature même, en mettant au jour, ne s'étoit pas souciée de fournir des choses nécessaires à le preserver, fût comme eux capable de raison" (25).

The travellers become the objects of universal curiosity; Gulliver is kept in a box, and Cyrano in a cage. Each is exhibited for money. Gulliver's master "demanded the rate of a full room, whenever he showed me at home, though it were only to a single family (26)." Cyrano's owner, likewise, makes capital out of his pet, "Il faisoit prendre à la porte un certain prix, de ceux qui me vouloient voir (27)." The function of the traveller in each case is to show off, perform tricks, and entertain the crowds in any way he can.

> "I turned about several times to the company, paid my humble respects . . . and used some other speeches I had been taught. I took up a thimble filled with liquor . . . and drank their health. I drew out my hangar and flourished with it . . . My nurse gave me part of a straw, which I exercised as a pike . . . I was that day shown to twelve sets of company, and as often forced to go over again with the same fopperies" (28).

At court, Gulliver's chief function is to divert the "Queen and her ladies, who thought themselves well entertained with my skill and agility (29)." Cyrano is similarly employed.

> "En attendant que la Reine m'envoyât quérir . . . ce bateleur me porta à son logis, où il m'instruisit à faire le godenot, à passer des culbutes, à figurer des grimaces . . . Mon bateleur s'aperçut que la chambrée commençoit à s'ennuyer de mon jargon . . . Il se remit de plus belle à tirer ma corde, pour me faire sauter, jusqu'à ce que, les spectateurs étants soûls de rire et d'assurer que j'avois presque autant d'esprit que les bêtes de leur pays, ils se retirèrent chacun chez soi" (30).

Both of the travellers are exhausted by the fatiguing exhibitions (31), in the course of which, by the way, both have

(25) *Histoire comique*, 277. See also, 143, where the Selenites conclude that God could have had no part in the creation of the traveller, as no care seemed to have been taken in forming the miserable creature.

(26) *Brob.*, 101.

(27) *Histoire comique*, 118.

(28) *Brob.*, 100.

(29) *Ibid.*, 123.

(30) *Histoire comique*, 117-8; **124.**

(31) *Ibid.*, 124; *Brob.*, 100.

to dodge huge nuts which are hurled at them by mischievous spectators (32).

In both stories, the traveller becomes the pet of the queen, and wins her favor against the unfriendly dwarf. In each case the king desires to have the traveller mate and propagate his own kind. Gulliver says,

> "He was strongly tempted to get me a woman of my own size, by whom I might propagate the breed" (33).

Cyrano is actually married to the unfortunate Gonzales by royal decree.

> "Le Roi commanda de nous ramener avec ordre exprès de nous faire coucher ensemble . . . pour faire en son royaume multiplier notre espèce" (34).

The affection felt for Gulliver by the Queen's maid, Glumdalclitch, is anticipated in the French romance.

> "Les filles de la Reine, entre autres, fouroient toujours quelque bribe dans mon panier; et la plus gentille de toutes, ayant conçu quelque, amitié pour moi, elle étoit si transportée de joie . . . qu'elle me protestait, les larmes aux yeux, que, si jamais je me trouvois en état de revoler en notre monde, elle me suivroit de bon coeur" (35).

The love of this giant maid for Cyrano is wholly chaste, but rumor is not. She is compelled to visit with him in secret to avoid the accusation of committing with him the unnatural sins practised with Gulliver by the Maids of Honour (36).

> "Elle ne m'entretint pas cette fois davantage, parce qu'elle craignoit d'être trouvée toute seule avec moi . . . Ce n'est pas qu'en ce pays l'impudicité soit un crime; au contraire . . . toute homme a pouvoir sur toute femme . . . Mais elle ne m'osoit pas fréquenter publiquement, à cause que les gens du conseil avoient dit . . . que c'étoient les femmes principalement qui publioent que j'étois homme, afin de couvrir sous ce prétexte le désir qui les brûloit de se mêler aux bêtes, et de commettre avec moi sans vergogne des péchés contre nature" (37).

Gulliver notices particularly that the birds in Brobdingnag are not afraid of him.

> "I cannot tell whether I were more pleased or mortified to observe . . . that the smaller birds did not appear to be at all afraid of

---

(32) *Histoire comique*, 142; *Brob.*, 100.
(33) *Brob.*, 144.
(34) *Histoire comique*, 133.
(35) *Ibid.*, 145. The affection of Glumdalclitch for Gulliver was celebrated in a poem by Gay, *The Lament of Glumalclitch*, included in all editions of Gay's complete works.
(36) *Brob.*, 120-6.
(37) *Histoire comique*, 149.

me, but would hop about within a yard's distance . . . with as
much indifference and security, as if no creature at all were near
them" (38).

With Cyrano, the enormous moon-birds are equally at ease.

"Ce qui me surprit davantage fut que ces oiseaux, au lieu de
s'effaroucher à ma rencontre, voltigeoient alentour de moi" (39).

At the close of their sojourn among the giants, both travellers
are borne away by native birds; Gulliver, by an eagle, which
carries him off in his box, and Cyrano, by a roc, which carries
him in his cage, suspended by a cord passed around its
neck (40).

The *Histoire de la lune* is quite inferior to the *Voyage, to
Brobdingnag*, as a story. No clear picture of the race inhabiting the moon, is given to the reader. The height of the people
is said to be eighteen feet (41), but there are times when the
proportions seem to be disregarded. The narrative interest
is not maintained by Cyrano as it is by Swift; the moon is
made a setting for lengthy and wearisome debates on meta-
physics. For us the main interest in the French romance must
consist in the relation which it bears to *Gulliver's Travels*.
This study makes it clear enough that the parallel is not alone
one in identical circumstances, and in similar turns of wit and
fancy, but in the main outline and sequence of the adventures;
and particularly in the attitude assumed and maintained by
a race of giants toward a human traveller (42).

(d) The Adventures of Hassân al Bassri (53).

Two years before the publication of *Gulliver's Travels*,
Galland's French version of the *Arabian Nights* was translated into English. It would be unreasonable to suppose that
a work of such universal popularity escaped the eye of Swift.
The renewed interest in pure marvels in fiction, which followed the *Arabian Nights* into Europe, is elsewhere dis-

---

(38) *Brob.*, 120.

(39) *Histoire comique*, 276.

(40) *Brob.*, 146; *Histoire comique*, 339.

(41) *Histoire comique*, 117: "La plupart d'entre eux ont douze coudées
de longueur." For the height of the Brobdingnagians, see, below 136-7.

(42) The best critical study of Cyrano's *Fantastic Voyages*, is the
excellent one by Pierre Brun, *Savinien de Cyrano* Bergerac.

(53) The parallels between this Abrabian tale and *Brobdingnag* were
first noted by Pietro Toldo, in the article referred to above, chapter 4,
note 7.

cussed (54). At this point we are concerned with only one
of the tales which affords a parallel to Gulliver's involuntary
intrigues with the Brobdingnagian Maids of Honour. The
story is an *Imaginary Voyage*, but not in any sense *Philosophic*. The extract quoted here is taken from the text of
Mardrus (55). I have not given it in English, because the
passage includes a good deal that by general (though wholly
illogical) consent is considered less objectionable in a foreign
language than in our own.

Having been captured by the giants and taken before their
king, Hassân is turned over to the princess as her pet.

"Lorsque la fille du roi vit Hassân, elle fut charmée de sa figure et
de ses formes jolies, et se mit à lui faire mille caresses et à le
gâter de toutes les façons. Et elle lui parlait d'une voix très
douce, pour l'apprivoiser, bien que Hassân ne comprît rien à son
langage. Mais, comme il voyait qu'elle ne lui voulait pas de mal,
il essaya de l'attendrir sur sa destinée, en pleurant et en gémissant.
Et la princesse prenait chaque fois ses gémissements et ses soupirs
pour des chants harmonieux; et elle éprouvait pour lui une inclination extraordinaire . . .

Or, un jour, la fille du roi tira Hassân de la cage pour le nettoyer
et le changer d'habits. Et lorsqu'elle l'eut déshabillé, elle vit, O
prodigieuse découverte, qu'il n'était pas du tout dépourvu de ce
qu'avaient les géants de son père, bien que tout cela fût, en
proportion, extrêmement menu. Et elle pensa: 'Par Allah, c'est
la première fois que je vois un oiseau avec des choses comme ça'.
Et elle se mit à manipuler Hassân et à le tourner et retourner dans
tout les sens. en s'émerveillant de ce qu'elle decouvrait en lui à
chaque instant. Et Hassân était dans ses mains exactement comme
un moineau entre les mains du chasseur. Et la jeune géante,
voyant que sous ses doigts le concombre se changeait en courge, se
mit à rire tellement qu'elle se renversa sur le côté. . . . Elle le prit
tout contre elle, et se mit à le caresser partout comme s'il était un
homme, lui faisant mille propositions, non en paroles, car un oiseau
n'aurait pu les entendre, mais en gestes et en actions, si bien qu'il
se comporta avec elle tout à fait comme un moineau avec sa
moinelle . . .

En le changeant d'habits, la fille du roi des géants lui avait
enlevé les objects précieux; et il avait beau les réclamer par signes
et par tous les gestes qu'on fait en arabe; elle ne comprenait point
ce qu'il lui demandait, et croyait chaque fois qu'il lui demandait la
copulation. Ce qui faisait chaque fois qu'il demandait le tambour,
c'était une copulation qui lui répondait, et chaque fois qu'il récla-
mait la touffe de poils, c'était une copulation qu'il lui fallait exé-

---

(54) Above, chapter I. The *Arabian Nights* would certainly have
attracted the attention of Swift. He admits having suspended urgent
business to read Perrault's *Contes des fées*, among the most famous of
the contemporary imitations of oriental fiction. *Prose Works*, II, 327.
Journal to Stella, Letter XL, Jan. 26, 1711-12.

(55) *Le livre des mille nuits et une nuit*, (16 vols.) by J. C. Mardrus,
Paris, 1917. *Les aventures de Hassân al Bassri*, X, 7-160.

cuter, tant et tant . . . qu'il n'osait plus faire un geste ni le moindre signe, de peur de voir la réponse en action de la terrible géante . . . " (56).

No other story corresponds so closely as this to the predicaments into which Gulliver is led by the Maids of Honour (57). Swift, however, does not describe his scene in a suggestive manner. The whole point of the incident is the loathsome effect upon Gulliver of the contact with the female giants. Their bodies are repulsive to his acute senses. Sex is exposed, stripped of all its charm. He is "disgusted, because to say the truth, a very offensive smell came from their skins" (58). In the Arabian story no such satire is intended; the intrigue is frankly and wholly obscene. And yet the parallel is an interesting one. The traveller is captured by the giants, taken to their king, and is made the victim of amorous attentions by a giantess at court. The "many other tricks" omitted by Swift are included in the oriental story. In both, a great deal is made of the traveller's unwillingness to reciprocate the passion of his admirer. The main difference between the two is in the importance of the incident. What in the story of Hassan constitutes his principal adventure in giant-land, is only a minor incident in *Gulliver*.

(e) *Wasobiyoe* (59).

One *Voyage* remains to be considered among the forerunners of Brobdingnag, and that is the anonymous story of Wasobiyoe to the Land of Giants. The narrative is much shorter than either Swift's or Cyrano's, and the adventures told are few. A remarkably close parallel to *Brobdingnag* is to be found in the details of Wasobiyoe's reception by the giants.

> "On alighting in Giant-land, Wasobiyoe espied a broad road running through a large bamboo thicket, which soon turned out to be merely a foot-path through a corn-field, where every stalk was as tall as one of the largest Japanese bamboos . . . Even the most

(56) *Ibid.*, pp. 113-8.

(57) *Brob.*, 120-1.

(58) *Ibid.* Swift seems to have been obsessed with a morbid delight in degrading the human body and its functions. Several of his poems are inexcusably revolting in this respect. See especially, *Strephon and Cloe*, and *A Beautiful Nymph Going to Bed. Poems*, by W. E. Browning, 1910, I, 200-211.

(59) For a discussion of the relation between this work and *Gulliver* see above, chapter 4.

ordinary little trees would be, some one-hundred-and-fifty, some one-hundred feet in circumference" (60).

It looks very much as though Wasobiyoe were describing Brobdingnag. Gulliver's adventures there begin as follows:

"I fell into a high road, for so I took it to be, though it served to the inhabitants only as a foot-path through a field of barley . . . I was an hour walking to the end of this field, which was fenced in with a hedge of at least one-hundred-and-twenty foot high, and the trees so lofty that I could make no computation of their altitude" (61).

Wasobiyoe is discovered by the inhabitants as follows:

"A sixty-five foot man picked him up, and putting him in his left hand and covering him up carefully with his right, as a child does who has caught a fly, carried him off to his house . . . 'What an extraordinarily tiny creature,' they cried, as they picked him up between thumb and fore-finger and made him stand upon their hands."

Very much the same thing happens to Gulliver.

"One of the reapers . . . looking about under him for some time, at last espied me as I lay on the ground . . . At length he ventured to take me up behind by the middle between his fore-finger and thumb and brought me within three yards of his eyes . . . He held me in the air about sixty foot from the ground, although he grievously pinched my sides for fear I should slip through his fingers . . .

He then sent his servants to their work, and taking his handkerchief out of his pocket, he doubled and spread it on his left hand, which he placed flat on the ground, with the palm upwards, making me a sign to step onto it . . . and in this manner carried me home to his house" (62).

In the Japanese tale the giants crowd about the traveller and ask,

" 'Where do you come from; are you a human being or an elf?' To which Wasobiyoe, stretching his legs wide apart as he stood upon the palm of one of them, and bawling at the top of his voice, made answer . . . 'If you despise me for my small stature, I will show you what feats can be performed by a fighting man brought up in the school of the Yoshitsune.' "

In Brobdingnag, Gulliver flourishes his hanger after the manner of fencers in England (63), and boasts to the King

---

(60) Quotations are from the partial translation by Basil Hall Chamberlain, Professor Emeritus of Japanese literature and philology in the Imperial University of Tokio, published in the *Journal of the Asiatic Society of Japan*, VII, 1879.

(61) *Brob.*, 87-8.

(62) *Ibid.*, 89-91.

(63) *Ibid.*, 100.

of the military prowess of his race (64). In the persons of
the Brobdingnagians he sees the ugliness of the human body
grossly magnified (65), while he pities them for their narrowness of intellect and their defective learning. So also,
Wasobiyoe concludes,

> " 'It would seem as if this foolish country were superior to the rest
> in nothing but size; tenanted as it is by such empty-headed folk.
> It is nothing more than a great, overgrown asparagus of a country.
> Diminutive as I am, why should not I . . . aspire to the glory of
> becoming a guide to this nation?' "

The circumstantial agreement of the Japanese story with
Gulliver's Travels may very well be a mere coincidence. Given
the situation of a human being, thrown among sixty or seventy
foot giants, the details that follow might easily appear
in stories of independent origin. The traveller would of course
walk along a road, which, if a giant's foot-path, must of necessity seem to him to be a broad high-way. The giants could
not pick him up more naturally than between thumb and
fore-finger; and, unless the giant were left-handed, it would
be done with the right hand, and the object placed upon the
left. The most interesting point of agreement is the idea of a
giant race differing from the traveller in nothing but size;
a conception not common to giant stories, but one that is
essential to the satire of *Brobdingnag* (66).

4. The Giant Type

It is to be regretted that it is impossible to trace through
the literature that has been discussed a unified tradition of
giant life. This is particularly true of the giant stories told
by sophisticated authors, by writers of *Imaginary Voyages*
in which the narrative is of secondary, and the moral, of primary importance. The giants that appear in *Wasobiyoe,
Gonzales, Gulliver,* and Cyrano, for example, have been
trimmed and groomed by their creators to suit the allegory
in hand. I believe, however, that it is possible to distinguish
something universal in the popular conception of giants that
will be found to run through a great deal of our literature.
This summary of a mere paragraph includes all that can be
asserted about the universal nature of the giant of fiction;
for the rest he conforms to the caprice of his creators.

It is not unlikely that the type of the giant of fiction is the
product of the character of his counterpart in real life. At

---

(64) *Ibid.*, 138-9.
(65) See, below, chapter 8.
(66) See, below, chapter 8.

all events, I find in the conclusions reached by a student of
actual giants a suggestion of what I want to say about the
giants of fiction.

> "Giants are almost always characterized by mental and bodily
> weakness; while dwarfs are generally active, intelligent, and
> healthy" (67).

I believe that a comparison of popular giants will show that,
as a rule, giants are creatures of low mentality, and of little
or no cunning; that they fall short of man intellectually, as
they exceed him physically. This proverbial stupidity of giants
may be set down as all but a universal trait. The Titans in
spite of their greater physical power are enchained by the
crafty gods of Olympus. David fells Goliath scientifically, to
the rapture of small boys, usually indifferent to their Sunday
lessons. Atlas is still carrying the world upon his shoulders,
because he was duped by Hercules. The neighbors of Polyphemus are easily deceived by a pun on the supposed name
of Ulysses. Giants fail to grasp any but the obvious meaning
of what they see and hear. *Double entendre*, strategy of any
kind, is too much for them. As Jack, the hero of the chapbooks
invariably discovered, giants have a one-track mind (68).

5.   Brobdingnag

The inhabitants of Brobdingnag share this intellectual defi-
ciency of giants in general. They are not guilty of the fallacies
of thought which are the rule in Laputa, partly because they
lack the faculty of thinking in more than one way about anything. Their merit is common sense, but not genius. The
King is horrified at Gulliver's account of Western civilization,
but it is also true that he cannot comprehend its complexity.
Gulliver orates, but the King does not. His ideas are few
and far between; he does not counter with any profound
philosophy of his own. Nowhere in the account of Brobdingnag
is there any evidence of intellectual power comparable to a
European's. The genius of the people is mute if not inglorious.
Gulliver discovers that their defects "have arisen from their
ignorance."

> "I remember very well, in a discourse I had with the King, when
> I happened to say there were several thousand books among us
> written upon the art of government, it gave him (directly contrary
> to my intention) a very mean opinion of our understandings. He

---

(67) E. J. Wood, *Giants and Dwarfs*, p. 109.
(68) No general rule about the good nature of giants can be laid
down. Though not generally as treacherous as dwarfs, giants are as
frequently brutal as friendly.

professed both to abominate and despise all mystery and refinement, either in a prince or a minister . . .

He confined the knowledge of government within very narrow
bounds . . . The learning of this people is very defective . . . As
to ideas, entities, abstractions, and transcendentals, I could never
drive the least conception into their heads . . .

No law in that country must exceed in words the number of
letters in their alphabet . . . but indeed few of them extend even
to that length. They are expressed in the most plain and simple
terms ,wherein those people are not mercurial enough to discover
above one interpretation" (69).

So the Flintshire giant was not mercurial enough to distinguish between Jack and a billet of wood. The libraries of
the Brobdingnagians are small, and their vocabulary is
limited (70). Gulliver is a constant source of information for
them. At no point in the narrative is Gulliver confronted with
superior intelligence or versatility on their part.

The King of Brobdingnag is an out and out pacifist. On
hearing Gulliver boast of the destruction brought about in
European warfare by means of gun-powder, the King,

"was struck with horror at the description I had given of those
terrible engines . . . He was amazed how so impotent and grovel-
ling an insect as I could entertain such inhuman ideas, and in so
familiar a manner as to appear wholly unmoved at all the scenes
of blood and desolation, which I had painted as the common
effects of those destructive machines, whereof, he said, some evil
genius enemy to mankind, must have been the first contriver" (71).

Even the better giants of fiction are not, as a rule, so humane
as the King. In this particular respect Swift seems to be
following Rabelais, with whose work, as we have seen, he was
familiar. Swift quotes anecdotes about Rabelais' giants no
less than three times, in the course of his correspondence (72).
In the person of Grangousier, the first of Rabelais' giants and
father of the more famous Gargantua, we find a real prototype for the pacifistic King of Brobdingnag: a kindly giant
king, who desires nothing so much as peace, and to whom
human warfare is inhuman. When asked by Touchefaucet
to comment on Picrochole's invasion of his kingdom, Grangousier replies,

"The time is not now as formerly to conquer the kingdoms of our
neighbour princes, and to build up our own greatnesse upon the
loss of our nearest Christian brother: this imitation of the ancient

(69) *Brob.*, 139.

(70) *Ibid.*, 140-1.

(71) *Ibid.*, 139.

(72) These references are discussed in full in chapter 4.

Herculeses, Alexanders, Hannibals, Scipios, Caesars, and other such heroes is quite contrary to the profession of the Gospel of Christ . . . And that which heretofore the Barbers and Saracens called prowesse and valour, we do now call robbing, thievery, and wickednes" (73).

As the invaders approach his kingdom, the old giant protests,

"All the dayes of my life I have laboured for nothing so much as peace" (74).

When asked to give his opinion of *Gulliver's Travels*, Dr. Johnson said, "When once you have thought of big men and little men, it is very easy to do all the rest (75)." This judgment will hardly satisfy those of us who do not share Johnson's constitutional dislike for Swift. As a matter of fact, the world of Brobdingnag is constructed with a great deal of art.

As in the case of Lilliput, the reader is informed of the scale of life by the description of the first inhabitant met by Gulliver.

"He appeared as tall as an ordinary spire-steeple, and took about ten yards at every stride, as near as I could guess" (76).

The average human stride is thirty inches, or exactly one-twelfth of ten yards. This twelve-to-one scale for Brobdingnag is definitely asserted by Gulliver in his account of the hailstones which struck him to the ground.

"Nature in that country observing the same proportions through all her operations, a hailstone is near eighteen hundred times as large as one in Europe, which I can assert upon experience, having been so curious to weigh and measure them" (77).

---

(73) *Rabelais*, Bk. I, ch. 46. Reprint of the Urquhart, Motteux translation, completed in 1694, in *Tudor Translations*, W. E. Henley, 1900.

(74) *Ibid.*, Bk. I, ch. 28.

(75) Boswell's, *Samuel Johnson*, under date, March 24, 1775. Aet. 66. Edition Birkbeck Hill, 1887, II, 318-9.

"He attacked Swift, as he used to do upon all occasions . . . I wondered to hear him say of *Gulliver's Travels*, 'When once you have thought of big men and little men, it is very easy to do all the rest.' I endeavored to make a stand for Swift . . . but in vain. Johnson at last, of his own accord, allowed very great merit to the inventory of articles found in the pocket of the *Man-Mountain* particuarly the description of his watch, which it was conjectured was his GOD, as he consulted it upon all occasions."

This grudging acknowledgment of merit illustrates the principle of damning with faint praise, so thoroughly and ineffectively applied by Bernard Shaw to the Scriptures.

(76) *Brob.*, 88.

(77) *Ibid.*, 118-9.

Accepting Gulliver's statement that nature's operations hold good for Brobdingnag, and applying the linear scale of twelve-to-one, we find that volumes, in Brobdingnag, should exceed ours 1728 times, the cube of twelve. A hail-stone 1728 times normal size might well be described as "Near eighteen hundred times as large as one in Europe." If this proof seem trifling and unnecessary in this place, I can only offer as my excuse, the fact that Gulliver was equally curious to verify the weights and measures of Brobdingnag. The scale stated will be found to satisfy most of the dimensions given in the narrative. The Brobdingnagians themselves average about seventy feet in height. For the most part, however, it will be found upon examination that most of the dimensions are stated in round numbers, lacking the precision shown in the measurement of rations and beds in Lilliput. For this vagueness in the second voyage there is a very good reason. Whereas it was easy for Gulliver to ascertain the proportions of smaller objects in Lilliput, to determine which he could employ the familiar units of his own arms and body, in Brobdingnag he is dependent upon conjecture. The point is that Swift is not less careful and consistent in his description of the giant country, but only less precise; and in that very lack of precision he shows a regard for his hero's ability to estimate distance (78). The story must appear to be Gulliver's, not Swift's. No pains are spared to convince the reader that Gulliver knows whereof he speaks. Of the great oven in the King's kitchen, Gulliver says,,

> "It is not so wide by ten paces as the cupola at St. Paul's: for I measured the latter on purpose after my return. But if I should describe the kitchen-grate ,the prodigious pots and kettles . . . perhaps I should be hardly believed; at least a severe critic would be apt to think I enlarged a little, as travellers are often suspected to do " (79).

The illusion of reality created is largely the result of the adoption by Gulliver of the Brobdingnagian point of view. On viewing the tower of the chief temple, Gulliver,

> "came back disappointed, for the height is not above three-thousand feet . . . not at all equal in proportion to Salisbury Steeple" (80).

Gulliver's accommodation to the giants' scale is humorously scored in his instructions to the English sailors who rescue him.

---

(78) In this way Swift hides his art, making the reader feel that Gulliver himself is responsible for the description of the countries visited.

(79) *Brob.*, 117.

(80) *Ibid.*, 116.

> "Let one of the crew put his finger into the ring and take the box out of the sea, and so into the captain's cabin" (81).

The box, it will be remembered, is sixteen feet square and twelve high.

> "Some of them, upon hearing me talk so wildly, thought I was mad; others laughed; for indeed, it never came into my head that I was now got among people of my own stature."

When taken aboard, Gulliver is "confounded at the sight of so many pygmies;" (82) actually in England again, he finds the illusion a serious inconvenience.

> "As I was on the road . . . I began to think myself in Lilliput. I was afraid of trampling on every traveller I met, and often called aloud to have them stand out of the way, so that I had like to have gotten one or two broken heads for my impertinence" (83).

I will not discuss Gulliver's adventures in Brobdingnag individually; in so far as they are concerned with the fact of giant life, their analogues have been noted already. For the most part they follow the sequence in Cyrano. There is a good deal, however, that suggests sources outside of giant literature.

(a) The Fable of the Rukh, or Roc

One of the oldest of fables is that of the rukh, or gigantic bird, which pounces upon men and elephants and carries them away. The question of its origin, which has been traced to the folk-lore of Arabia, does not concern us here (84). Cyrano is borne away from the moon by a roc, and Gulliver is carried away from Brobdingnag by an enormous eagle. In the French *Philosophic Voyage, Jacques Sadeur*, the traveller is carried by a gigantic bird, called the Urg, from the land of the hermaphrodites to Madagascar (85). Atkinson is of the opinion (86) that this incident in *Sadeur*, which is described with great detail, is based on the following in the *Travels* (1166-1171) of Benjamin of Tudela.

> "Zin is in the uttermost East, and some say that there is the Sea of Nikpa . . . Many a ship has been lost, but people eventually

(81) *Ibid.*, 148.
(82) *Ibid.*, 149.
(83) *Ibid.*, 154.
(84) The origin and spread of this fable are discussed by Henry Yule in the notes to his edition of *Marco Polo*, 1871, II, 349-353, where copious references to accounts of the Roc in ancient and medieval literature are given.
(85) *Voyages Imaginaires*, XXIV, 391 ff.
(86) Dr. Atkinson, author of *The Extraordinary Voyage in French Literature*, stated this opinion in a letter to me.

discovered a device by which to escape from this evil place. The
crew provide themselves with hides of oxen, and when the evil
wind blows . . . they wrap themselves up in the skins and . . .
plunge into the sea. A great bird called the Griffen spies them
out, and in the belief that the sailor is an animal, the Griffen sizes
hold of him, brings him to dry land, and puts him down on a
mountain" (87).

Several authors locate the bird in Madagascar (88), as does
the author of *Sadeur*. In the *Travels of Marco Polo*, the following occurs in the chapter entitled, "Concerning the Island
of Madagascar."

> " 'Tis said that in those islands . . . is found the bird Gryphon
> . . . For persons who had been there and seen it told (us) . . .
> that it was for all the world like an eagle, but one indeed of
> enormous size; so big in fact that its wings covered an extent of
> 30 paces, and its quills were 12 paces long, and thick in propor-
> tion. And it is so strong that it will seize an elephant in its
> talons, and carry him high into the air . . . The people of those
> isles call the bird 'Roc' and it has no other name" (89).

Interest in the rukh was no doubt heightened by the introduction into Europe of the *Arabian Nights* in the seventeenth
century. The collection contains at least two accounts of
travel by means of a monstrous bird; one of these, the story
of Sinbad's escape by tying himself to the rukh's feet with
his turban, is too familiar to need quotation here (90). To me
it seems highly probable that the incidents in Cyrano and
Brobdingnag are based ultimately upon these Arabian stories.

(b) Domestic Dwarfs

Gulliver's performances at the court of Brobdingnag have
their parallels in contemporary life, as well as in earlier liter-

---

(87) Quoted from the translation of the *Travels of Benjamin of
Tudela*, by M. N. Adler. *Jewish Quarterly Review*, XVIII, pp. 100-1.
The translation is complete in ten installments, XVI-XVIII.

(88) See remarks by Yule, referred to in note 84, above.

(89) Henry Yule, *The Book of Ser Marco Polo*, 1871, II, Book III,
chapter xxxiii, pp. 345-7.

(90) R. F. Burton, *The Book of the Thousand Nights and A Night*,
Re-edited by L. C. Smithers, 1897, IV, 377-8. E. W. Lane, *The Thousand
and One Nights*, III, 88. Edited by E. S. Poole, 1859.

In the eighteenth century chapbook ballad (printed in 1700) discussed
in note 13 above, there is the following:

> "Now by a raven of great strength,
>   Away poor Tom was borne,
> And carried in the Carrion's beak,
>   Just like a grain of corn."

An accompanying illustration shows Tom upside down in the raven's beak.

ature. Not only in courts, but also in the homes of the nobility,
the practice of keeping a dwarf was a common one. Frequently a giant and a dwarf were kept together to provide
amusement. Anecdotes of these domestic dwarfs, very much
like those in Gulliver's second voyage, have been collected by
E. J. Wood in his interesting book, *Giants and Dwarfs*. No
one, however, has suggested that the incidents in Brobdingnag
might have been based upon them. The following is quoted
from the account of a dwarf who lived at the court of the
Archduke Ferdinand in the Tyrol, in the middle of the eighteenth century:

> "Aymon, a giant, frequently bantered the dwarf on his diminutive
> figure; and out of revenge the latter privately desired the duke,
> that, when at table, he would drop one of his gloves, and order
> Aymon to take it up. The dwarf in the meantime crept under the
> Duke's chair, and while Aymon was stooping for the glove, the
> dwarf gave him a blow on the face, to the great diversion of all
> the company" (92).

Byron, in *Don Juan*, has quite a little to say about the dwarfs
who were kept for amusement and ornament in oriental
countries (93). One English dwarf was written into history
and poetry before Swift's time, and so clearly falls within the
field of this study, and that is Jeffrey, the court dwarf of
Charles I. The following account of Jeffrey is extracted from
his biography in Thomas Fuller's *History of the Worthies of
England*, 1662:

> "Jeffrey Hudson, the famous dwarf, was born in 1619 at Oldham
> in Rutlandshire. His father was a very proper man, broad-
> shouldered and chested, though his son never arrived at a full ell in
> stature . . . Jeffrey was presented by his father to the Duchess
> of Buckingham, when he was . . . scarce a foot and a half in
> height. Instantly Jeffrey was heightened (not in stature but in
> condition) from one degree above rags, into silk and satin, and
> two tall men to attend him . . .
> An old gossip having invited some tattle-baskets to a junketing
> court, some arch wags stole her cat, Rutterkin, flayed him, dressed
> Jeffrey in his skin, and conveyed him into the room. When the
> feast was near over, and cheese set upon the table, one of the
> females offered Rutterkin a bit. 'Rutterkin can help himself, when
> he is hungry,' said Jeffrey, and so nimbly made downstairs. The
> women all started up in the greatest confusion and clamour imagin-
> able, crying out, 'A witch, a witch' . . .
> Soon after the marriage of Charles I, that king and his queen
> were entertained at Burleigh . . . on which occasion Jeffrey was
> served up to table in a cold pie, armed and accoutred, and pre-
> sented by the Duchess to Henrietta Maria, who kept him as her
> dwarf many years afterwards. The ladies of the court were very

(92) *Giants and Dwarfs*, 88.
(93) Canto, III:xxxiv, lxviii, lxxviii, ci.   Canto, V:lxxxvii-xc.

fond of him. He is said to have scraped an acquaintance with the Queen's monkey, with whom as a source of amusement he was an equal. He was much teased by the courtiers and domestics of the royal palace, and had many squabbles with the giant porter thereof. It was a strange contrast to see him and the King's gigantic porter, William Evans, together; particularly in that anti-masque at court where the porter lugged out of one pocket a long loaf, and little Jeffrey instead of a sliver of cheese out of the other . . . first to the wonder, and then to the laughter of the beholders . . . Once as he was washing his face and hands he had like to have been drowned in his basin . . . " (94).

The life of Jeffrey suggests at many points the *Voyage to Brobdingnag.* *Gulliver* is also a queen's pet, associates with her monkey, is teased by domestics, fondled by court ladies, and nearly drowns in a bowl. He is handled by the giants much as Jeffrey is manipulated by Evans. It is not at all unlikely that Swift knew of Jeffrey, either from Fuller's *History* or from some other source; certain it is that the stories about Jeffrey and his fellow dwarfs were familiar to many of Swift's contemporaries (95). The *Voyage to Brobdingnag* differs from other stories of a traveller among giants, in the emphasis placed upon the position of Gulliver as a court toy and royal pet. I cannot help but feel that this stress upon the domestic exhibitions of Gulliver is a very distinct echo of the contemporary vogue of the household dwarf.

In 1638, Sir William Davenant wrote a poem entitled *Jeffreidos,* one of the worst pieces of verse ever written by a poet laureate, in which a battle between Jeffrey and a turkey-cock is described (96). The poem has no merit whatsoever,

---

(94) *History of the Worthies of England,* 1662. By Thomas Fuller, 1608-1661, II, pp. 439-440; III, 40-41.

(95) See Edmund Waller's poem, *Of the Marriage of the Dwarfs,* celebrating the wedding of the court dwarfs Richard Gibson and Anne Shepherd (Gibson lived 1615-1690), *Waller's Poems,* 1784, I, 98.

Wood gives a number of contemporary allusions to the dwarf Jeffrey. See *Giants and Dwarfs,* 281-2, whence I quote the following:

"A very diminutive, singular, and extremely rare volume written in defense of Jeffrey, was published in 1636. It was entitled, 'The New Year's Gift, presented at court from the Lady Parvula to the Lord Minimus (commonly called Lord Jeffrey). Written by Microphilus.' "

(96) Swift was evdiently familiar with the poems of Davenant. See *Prose Works,* I, 178, (Battle of the Books). The poem *Jeffreidos* was based on the following incident. In 1630, Jeffrey was sent to France to fetch a midwife for Queen Henrietta Maria. On his return with the lady in question, he was taken prisoner at sea by Dunkirk privateers. The poem describes his capture and examination by the Dutchmen, who found him under a candlestick, his release from the charge of conspiracy

and fully deserves the oblivion into which it has fallen. It illustrates for our purposes, however, the popularity of Jeffrey, and affords something of a parallel for the description

---

against the state, his journey to Brussels, his danger from a turkey-cock, who determined to swallow him like a grain of wheat, the battle which ensued, and the timely intervention of the midwife. I quote here about one-fourth of the poem:

"Jeffreidos, or The Captivity of Jeffrey

" .   .   .
Each eye was now employed; no man could thinke
Of any uncouth nooke or narrow chinke,
But strait they sought him there; in holes not deep
But small, where slender maggots used to creep;
At last, they found him close, beneath a spick
And almost span-new-pewter-candlestick.
A sapient Diego, that had now command
Of ships and victorie, tooke him in hand;
Peis'd him twice, tasted his discourse; at length
Beleev'd that he dissembled wit, and strength:
Quoth he, 'Victors and vanquished, I bid
You all give eare to wisdom of Madrid.
This that appeares to you a walking-Thumbe
May prove, the general spie of Christendome.'

  .   .   .
The people view him round; some take their oath
He's human issue, but not yet of growth;
And others (that more subt'ly did conferre)
Thinke him a small, contracted conjurer;

  .   .   .
.   .   .   . he scarce had driven
Along that coast the length of inches seven,
But downe his Izeland fell; some authors say
A burly oake lay there disguis'd in's way;
Others, a rush; and some report, his steed
Did stumble at the splinter of a reed;
And some, far more authentick, say again
'Twas at a haire, that drop'd from humane chin.

  .   .   .
And Diego too, whose grave and solemne brow,
Was ever knit, grew loud, and wanton now.
'O for a guard,' quoth he, 'Of Switzers here
To heave that GIANT up, but come not neere;
For now enraged, he may perchance so tosse us,
As you would thinke, you touched a live Colossus.'
This Jeffrey heard, and it did stir his gall,
More than his courser's death, or his own fall.

  .   .   .
.   .   .   . for now behold
A foule of spatious wing, bloody and bold
In his aspect; haughty in gait, and stiffe on
His large spread clawes he stood, as any griffon;
Though by kinde a turkey; whose plot that way
Was like a subtle scowt to watch for prey;

of Gulliver's desperate battle with the gigantic linnet which is "somewhat larger than an English swan (97)."

Such as is blowne about by every wind;
But here's the dire mistake; this foule (halfe blinde)
At Jeff'ry pecks, and with intent to eat
Him up, instead of a large graine of wheat.
Jeff'ry (in duell nice) ne're thinkes upon't
As the turkey's hunger, but an affront.
His sword he drew, a better none alive
E're got from Spanish foe, for shillings five.
. . .
Jeff'ry the bold, as if he had o'reheard
Those instruments of warre, his arme uprear'd,
Then cryes, 'St. George for England,' and with that word
He mischief'd (What I pray?) nought but his sword.
Though some report he notched the foe's left wing;
And poets too, who faithfully did sing
This bataille in Low Dutch, tell of a few
Small feathers there, which at the first charge flew
About the field, but doe not strictly know
That they were shed by fury of that blow.
. . .
Jeff'ry retorts each stroke, and then cries, 'Mauger
Thy strength, I will dissect thee like an augure'
. . .
For Jeff'ry strait was throwne; whilst faint and weake,
The cruell foe assaults him with his beake."
. . .

(97) *Brob.*, 120.

Before leaving the subject of Swift's literary models for the story of Brobdingnag, it should be of interest to note that in the description of the storm at sea, Swift was copying verbatim a passage in Samuel Sturmy's *Mariner's Magazine*, published at London, 1679. This is the only instance in *Gulliver's Travels* in which Swift seems to have copied out of a book that was before his eyes as he wrote. The first to notice the debt was E. H. Knowles, *Notes & Queries*, March 7, 1868, Ser. IV, vol. 1, page 223. I have reproduced the parallels from Churton Collins' *Jonathan Swift*, 1902, pp. 107-8.

The quotation from *Brobdingnag* is in capitals with the source in the *Mariner's Magazine* underneath. Except for the two places indicated by dots, the extract from *Brobdingnag* is continuous in the text. In the first case four words are omitted; in the second, three sentences.

"FINDING IT WAS LIKELY TO OVERBLOW, WE TOOK IN
"It is likely to overblow, take in

OUR SPRIT SAIL, AND STOOD BY TO HAND THE FORE
your sprit sail, stand by to hand the fore

SAIL; BUT, MAKING FOUL WEATHER, WE LOOKED THE
sail . . . We make foul weather, look the

GUNS WERE ALL FAST, AND HANDED THE MIZEN. THE
guns be all fast, come hand the mizen. The

SHIP LAY VERY BROAD OFF, SO WE THOUGHT IT BET-
ship lies very broad off; it is bet-

TER SPOONING BEFORE THE SEA THAN TRYING OR
ter spooning before the sea than trying or
HULLING. WE REEFED THE FORE SAIL AND SET HIM,
hulling. Go reef the fore sail and set him;
AND HAULED AFT THE FORE SHEET; THE HELM WAS
haul aft the fore sheet. The helm is
HARD AWEATHER . . . WE BELAYED TH FORE-DOWN-
hard aweather. Belay the fore-down-
HAUL, BUT THE SAIL WAS SPLIT, AND WE HAULED
haul. The sail is split: go haul
DOWN THE YARD, AND GOT THE SAIL INTO THE SHIP,
down the yard and get the sail into the ship,
AND UNBOUND ALL THE THINGS CLEAR OF IT. IT WAS
and unbind all things clear of it.
A VERY FIERCE STORM; THE SEA BROKE STRANGE AND
A very fierce storm. The sea breaks strange and
DANGEROUS. WE HAULED OFF UPON THE LANYARD OF
dangerous. Stand by to haul off above the lanyard of
THE WHIPSTAFF, AND HELPED THE MAN AT THE HELM.
the whipstaff, and help the man at the helm.
WE COULD NOT GET DOWN OUR TOP-MAST, BUT LET ALL
Shall we get down our top-masts? No, let all
STAND, BECAUSE SHE SCUDDED BEFORE THE SEA VERY
stand: she scuds before the sea very
WELL, AND WE KNEW THAT, THE TOP-MAST BEING
well; the top-mast being
ALOFT, THE SHIP WAS THE WHOLESOMER AND MADE
aloft the ship is the wholesomer and maketh
BETTER WAY THROUGH THE SEA, SEEING WE HAD
better way through the sea, seeing we have
SEA-ROOM . . . WE GOT THE STARBOARD TACKS ABOARD,
sea-room. Get the starboard tacks aboard,
WE CAST OFF OUR WEATHER BRACES AND LIFTS; WE
cast off our anchor, braces and lifts;
SET-IN THE LEE-BRACES AND HAULED FOREWARD BY
set-in the lee-braces and
THE LEATHER-BOWLINGS, AND HAULED THEM TIGHT,
haul them taught
AND BELAYED THEM, AND HAULED OVER THE MIZEN-
and belaye them, and haul over the mizen-
TACK TO WINDWARD, AND KEPT HER FULL AND BY AS
tacks to windward and keep her full and by as
NEAR AS SHE WOULD LIE."
near as she would lie."

CHAPTER 8

Brobdingnagian Views of Life

Critics have differed widely in their attempts to explain the judgments of life implied in the *Voyage to Brobdingnag,* and I dare say that not many of its readers would agree off-hand in an analysis of the allegorical scheme. Leslie Stephen, while recognizing the incompleteness of his view, asserts the second voyage to be the counterpart of the first, a supplementary picture of man's contemptible qualities. He says,

> "He strikes the keynote of contempt by his imagery of giants and dwarfs; we despise the petty quarrels of beings six inches high; and therefore we are prepared to despise the wars carried on by a Marlborough and a Eugene. We transfer the contempt based upon mere size to the motives, which are the same in big men and little . . . In Brobdingnag Swift is generally said to be looking, as Scott expresses it, through the other end of the telescope. He wishes to show the grossness of men's passions, as before he had shown their pettiness" (98).

The same interpretation is made by a German critic who declares that the moral of the voyage is,

> "Whether man is three inches or three miles high, he remains man, that is, a presumptuous zero" (99).

The view more commonly held, however, is that the Brobdingnagians are an idealized race, contrasted sharply with the miserable creatures represented by the human being, Gulliver. Walter Scott says,

> "As he had held up to the derision of ordinary beings the intrigues, cabals, wars, and councils of a Lilliputian court and ministry, he now shows us . . . a people of immense stature and gifted with a

---

(98) Leslie Stephen, *Jonathan Swift,* 1882, chapter viii, pp. 175-6 (*Eng. Men of Letters,* Series). Much the same view is held by William Hazlitt, *Lectures on the English Poets,* Lecture vi. *Collected Works of William Hazlitt,* by A. R. Waller, 1902, V, 110-2.

"His object was to strip empty pride and grandeur of the imposing air which external circumstances throw around them, and for this purpose he has cheated the imagination of the illusions which the prejudices of sense and of the world put upon it, by reducing everything to the abstract predicament of size. He enlarges or diminishes the scale as he wishes to show the insignificance or the grossness of our overweening self-love."

(99) Richard M. Meyer, *Jonathan Swift und G. Ch. Lichtenberg.* (Monograph, Berlin, 1886, pp. 20-1.)

> soundness and coolness of judgment . . . Swift's King of Brob-
> dingnag is a patriot monarch . . . a stoic in appetite and ambi-
> tion; holding everything of little importance, except what directly
> tended to the real benefit of his subjects. This vision, as vain and
> improbable as the size of the personage so gifted, is maintained
> with singular art through the whole section" (100).

There is, of course, plenty of justification in the *Voyage to Brobdingnag* for this interpretation, though Scott's last statement is quite incorrect. More recently, another writer has expressed this latter point of view, though he admits that there are objections to it.

> "Swift is at least consistent in keeping generally upper most the
> idea that littleness is the trivial thing and bigness the important
> one" (101).

My main effort in this chapter will be devoted to an attempt to clear up this dilemma.

One point is fundamental. The satire of the second voyage is not so simple as that of the first; a two-fold method is evident. In the first voyage, with a few minor exceptions previously noted (102), Swift's contempt for mankind is unfolded objectively in the thoughts and actions of the Lilliputians themselves. Gulliver is an outsider, whose function is merely to describe the race as it appeared to him. Not so in Brobdingnag. In the earlier chapters of the second *Voyage* the same method does indeed prevail. There the reader's interest is centered upon the Brobdingnagians, in whom is mirrored another aspect of the human race, one complementary to the Lilliputian and equally unfavorable (103). This

---

(100) *Works of Swift*, XI, 7.

(101) *The Nature of Allegory as Used by Swift*, H. M. Dargan, *Studies in Philology*, July, 1916, XIII, 174 ff.

(102) See above, chapter 6, section iii.

(103) The metaphor of the telescope is not, as many assume, original with Walter Scott. The following is quoted from the preface to the French translation of *Gulliver*, 1727, by DesFontaines, pp. xix-xx:

> "Les deux premiers *Voyages* sont fondés sur l'idée d'un principe de
> physique très certain, savoir, qu'il n'y a point de grandeur absoluë,
> et que toute mesure est relative . . . Dans ces deux *Voyages*, il
> semble en quelque sorte considerer les hommes avec un telescope.
> D'abord il tourne le verre objectif du côté de l'oeil, et les voit par
> conséquent très petits: C'est le *Voyage de Lilliput*. Il tourne ensuite
> son telescope, et alors il voit les hommes très grands: C'est le
> *Voyage de Brobdingnag*."

I believe that Scott had the above words in his mind, when he wrote the following:

> "In fact, the work rests upon an axiom, in itself certain, that there
> is no such thing in nature as an absolute standard of size, and that
> all our ideas upon the subject as relative."
> (*Works of Swift*, XI, 8.)

explains the opinions of Leslie Stephen and Meyer. Later, however, Gulliver himself mounts the stage to show off the qualities of the human race, while the Brobdingnagians apparently step out of their disguise and proceed to sit in judgment upon the traveller, as representatives of a superior race. The satiric method is thus a double one: both the Brobdingnagians and Gulliver represent man, and are made the objects of Swift's satire. The failure to recognize this fact has led to the charge of inconsistency on Swift's part. Any study of the philosophic import of *Brobdingnag,* to be successful, must keep the two departments of the satire carefully separated. To judge fairly, therefore, of Swift's intentions, let us first consider the aspect of human life, which Gulliver sees in the Brobdingnagians; and later consider what aspect of it they see in him.

I

Is there any inconsistency in Swift's use of the Brobdingnagians? Does he forget that he has caused them to represent humanity, and make them an ideal race of the kind met in Utopias by travellers in other *Imaginary Voyages?* I believe not.

There may be difference of opinion as to whether the giants are admirable, but there is no real conflict in the statements about them. A person or a race, may be physically disgusting and yet be well disposed toward others. Coarse manners are not necessarily incompatible with humility and honesty; lack of culture does not exclude common sense. The King's abhorrence of gunpowder, so frequently quoted ,is not sufficient to mark him as a superior being, for in the world to-day, lofty and high-sounding ideals of pacifism are proclaimed as frequently by the ignorant and by the immoral, as by misguided idealists. It is not unlikely that the Yahoos would shudder at the idea of going to war, as well as the King. There is, in short, nothing contradictory about the Brobdingnagians. For certain very good reasons, Gulliver dislikes them, and for other and better ones they despise him. Neither is represented as a model of perfection. Swift might have made the Brobdingnagians thoroughly ridiculous. In them he could have shown all of man's worst impulses and practices, had he chosen to do so. Instead, he represents in this race of giants the human race in its better mood, a mixture of good and bad, of attractive and undesirable qualities, inconsistent only as man himself is an inconsistency. The qualities of the race are exaggerated, but that is all. Morally, the giants are better than the best of men, and personally, they are coarser and more forbidding than the worst.

There is no precedent anywhere in the literature of the *Philosophic Voyage* for this magnification of the human race, or for the allegorical use of a giant race to represent mankind. Nor do I know of any giant story of any kind or origin in which the giants stand for man. They go with him as his friends, or oppose him as his enemies, but they are not identified with man himself.

Other writers had, however, employed giant races for satiric effect, as I pointed out in the preceding chapter. These giants were, as a general rule, idealized beings, vastly superior to the traveller. Swift's idea that the giants embody the exaggeration of common defects as well as merits, is paralleled in the conclusion reached by the Japanese traveller, Wasobiyoe.

> "It would seem as if this foolish country were superior to the rest in nothing but size; tenanted as it is by such empty-headed folk. It is nothing more than a great, overgrown asparagus of a country."

Swift's implication is not in exact agreement with the conclusion reached by Wasobiyoe. The Brobdingnagians differ from the Lilliputians in other respects as well as in size, and it will be our business before we are done to determine just what characteristics of the race Swift conceived would be altered by an increase in the scale of being (104). The Japanese story does, however agree with the account in *Gulliver* in the circumstance of the travellers' disgust with, and contempt for, the giants.

Swift was no doubt influenced by literary tradition, when he decided to attribute commendable qualities to the giants. Pygmy life frequently had been treated as laughable. The physical smallness of the people implied corresponding mentality. Nothing great was expected from a petty creature. Giants, on the other hand, had often been credited with superior qualities. As stated fully in the preceding chapter, the giants met by Gonzales on the moon were of differing size and of corresponding mental and moral vigor. Cyrano's account of the Selenites, eighteen feet tall, credits them with the same superior virtues that the Brobdingnagians possess. Henrion's thesis assumes a connexion between human depravity and the dwindling proportions of the human body. It was therefore in conformity to literary usage that Swift chose to ennoble the Brobdingnagians instead of the Lilliputians.

---

(104) See below, pp. 154-5.

What, then, as Swift conceived it, would be the effect of magnifying the proportions of life? In the answer to this question will be seen the reason for the mixture of good and bad qualities in the Brobdingnagians, as well as the reason for their differing from the Lilliputians in character as well as in size.

The effect of reducing the scale of life in Lilliput is to strip human affairs of their self-imposed grandeur. Rank, politics, international war, lose all of their significance. This particular idea is continued in the second voyage, not in the picture of the Brobdingnagians, but in Gulliver himself, who is now a Lilliputian. The King laughs heartily at Gulliver's account of English "trade and wars by sea and land, of schisms in religion, and parties in the state" (105). But the affairs of Brobdingnag are not the objects of ridicule, for they are not petty. Swift was wise enough to realize that the same defects of the race could not be exposed to equal advantage in both pygmies and giants.

The enlargement of human life, Swift would say, does not reflect discredit upon human institutions, but it does rob personality of its grace, and expose the human form as anything but a thing of beauty. Human ideas suffer nothing when attributed to a gigantic race; human claims to physical beauty and charm suffer a great deal. Swift dwells upon the grossness of the body and of its passions. The farmers in Brobdingnag are clumsy, awkward louts. Gulliver cannot restrain his laughter at the old man with spectacles, whose "eyes appeared like the full moon shining into a chamber at two windows." The old man "was fool enough to be angry and out of countenance" (106). Of the revolting aspect of the bodies of the Maids of Honour I have written before. Swift here discredits not only feminine beauty, but sex relations in and for themselves. Gulliver cannot comprehend the attraction of those girls for their lovers; for to him they are "far from tempting," or, "from giving any other emotions than those of horror and disgust" (107). Several of Swift's poems echo this attempt to rob sex of its conventional charm. But if the lovely Maids of Honour, the pick of the land, can be so repulsive, what would a diseased person look like in Brobdingnag? Swift gives a ghastly picture of the "horrible" beggars who crowded about Gulliver in the streets of the capital.

"There was a woman with a cancer in her breast, swelled to a monstrous size, full of holes, in two or three of which I could have

(105) *Brob.*, 109.
(106) *Ibid.*, 98.
(107) *Ibid.*, 121.

easily crept, and covered with my whole body. There was a fellow
with a wen in his neck, larger than five wood packs . . . But the
most hateful sight of all was the lice crawling on their clothes. I
could see distinctly the limbs of these vermin with my naked eye,
much better than those of a European louse through a microscope,
and their snouts with which they rooted like swine" (108).

The implication clearly is that a microscope would disclose
the similar appearance of lousy Europeans. Gulliver remem-
bers how a Lilliputian courtier had described the repulsive
appearance of the Man-Mountain, and he reflects that the
Lilliputians appeared fair and dainty to him, only because he
overlooked their imperfections (109). Aristotle had expounded
the same theory of beauty in the following passage, which
may well have been known to Swift:

"Whatever is beautiful, whether it be an animal or any other thing
composed of different parts, must . . . be of a certain magnitude
. . . One of prodigious size cannot be beautiful, because as all its
parts cannot be seen at once, the whole, the unity of the object is
lost to the spectator . . . The magnitude must be such as to present
a whole, easily comprehended by the eye" (110).

So Gulliver finds that the ordinary attractions of a public
execution do not exist for him in Brobdingnag, where the
flow of blood and the fall of the huge head exaggerate the
brutality of the whole affair (111). In a word, all the transactions of life, all passions and all social amenities, which
involve the body, lose their respectability in Brobdingnag. All
values that arise from our physical natures are unsound ones.

Not so, however, with moral values. There is nothing
absurd or disreputable about the honest labor of the farmers
in Brobdingnag. Industry, reliability, and kindheartedness,
are eternal values, not affected by the scale of life in which
they are practised. When Gulliver stumbles against a crust,
he observes "the good people to be in much concern," and is
grateful for their solicitude (112). There is nothing grotesque
about the affection of Glumdalclitch for Gulliver, because, unlike the Maids of Honour, her motives are spiritual and not
physical. The spiritual nature of the giants is not idealized,
nor has it been altered in any other way. Their boys are
sometimes mischievous and cruel to animals, their misers are

---

(108) *Ibid.*, 115.

(109) *Ibid.*, 94.

(110) Aristotle's *Poetics*, Part II, Section 4, paragraph 2. Translation by Daniel Twining, 1812, Vol. I, p. 123. (First pointed out in *Notes
& Queries*, Jan. 18, 1868. Ser. IV, Vol. I, p. 51.)

(111) *Brob.*, 122.

(112) *Ibid.*, 92.

mean and stingy as misers are everywhere (113). Altruism and selfishness are the same in a giant as in a pygmy. The administration of government in Brobdingnag is excellent, not because the people are free from corrupt instincts, but because the principles are beneficent, and therefore as effective in Brobdingnag as in Houyhnhnmland, or anywhere else. Man's physical nature is an accident of birth, but his moral nature is of changeless quality and value, admirable or contemptible alike, in Brobdingnag as in Europe.

II.

So much for what Gulliver discovers in the Brobdingnagians; the other half of Swift's satire in this voyage is contained in Brobdingnag's opinions of Gulliver.

In the attitude of the giants toward Gulliver there is nothing new, but only a more direct condemnation of the "tiny race, and nation void of brain" previously ridiculed in the first voyage. In point of size, Gulliver is now the small creature "not six inches high," in this bigger and better world. It is as though the parable had been turned upon him by some Old Testament prophet. The insignificant nature of man is first presented to him in a fable of pygmy life. He is amused and interested. In the sequel, the prophet draws himself up to his full height, and, pointing a finger of scorn, says, "Thou art the man."

The objections of the King of Brobdingnag to Gulliver coincide with the objects of satire in Lilliput. Not man's physical grossness is exposed, but the narrowness of his pride, and the folly of his actions. With greater vision and with far-reaching intelligence, the King is unresponsive to Gulliver's boasts of the glory of his own dear country. Seen by him in true perspective, European pomps and cares are contracted to a span. There is no need to rehearse the scene, for it is merely the moral of the story of the "great and glorious Empire of Lilliput," to which the reader is referred. In the second voyage the satire is more biting; mild ridicule has given place to savage contempt. In the beginning the King laughs at the grandeur mimicked by such a diminutive insect (114); but as

---

(113) *Ibid.*, 98.

(114) *Ibid.*, 109.

"After I had been a little too copious in talking of my own beloved country, of our trade, and wars by sea and land, of our schisms in religion, and parties in the state; . . . He could not forbear taking me up in his right hand, and stroking me gently with the other, after a hearty fit of laughing, asked me, whether I was a Whig or a Tory."

he listens to Gulliver's patriotic orations, his brow darkens
and his tone begins to threaten, until in the end his indignation is thoroughly aroused.

> "He was perfectly astonished with the historical account I gave
> him of our affairs during the last century, protesting it was only
> an heap of conspiracies, rebellions murders, massacres, revolutions,
> banishments, the very worst effects that avarice, faction, hypocrisy,
> perfidiousness, cruelty, rage, madness, hatred, envy, lust, malice, or
> ambition could produce" (115).

He dismisses Gulliver with the following:

> "I cannot but conclude the bulk of your natives to be the most
> pernicious race of little odious vermin that nature ever suffered
> to crawl upon the surface of the earth" (116).

The condemnation of Gulliver by the giants occupies the
later chapters of *Brobdingnag*, and it is this part of the *Voyage*
which corresponds so closely to Cyrano's *Histoire de la lune*,
as may be seen by referring to the parallels in chapter seven
above. The general situation is no longer one of allegory, but
one of contrast between the traveller and his hosts. This
situation, almost the invariable rule in earlier *Philosophic
Voyages*, exists in *Gulliver* only in the latter part of *Brobdingnag* and throughout the *Voyage to Houyhnhnmland*. A
certain common factor for the satire of situations of this type
may be distinguished. The traveller is led into the presence
of the king, where he is questioned and examined about his
race and training. It is concluded that he is not a reasonable
creature, or, at best, a potentially reasonable creature perverted through "civilization." He, in turn, discovers there a
high state of virtue and tolerance unknown in the world from
which he has come. He is treated with clemency that he does
not deserve, and returns at length to his native land, a sadder
and a wiser man. Gulliver is not so teachable as most of his
fore-runners, but the truth does dawn upon him. At first his
color comes and goes with indignation at hearing his noble
country, the mistress of arts and arms, so contemptuously
treated, but he says later, "Upon mature thoughts, I began
to doubt whether I were injured or no," and decides, with
rather unusual candor, that he would be tempted now to laugh
at his own countrymen as much as the king and his grandees
did at him (117).

Many of the earlier *Voyages* of this kind anticipate the
satire on courts of justice, government, and war. The topics

---

(115) *Ibid.*, 135.

(116) *Ibid.*, 136.

(117) *Ibid.*, 110.

are among the commonest (118). As far as the device employed is concerned, that of a giant race looking down upon
man, the source is Cyrano, as must be clear from the parallels
noted in the preceding chapter. Swift's method is rather unusual, however, in regard to the traveller's extended orations
to the king of the people visited. The situation more typical
of *Philosophic Voyages* is that in which the traveller is taken
in hand by a native who expounds to him, often at wearisome
length, the superior virtues of his country (119). A close
parallel to *Brobdingnag* in this respect is to be found in the
Journey of Klimius to the World Underground. His Serene
Highness, King of Potu, grants Klimius an audience, and
expresses a desire to know "something respecting the manners
and customs of our globe."

> "I (Klimius) expatiated with much warmth on the intellect and
> virtues of man; and on the morals, good-breeding, and other accom-
> plishments, of which mankind in general are accustomed to pride
> themselves. But he was quite indifferent at the recital, and even
> yawned at several circumstances, which I conceived most likely to
> excite his admiration. Alas, thought I, . . . that which is the most
> charming and agreeable to us, awakens in this people nothing but
> disgust and nausea. What appeared to grate most on his princely
> ear, was that which I related to him concerning our method of
> pleading causes at the bar; respecting the eloquence of our barris-
> ters; and the alacrity of our judge in deciding questions, and pro-
> nouncing verdicts" (120).

The Potuans are, like the Brobdingnagians, tolerant of religious differences, and hold that "every persecution on account
of thoughts and opinions, or errors . . . has its origin entirely in pride; since one person foolishly imagines that he is
able to see deeper into matters of religion than another."
Another parallel to Brobdingnag is to be found in the constitution of Potu, which assigns the highest honor in the state
to peasants, and the lowest to the court and the royal
family (121). So also the King of Brobdingnag

> "gave it for his opinion that whoever could make two ears of corn,
> or two blades of grass, grow upon a spot of ground where only
> one grew before, would deserve better of mankind, and do more
> essential service to his country than the whole race of politicians
> put together" (122).

---

(118) See above, chapter 3.

(119) This is the method followed in *Sadeur, Séverambes, Mundus
Alter, Consolidator, Gonzales,* and *Cyrano.* See chapter 3.

(120) *Journey to the World Underground,* from the original of Lewis
Holberg. London, 1828, pp. 66-7.

(121) *Ibid.,* 108-9.

(122) *Brob.,* 140.

In general, the specific objects of satire in *Brobdingnag* are
not original with Swift. From Lucian down to Holberg, the
writers of *Philosophic Voyages* had found the same faults in
civilization. For the most part they agreed in shifting the
guilt to the shoulders of lawyers, legislators, and soldiers.
Man, they insisted, is the unfortunate victim of his inhuman
institutions. This is the text from which the king preaches
in the second voyage of Gulliver. The sermon is based on a
platitude. A deeper logic is reserved by Swift for the fourth
voyage, where the inhuman institutions are shown to be the
logical expression of man's inherent depravity.

III.

Before closing this study, I wish to say a final word about
Swift's theory of the relativity of values set forth in the first
two voyages. I have explained the devices by which it is
worked out; and the transfiguration of life that follows upon
each change in the scale. The larger question arises, what
does Swift mean by it all? Is he a complete skeptic? Is all
vanity? Let us see.

I believe that the philosophy of *Lilliput* and *Brobdingnag*
rests upon one clear axiom: the true values of the human
drama are those which are wholly independent of the size of
the actors; all others are purely relative and ultimately false.

If this be true, it is useless to argue whether Swift means
the big men to be more admirable than the little ones. Nothing
is admirable but what will endure the test of its practice by
men of any size. But is there anything which will do this?

Certain common values are at once rejected when the test
is applied. Personal endowments will not endure. When magnified, the handsomest face in the world becomes ugly.
Polished manners may appear agreeable in Lilliput, but they
would be clumsy in Brobdingnag; the Queen's table manners
are disgusting (123), and still she is the Queen, the dictator
of fashions. Physical passion appears gross when indulged
in by the giants. There is nothing essentially good or bad
about the human body and its wants, but thinking makes it so.

Conversely, public and official life with its honors and titles
is contemptible in Lilliput. The grandeur of our civilization,
as we have been told so often, is a mere illusion. Temporal
dominion is a doubtful source of pride; party-strife is a ridiculous absurdity on this little planet of ours. Those causes of
pride and dissension, which we think so great, seem foolish to
those powers who look down upon us from above.

---

(123) *Ibid.*, 108.

Intellectual achievement is also of questionable finality. The opinions of the Lilliputians are provincial, their observations are confined to narrow limits, and their deductions are unsound. The Brobdingnagians see the larger issues of life more clearly, but their minds lack fineness. Complicated ideas are distasteful to them, distinctions and shades of thought are overlooked, subtleties are not comprehended, even government is confined by law to a few general principles. The philosophers fail to classify Gulliver correctly because he is so small. The intelligence of a race, Swift implies, is at best limited and fallible.

Of all human values, those which we commonly call altruistic, would appear alone to equal advantage in both Lilliput and Brobdingnag; and the reason for this will become clear upon reflection. Self interests change their aspect as the importance of self varies. Altruism is a negation of self, as that is commonly conceived. Unfortunately, the Lilliputians do not exhibit any altruistic qualities by which I could illustrate my point. To have them perform noble and unselfish deeds would have interfered with Swift's plan of consistent ridicule which he employs in the first voyage. If a Lilliputian had rescued a child from the fire at the palace, at great personal risk, would the act have appeared ridiculous? I think not. It is certain at least that the devotion of Glumdalclitch for Grildrig is a sincere, touching affection, not at all grotesque; and that the benevolence of the King of Brobdingnag is wholly admirable.

This interpretation may, finally, throw some light on the omission of religion from the list of objects satirized. Many of Swift's fore-runners had specialized in the abuse of Christianity, but for some reason he breaks with their practice at this point. The reason, of course, is that Christianity is not a by-product of civilization, but an ideal, which does not depend for its respectability upon the physique of its worshippers. The religions of Lilliput are not ridiculed, though the religious quarrels are. The faults of religion are faults of corruption. The King of Brobdingnag is thoroughly disgusted with all but one of the institutions described by Gulliver; in that solitary exception I believe we may discern the reverence of a Dean for his Church, and his regret for its decline in purity. The King says, of this otherwise pernicious race of odious vermin,

"I observe among you some lines of an institution, which in its original might have been tolerable, but these, half-erased, and the rest wholly blurred and blotted by corruptions" (124).

---

(124) *Ibid.*, 136.

The Travels of Lemuel Gulliver

III

Laputa, Balnibarbi, Luggnagg, Glubbdubdrib, and Japan

"Those people suppose, that because the smallest circle hath as many degrees as the largest, therefore the regulation and management of the world require no more abilities than the handling and turning of a globe."

(*Laputa*, chapter 2.)

CHAPTER 9

A Voyage to Laputa, Balnibarbi, Luggnagg, Glubbdubdrib, and Japan.

The third part of *Gulliver's Travels* is at once the longest and the worst. It is a miscellany of unrelated situations that are, with one exception, Struldbruggland, uninspired and dull. There is here no attempt to create an agreeable world of the imagination, but only a collection of brief and imitative voyages, in which the satire is of contemporary rather than of abiding interest. When we add to this statement, the further one that the contemporary readers themselves were bored (1), it is not surprising that posterity has been indifferent. In short, it would be the apotheosis of pedantry for me to attempt to enlist interest where Swift himself has failed. The *Voyage to Laputa* is too long as it stands; the satire is inexcusably obvious. I shall attempt, only, to present the materials for such further study as readers may desire to follow for themselves.

I.

Laputa.

In his first adventure, Gulliver is taken up into the Flying Island, Laputa, whose inhabitants are absent-minded, impractical mono-maniacs on the subject of mathematics. Their food is served in geometrical shapes, "A shoulder of mutton, cut into an equilateral triangle, a piece of beef into a rhomboides, and a pudding into a cycloid . . . The servants cut our bread into cones, cylinders, parallelograms, and several other mathematical figures" (2), *etc.* Gulliver is measured for a suit of clothes by a Laputan tailor by means of a quadrant and a rule and compass (3). Music and astrology form the chief amusements of the people. The King of Laputa keeps his subjects (on the earth) in subjection by steering his island about as needed, hovering over rebellious provinces to deprive the rebels of sunshine and rain, until they capitulate (4).

---

(1) See, above, ch. 4, note 24.

(2) *Laputa*, 165.

(3) *Ibid.*, 166-7.

(4) *Ibid.*, 178-9.

There seems to be no motive for the story beyond a pointless and not too artfully contrived satire on mathematicians; for whom Swift entertained, apparently, a pet aversion. The clothes made by the tailor are "very ill made, and quite out of shape, by happening to mistake a figure in the calculation." The houses of the Laputans are "very ill built . . . without a right angle in any apartment" (5). The people "although they are dexterous enough upon a piece of paper . . . yet in the common actions and behavior of life, I have not seen a more clumsy, awkward, and unhandy people . . . They are very bad reasoners, and vehemently given to opposition, unless when they happen to be of the right opinion, which is seldom the case." Now, granting the justice of the remarks about the futility of abstract, mathematical thinking in the affairs of life, we may still object that the theme lacks interest. Why so much ado about nothing? The average reader is not likely to be greatly affected by Gulliver's statement,

> "I have indeed observed the same disposition among most of the mathematicians I have known in Europe . . . Those people suppose that because the smallest circle hath as may degrees as the largest, therefore the regulation and management of the world require no more abilities than the handling and turning of a globe."

For this attack on theoretical science I can find no literary source or analogue, and conclude that it must have been inspired by one of Swift's ideocyncracies. Attempts have been made (6) to detect allusions to the work of Newton and other contemporary scientists, but these, however successful, cannot greatly increase for us the slight importance of the satire of Laputa.

From the narrative point of view, it is difficult to explain the gratuitous violation of natural laws in the case of the Flying Island. When Swift contrives pygmies, giants, or horses, he does so to good purpose, and the fictions are appropriate, nay indispensable, to the satire. There is not, however, any need for the magical apparatus of Laputa; nothing is gained, while Probability, the patron saint of the popular fabulist, is offended. The explanation, such as it is, seems to be that Swift felt obliged to sustain the marvellous interest already created in the first two voyages; and, having nothing apt in mind, proceeded to copy the aerial adventure in Lucian's *True History*, from which he had already borrowed heavily for

---

(5) *Ibid.*, 168.

(6) *Laputa*, 164 note, 166 note, and 167 note.

Gulliver. In the latter work, Lucian and his companions sail on a ship through the air, until,

> "We continued thus our course through the sky for the space of seven days and as many nights. At last on the eighth day we discover'd a great land in the sky, like a shining island, round and bright, where . . . we went ashore, and soon found it to be inhabited . . . Below us was another earth, containing cities and rivers and seas and woods and mountains, which we conjectured to be the very same with that which is inhabited by us" (7).

Gulliver says,

> "The sky was perfectly clear . . . when all on a sudden it became obscured, as I thought, in a manner very different from what happens by the interposition of a cloud. I turned back and perceived a vast, opaque body between me and the sun . . . It seemed to be about two miles high, and hid the sun six or seven minutes . . . As it approached nearer over the place where I was, it appeared to be a firm substance, the bottom flat, smooth, and shining very bright from the reflection of the sea below" (8).

Lucian discovers that the inhabitants of the aerial island are at enmity with the sun. The King informs him,

> "At present I am engaged in a war with the inhabitants of the sun . . . Phaeton, the king of those people, has, for this long while, carried on a fierce war against us" (9).

Phaeton brings the enemy to terms by cutting off his supply of sunbeams, leaving him in total darkness (10). In the same way the King of Laputa subdues the Balnibarbes. The only fear of the Laputans is that they may be annihilated by their greatest enemy, the Sun (11). Both Lucian and Swift describe, in the center of the island, a well, or chasm, stored with astronomical instruments (12). When he descends from the island to *terra firma*, Lucian says,

> "On the fourth day about noon, having a fair and gentle gale, we were let down upon the sea. As soon as we touch'd water, you cannot imagine how greatly we rejoiced" (13).

Gulliver is equally relieved to be lowered to the earth.

> "The island being then hovering over a mountain . . . I was let down from the lowest gallery in the same manner as I had been taken up . . . I felt some little satisfaction in finding myself on firm ground" (14).

---

(7) *Dryden Lucian*, III, 128-9.
(8) *Laputa*, 160-1.
(9) *Op. cit.*, III, 130.
(10) *Ibid.*, III, 136.
(11) *Laputa*, 169.
(12) *Laputa*, 173. *Dryden Lucian*, III, 140-1.
(13) *Op. cit.*, III, 143.
(14) *Laputa*, 181.

I think we may safely ascribe the Flying Island to a direct
imitation of the *True History* (15).

II.

Lagado.

In Balnibarbi, Gulliver spends his time among the projectors of the Academy of Lagado, the metropolis. The ridicule,
previously concentrated on the mathematicians of Laputa, is
here extended to scientists and academicians in general. Now
a satirical parody of European learning was one of the commonest of themes in the *Philosophic Voyages*. Lucian rules
the academicians out of the Island of the Blessed because on
earth they had attempted to disprove the existence of the place,
and of all future life (16). Joseph Hall, in his *Mundus Alter*,
describes an academy of impractical innovators, of whom
some account has been given already (17). There is a very
entertaining satire on a community of philosophers in Holberg's *Klimius*, which has escaped the notice of critics altogether. In the general satirico-comic tone, Holberg is very
near to Swift.

> Klimius visits the Land of the Philosophers (Maskattia), which
> adjoins Koleku. He finds travel difficult as "the roads through the
> country were very stony and full of holes," so that Klimius gets
> "both besmeared and ulcerated legs." He asks a peasant how far
> it is to the Land of the Philosophers, to which the peasant replies,
> "You ought rather to ask how far you have to go before you get
> out of it, for you are now just in the midst of it." The astounded
> Klimius replies, "How is it, then, that this country, which is in-
> habited by nobody but philosophers, should be more like a haunt for
> wild beasts, than a cultivated and inhabited kingdom?" The native
> explains that the inhabitants have "little leisure to attend to such
> like bagatelles. For the present we must excuse their suffering
> the fields and meadows to remain untouched, as they have some-
> thing very celestial and sublime in their heads, and are speculating
> on discovering a way up to the sun." Klimius concludes his de-
> scription as follows: "Through the streets I saw promiscuously
> walking herds of swine and philosophers, which were only to be
> distinguished from each other by their form; for the latter were
> equally besmeared and filthy with the former. All the philosophers
> wore a sort of gown or cloak; but of what colour I was not able to
> discern, as it was impossible to discover it through so much dust

---

(15) This debt was first pointed out by Hime, *op. cit.*
"In connexion with Swift's Laputa, the Flying City, Saubha, of
the *Mahabharata* should be remembered." (Dunlop, *op. cit.*, 536,
note.)

(16) *Op. cit.*, III, 165.

(17) See, above, ch. 3.

and filth as were hanging upon them. I stopped before one of these sages, who, quite entranced and absorbed in contemplation, ran directly against me. 'I beg your pardon, Sir,' said I, 'May I ask the name of this city?' He remained immovable for a length of time in a standing position, with his eyes closed, as if his immortal part had taken leave of his body; but came at last again to himself, and answered with a look toward heaven,—'It is not far from midday.' This unseasonable answer, which betrayed a perfect insensibility and inattention, proved to me, that it was much more advisable to study with moderation, than to become deranged from too great a store of learning" (18).

Klimius, like Gulliver, pays a special visit to the national academy, where he listens dispassionately to an Inaugural Dissertation upon the subject: "Whether Humming and Buzzing Noise of Flies and Other Insects, Be Made with their Mouths or their Rumps" (19). The debate became a quarrel, "which at one time assumed an appearance of murder and bloodshed, terminated with mutual eulogies and congratulations, in the same manner as in our Academies, where, according to an anciently-allowed-of custom, the President always quits the rostrum victoriously." Klimius describes the Martinian projectors as follows:

"The repute in which projectors stand in this place, surpasses description; and the more preposterous and impractical a proposal is, the surer it is of meeting with general approbation . . . Notwithstanding the injury and loss which this plan had brought upon the country, the projector not only received no punishment, but, on the contrary, . . . was everywhere loaded with praise, for the Martinians are accustomed to say on such occasions,

'If the result has turned out sad,
The idea was still not bad' " (20).

Klimius proceeds to make his own fame and fortune in Martinia by the invention of Perriwigs made out of goats' hair, which become the fashion at once. "The whole nation made so much of this invention, that a new chronology was in consequence introduced; and from that time, according to Martinian annals, begins the *Age of Perriwigs*" (21).

The actual setting for the satire of Lagado, a succession of descriptions of the occupations of the professors, is based on Rabelais, Bk. V, ch. 21, 22, for which see, further, chapter four above. Swift has followed his model in the comic distortion of ideas, and in the exaggerated caricature, which run

(18) *Klimius*, 167-170.

(19) *Ibid.*, 247.

(20) *Ibid.*, 254.

(21) *Ibid.*, 257.

throughout the account of Lagado, besides borrowing directly from Rabelais the following specific occupations:

(1) Lagado	(2) Rabelais
Oldest professor, busy refining human ordure, separating its constituents.	Archasdarpenin engaged in distilling human excrement.
Professor writing treatise concerning the malleability of fire.	Others cut fire into steaks with a knife.
New method of building houses, by beginning at the roof and working downward to the foundation.	Others built churches to jump over the steeples.
Ground to be ploughed by hogs.	Others with three couples of foxes ploughed a sandy shore.
Condensing air into a dry, tangible substance.	Others pitched nets to catch the wind.
Physician attempting to resuscitate a dead dog with an anal pump.	A spodizator very artificially getting farts out of a dead ass.

This last was quoted from Rabelais by Swift, verbatim, in one of his minor prose writings in 1728 (22).

Several hints for the Academy of Lagado were also borrowed from the chapter in Tom Brown's *Amusements Serious and Comical* (with which, as we have seen (23), Swift was quite familiar) entitled, *The Philosophical or Virtuosi Country*, in which the East Indian visits an English academy. There is the same Rabelaisian list of grotesque inventions and pursuits, with this added resemblance to Lagado, that the Academy described by Brown is divided into two departments, 1.—Experimental Philosophy (Science), and 2.—Contemplative Philosophy. The Academy of Lagado likewise divides itself into 1.—The Projectors, and 2.—Advancers of Speculative Learning. There is no such departmental distinction in Rabelais.

Another parallel, closer than any between Lagado and Rabelais is the following, though it should be remembered that

(22) See, above, ch. 4.

(23) *Ibid.*, 64-5.

in all probability Rabelais' churches that jump over the steeples
were the ultimate origin of both:

Tom Brown	Lagado
"They lay their foundation in the air, and when they think they are come to solid ground, the building disappears, and the architects tumble down from the clouds" (24).	"There was a most ingenious architect who had contrived a new method for building houses, by beginning at the roof, and w o r k i n g downwards to the foundation."

Neither of these parallels have ever been noted before. To
them should be added the resemblances between the two academies, pointed out by Thompson (25) ; the total being, I believe,
sufficient to establish the influence of Tom Brown at this point.

Attempts have been made (26) to show that the experiments
carried on in Lagado allude to inventions produced by members
of the Royal Society and other scientists, in the first quarter
of the eighteenth century. It is, of course, conceivable that
Swift was making game of some of his contemporaries. On
the whole, however, in view of the obvious imitation of
Rabelais and Tom Brown, it seems more reasonable to suppose that Swift simply tortured his memory and his fancy to
invent or recall grotesque illustrations of scientific pedantry.
We cannot say that the effort was successful. *Klimius* contains the only thoroughly delightful satire on "highbrows;"
Tom Brown's is witty and laughable; Swift's, inferior to both,
is only occasionally brilliant; while Rabelais' conglomeration
involves a waste of printer's type and readers' time.

III.

Tribnia.

Gulliver's account of the Kingdom of Tribnia (27) is the
only instance in *Gulliver's Travels* of the satire of anagram
names, so popular in France in the sixteenth and seventeenth
centuries. Tribnia, is Britain, with the letters transposed,
Langden is England, *etc.* The section is itself a satire on the
anagrammistic and acrostic devices in literature. The youthful Fontenelle was the first, as far as I can determine, to employ these devices in the description of a supposedly strange

---

(24) Brown, *op. cit.*, III, 86-8.

(25) See, above, ch. 4, note 68.

(26) *Laputa*, 189 note, and 190 note.

(27) *Ibid.*, 199-201.

land. His *Relation de l'île de Borneo* (28) is a thinly veiled
satire on the Huguenots, in which MREO is the anagram of
ROME, and EENEGV the anagram of GENEVE. Louis Fontaines' *Pays de Jansenie* (29), in which the provinces are
named after religious sects of France, is another example of
the same general type of the satire of names, though the letters are not transposed. The voyage of discovery in all of
them is a transparent subterfuge, much as is Christian's pil-
grimage from the City of Destruction to the Celestial City.
The journey is only an elaborate metaphor.

IV.

Glubbdubdrib.

Gulliver's visit with the departed spirits in Glubbdubdrib is
modelled on Lucian's *Dialogues of the Dead*, and their imitations by Tom Brown, Lyttleton, Pryor, and many others. Certain passages echo more especially ideas in that part of the
True History, which describes the Island of the Blessed. In
both cases, the traveller converses with Homer and Aristotle,
who discourse on the stupidities of their commentators (30).
The dominant theme of the *True History* is the misrepresenta-
tions and wilful lies of historians, whose accounts are refuted
in the Island of the Blessed by the great men of history themselves. Precisely the same thing takes place in Glubbdubdrib,
and Gulliver concludes, at the close of his interviews with
Hannibal, Homer, Aristotle, Brutus, and others,

> "I was chiefly disgusted with modern history. For having exam-
> ined all the persons of greatest name in the courts of princes . . .
> I found how the world had been misled by prostitute writers, to
> ascribe the greatest exploits in war to cowards, the wisest counsel
> to fools, sincerity to flatterers, Roman virtue to betrayers of their
> country, piety to atheists, chastity to sodomites, truth to informers
> . . . Here I discovered the roguery and ignorance of those who
> pretend to write anecdotes, or secret memoirs, who send so many
> kings to their graves with a cup of poison; will repeat the dis-
> course between a prince and chief minister, where no witness was
> by; unlock the thoughts and cabinets of ambassadors and secre-
> taries of state, and have the perpetual misfortune to be mis-
> taken" (31).

Here, in this single paragraph is the burden of Lucian's *True
History*, as well as of his introductory essay, *How to Write*

(28) *Nouvelles de la république de letters.* Amsterdam, Jan., 1886.
(29) Paris, 1664. See Appendix, C2, below.
(30) *Op. cit.,* III, 166-7. *Laputa*, 206-7.
(31) *Laputa*, 208-9.

History (32). Here also is the substance of H. G. Wells' pon-
derous *Outline of History,* for those who do not care to waste
their time, nor squander their dollars, on the two-volume elaboration of the ideas which Swift compressed into two pages.

V.

The Struldbruggs of Luggnagg.

The only immortal part of the third part of *Gulliver* is the
chapter on the immortal Struldbruggs. Here there is originality, sound philosophy, and real pathos. No race just like
the Struldbruggs is to be found in literature, though the general idea of undesirable immortality is not original with Swift.

Two elements in the story will be distinguished in this study,
as they have divergent sources and do not always appear in
conjunction elsewhere as they do in Struldbruggland: 1.—The
hatefulness of old age and of prolonged existence; 2.—A *Philosophic Voyage* to a race of immortals.

The hideousness of old age found perhaps its oldest expression in the myth of Tithonus, related in the Homeric *Hymn
to Aphrodite* (33), from which I quote the following:

> "So too did Dawn of the Golden Throne carry off Tithonus . . .
> one like unto the immortals. She went to pray to Cronion . . .
> that her lover might be immortal and exempt from death forever.
> Thereto Zeus consented and granted her desire, but foolish of heart
> was the lady Dawn, nor did she deem it good to ask for eternal
> youth for her lover, and to keep him unwrinkled by grievous old
> age . . . So soon as grey hairs began to flow from his fair head
> and goodly chin, the Lady Dawn held aloof from his bed . . . But
> when hateful old age had utterly overcome him, and he could not
> move or lift his limbs . . . she laid him in a chamber and shut the
> shining doors, and his voice flows on endlessly, and no strength
> now is his such as once was in his limbs."

The myth is alluded to in the *Iliad* (34), and is quoted half a
dozen times or more by various classical authors (35), most of
whom were well known to Swift.

A much more popular story of an old man doomed to miserable immortality is to be found in the medieval legend of the
Wandering Jew. This curious Methusaleh, it appears, turned
up in various countries in every century of the Christian era,

---

(32) *Op. cit.,* IV, 12-33.
(33) *The Homeric Hymns.* Translated and edited by Andrew Lang.
London, 1899, pp. 178-9.
(34) XI, 1.
(35) Among others: Appollodorus, III, 12, 4; Horace, *Odes,* II, 16, 30;
Propertius, III, 10 (18). For bibliography of the myth, see article,
Tithonus in Pauly-Wissova's *Realencyclopädie.*

though under different circumstances each time. Indeed, the score or more accounts of his appearance, so interestingly reviewed by Baring-Gould (36), agree only in the single circumstance that relates the legend to the Struldbruggs: "An individual exists in an undying condition, wandering over the face of the earth, seeking peace, but finding none." During Swift's lifetime a chapbook was sold in London, entitled, "The Wandering Jew, or the Shoemaker of Jerusalem," in connexion with which the editor, John Ashton, gives the following account of the legend:

> "This famous myth seems to have had its origin in the gospel of St. John (xxi, 22) which, although it does not refer to him, evidently was the source of the idea of his tarrying on earth till the second coming of our Saviour . . . His name is generally received as Cartaphilus, but he was known, in different countries and ages, also as Ahasuerus, Josephus, and Isaac Lakedion. The usual legend is that he was Pontius Pilate's porter, and when they were dragging Jesus out of the door of the judgment-hall, he struck him on the back with his fist, saying, 'Go faster, Jesus, go faster; why dost thou linger?' Upon which Jesus looked at him with a frown, and said, 'I, indeed, am going; but thou shalt tarry till I come.' He was afterwards converted . . . He is believed every hundred years to have an illness, ending in a trance, from which he awakes restored to the age he was at our Saviour's Crucifixion" (37).

The Wandering Jew must have been well known to Swift, not only because his misery was proclaimed in street-ballads of the time, but because he appeared in Munich, on the 22nd of July, 1721, as well as in England when Swift was a boy. Concerning this visit Baring-Gould writes,

> "About the end of the seeventh century . . . an impostor, calling himself the Wandering Jew, attracted attention in England; and was listened to by the ignorant, and despised by the educated . . . He declared that he had been an officer in the Sanhedrin, and that he had struck Christ as He left the judgment-hall of Pilate. He remembered all the Apostles, and described their personal appearance, their clothes, and their peculiarities. He spoke many languages, claimed the power of healing the sick, and asserted that he had travelled nearly over all the world . . . Oxford and Cambridge sent professors to question him, and to discover the imposition, if any . . .
>
> Some impostors assuming to be the mysterious Jew, or lunatics actually believing themselves to be him, appeared in England in 1818, 1824, and 1840" (38).

---

(36) *Curious Myths of the Middle Ages.* S. Baring-Gould. London, 1869, pp. 1-31, and 637-640.

(37) *Chapbooks of the Eighteenth Century.* John Ashton. London, 1882, pp. 28-9.

(38) *Op. cit.*, 24-5.

In our own times, the legend has been expanded, but not improved, in the romance of Eugène Sue (Le Juif Errant), and of Dr. Croly (Salathiel), as well as in the more obscure "St. Leon," "The Undying One," and "Tarry Thou Till I Come" (39). From the first to the last, the versions all represent the Wandering Jew as an animated corpse, and his immortality as a hellish curse.

The sentiments of the Struldbruggs concerning death are anticipated in two satires of Lucian. In one of these, entitled, *On Mourning For The Dead*, a deceased son remonstrates with his father for his unreasonable grief:

> "O wretched man, why dost thou create so much trouble for me? Forbear to pull off thy hair, and tear the skin from thy face . . . Dost thou think it a misfortune to me that I did not live to become such an old man as thyself, with a bald pate, a wrinkled face, stooping in the back, feeble knees, and almost wholly rotten with age, having lived many Olympiads, and at length brought to dotage before so many witnesses?" (40)

I have quoted only one passage, but the entire satire is an elaboration of the same theme. In the sixth *Dialogue of the Dead*, Lucian makes Terpsio say,

> "In my opinion (Oh Pluto) the oldest ought to die first, and the rest successively in their turn, without permitting an old gouty dotard to live, after he has lost the use of his senses, and is at

---

(39) The early versions of the legend are reviewed by Baring-Gould, *op. cit.* They are reprinted verbatim in *Chronicles Selected from the Originals of Cartaphilus, The Wandering Jew. Embracing a Period of Nearly XIX Centuries.* Edited by David Hoffman. London, 1853, 6 vols. Among the novels which deal with the theme of the Wandering Jew, are the following:

Le juif errant. Eugène Süe. *Oeuvres*, Paris, (no date) XIV-XVII. (English translation, Boston, 1889.)

In the Track of the Wandering Jew. H. S. Merriman. In *Tomaso's Fortune, and Other Stories.* New York, 1904.

The Prince of India, or, Why Constantinople Fell. Lewis Wallace. New York, 1893.

St. Leon, A Tale of the Sixteenth Century. William Godwin. London, 1799.

Melmoth, The Wandered. C. R. Maturin. London, 1892, 3 vols. *Salathiel, The Immortal.* George Croly. Philadelphia, 1827. (Republished under the title *Tarry Thou Till I come.* New York, 1900.)

For bibliography of the Wandering Jew, see Gustave Brunet, *Notice historique et bibliographique sur les juifs-errants.* Paris, 1845. Also, P. L. Jacob (Paul Lacroix) *Curiosités de l'histoire des croyances populaires.* Paris, 1859.

(40) *Op. cit.*, I, 187-8.

> best but an animated tomb . . . The grievance would be somewhat
> alleviated, if one could but know how long they were to live, that
> one might avoid a tedious and fruitless courtship" (41).

So much for the simple idea of death as a boon. The account
of the Struldbruggs includes, besides, the narrative of a journey to a race of immortals, of which there is no hint in the
Tithonus myth, the Wandering Jew, nor in Lucian.

Brief mention of a deathless race is made in a rare little
book by Philippe d'Alcripe, *La nouvelle fabrique des excellens
traits de verité.,* Paris, 1579.

> "Un autre racontoit qu'en Iberie les hommes ne peuvent mourir,
> pour la bonne disposition de l'air, et qu'ils les convenoit transporter
> en une autre region pour les faire mourir, quand ils sont vieux et
> ennuyez de vivre" (42).

These Iberians could escape from life by moving to another
climate, but for the Struldbruggs there is no such refuge. In
both cases, however, long life is dreaded.

A race, cousin to the Struldbruggs, is found underground by
Klimius, in the province, Spelek, whose inhabitants, though
not immortal, yet live over 400 years, long enough to suffer
the horrors of old age.

> "The distinction between the Cambarrans and the Spelekans is
> that those in the first province never become more than, at the
> highest, four years old, while those in the second, on the contrary,
> live to above four hundred years . . . As much as I pitied the fate
> of the former, I, on the other hand, highly extolled the happy
> state of the latter. But when I maturely reflected on the real
> condition of both, I noticed that I was completely out in my judg-
> ment . . . This prolongation of life has a very lamentable effect.
> Those persons who, through unfortunate events, lose their prop-
> erty, receive hurts in their limbs, or fall into incurable sickness,
> are accustomed to curse intolerably their existence, and at last
> to commit suicide; as they, because of their long lives, see no end
> to their sufferings. The shortness of life is the most efficacious
> consolation to all wretched people. Both these countries greatly
> excited my admiration, and I quitted them with my head filled
> with philosophical contemplations" (43).

Swift goes much further than the author of *Klimius* in the
condemnation of long life. Only those Spelekans who are
impecunious, crippled, or sick, desire an early death; it is
prolonged misfortune, rather than long life itself which they
dread. The Struldbruggs are all equally miserable. With
them, under the most favorable circumstances, life is still an
unmitigated evil. Its horrors do not terminate after 400 years,

(41) *Ibid.,* III, 442-3.
(42) *Bibliothèque Elzévirienne.* Paris, 1853, CVII, 86.
(43) *Klimius,* 185-8.

nor may the unhappy immortals resort to suicide. Klimius, like Gulliver, envies the inhabitants their long life, at first; but is later converted from that absurdity by the spectacle of the ghastliness of indefinite old age.

An interesting analogue to the Struldbruggs is to be found in the anonymous Japanese work, *Wasobiyoe*, some account of which has been given in chapter seven, above. As I pointed out at the close of chapter four, above, Gulliver asserts, "It is very probable that the Japanese authors may have given some account of the Struldbruggs" (44). Swift may have been referring to the author of *Wasobiyoe*, when he wrote that.

Wasobiyoe visits the Land of Perennial Life, whose inhabitants are described, in part, as follows:

> "One death might indeed occur once in every thousand years, and would be compensated by one birth, but this was only a rare exception . . . These inhabitants were filled with quite a desperate admiration for death, and a distaste for their own never-ending existence . . . Wasobiyoe at first laughed this mania to scorn, but at last found that the prospect of never-ending life, year after year, and century after century, began to pall on him, . . . and so became slowly converted to the native notions on the subject of death" (45).

In this spirit, Wasobiyoe several times attempts suicide without success. Gulliver's experience is much the same.

> "I cried out, as in rapture, 'Happy nation where every child hath at least a chance for being immortal . . . Happiest beyond all comparison are those excellent Struldbruggs, who being born exempt from that universal calamity of human nature, have their minds free and disengaged, without the weight and depression of spirits caused by the continual apprehension of death . . . Whenever they see a funeral, they lament and repine that others have gone to a harbour of rest, to which they themselves can never hope to arrive . . . The reader will easily believe, that from what I had heard and seen, my keen appetite for perpetuity of life was much abated" (46).

The two narratives are not perfect parallels. The race met by Wasobiyoe derives its immortality from drinking the water of the rivers, "a dark red fluid," while the Struldbruggs are doomed to perpetual life from the hour of their birth. The philosophy involved, however, is much the same. Man's normal and habitual dread of death is exposed as the height of folly.

In the picture of the Struldbruggs, Swift paints life in its darkest colors. His theme here is no mere misanthropy, as

(44) See, above, ch. 4, 71. *Laputa*, 224.
(45) B. H. Chamberlain, *op. cit.*, VII, 1879.
(46) *Laputa*, 217-223.

with the Yahoos, later. Life is pleasant for Gulliver among the Houyhnhnms, despite human depravity. With the Struldbruggs, on the contrary, life itself is erased from the scanty list of things to be desired, and Death is hailed as the Great Deliverer. Here is no attempt to reform the race, no sneering slur at human vanity, but only a melancholy renunciation of life itself. There is no denying that Swift has done this chapter well. There is iron in the slow but powerful movement of the paragraphs describing the shades of the prisonhouse lengthening around the decaying Struldbruggs, for whom there is no escape to the world of youth and energy without, and no chance to lie down to pleasant dreams:

> "They were the most mortifying sight I ever beheld. Besides the usual deformities in extreme old age, they acquired an additional ghastliness in proportion to their number of years, which is not to be described . . . I grew heartily ashamed of the pleasing visions I had formed, and thought no tyrant could invent a death into which I would not run with pleasure from such a life."

The Travels of Lemuel Gulliver

IV

Houyhnhnmland

"I should never have attempted so absurd a project as that of reforming the *Yahoo* race in this kingdom; but I have now done with all such visionary schemes forever."

(*A Letter from Captain Gulliver to his cousin Sympson.*)

CHAPTER 10

A Voyage to the Houyhnhnms.

The *Voyages* to Lilliput and Brobdingnag are closely related in theme and story; Laputa is a miscellany of situations, paralleled in earlier satire; the *Voyage, to the Houyhnhnms* is a distinct unit, differing radically from the earlier *Voyages*, and complete in itself. It is marked by unreality of method and grotesqueness of conception, which have won for it vehement opinions from all sorts of people. Daring and unsparing in its criticism it surely is, but also, unconvincing and unpopular with all but the professional misanthrope.

I.

The Beast-Fable

The machinery employed by Swift (a race of horses endowed with the gift of tongues) connects the fiction of the Houyhnhnms with the venerable beast-fable, a literary convention as old as civilization, but no older. The animal fable, like the *Philosophic Voyage,* is not a primitive nor naïve form. It represents a conscious circumlocution for plain truth, a veiled attempt to moralize. The essence of the fable is an argument by analogy; the characteristics of the animals in the anecdotes representing human traits.

In its more common form the beast-fable appeared in short anecdotes. Its origin is still a battle ground for scholars and antiquaries. On the whole it seems fairly clear that our oldest fables came from northern Africa, more particularly, Egypt and the Nile valley (1). We must especially shun that Indogermanic school which goes to India for its origins. The African and Arabian fables lack the simple unity and terseness of Aesop. They are frequently long-continued *novelle,* involving a variety of events reflecting some phase of social life. The moral, usually, is not heavy, while the narrative is usually of high interest. Half a dozen fables of this type are preserved for us in the *Arabian Nights.*

The fables of Aesop, undoubtedly the best-known, may be predicated as the common source of most of the subsequent

(1) See, section III of the notorious *Terminal Essay* of Sir Richard Burton. *Arabian Nights.* London, 1886, X, 115-123.

collections known to the Western world. They are laconic tales, each containing a single event, and pointing a single moral. This element of clarity and simplicity made for permanent popularity; the epigrammatic moral became a proverb, as in the case of the fable of *The Fox and the Grapes*, which gave rise to the colloquial "Sour Grapes." Aesop's *Fables* were versified by the witty La Fontaine (2), and copied by a host of imitators. They appeared in prose form in London, accompanied by illustrations, in eighteenth century chapbooks (3). In fact, the bibliography of Aesop is itself a good-sized volume, which occupied the best years of at least one scholar to prepare (4).

Second only to Aesop is popularity were the *Fables of Bidpai*, of which a charming translation into Tudor English was made by Thomas North, under the title *The, Morall Philosophie of Doni* (5), consisting, largely, of Bidpai with original accretions. The popularity of Bidpai's *Fables* was great, and their versions many, but their influence upon European fabulists must not be exaggerated. After much time and type had been wasted in the effort to trace all fables to Bidpai and to India, a recent and more enlightened student has demonstrated the interesting fact that not more than one in ten of the beast-fables known in Europe can be traced to Indian origin (6). So that while we note here the most important collections of fables, it must not be supposed that we are tracing the rise and dissemination of the beast-fable. It seems to have developed independently in all parts of the world. If the best opinion today asserts that man was not once confined to the Garden of Eden, it is none the less certain that beast-fables did not all start from Noah's Ark.

In the Middle Ages, the beast-fable assumed an epic form in the cycle of *Reynard the Fox*, an extended satire on human civilization, which passed through many versions in Latin, French, German, and English (7). In the cycle of *Reynard*

---

(2) *Fables de la Fontaine*. Paris, 1779, 2 vols.

(3) *Chapbooks of the Eighteenth Century*. John Ashton. London, 1882, pp. 463-471.

(4) *A Manuel of Aesopic Fable Literature*. G. C. Keidel. Berlin, 1896.

(5) *The Morall Philosophie of Doni. Drawne out of the Auncient Writers*. By Thomas North. London, 1570. (Reprint in *Bibliothèque des Carabas*, with introduction by Joseph Jacobs. London, 1888.)

(6) Joseph Jacobs, *loc. cit.* See also, *Fables Turques*, J. A. Decourdemanche. Paris, 1882. (*Bibliothèque Orientale Elzévirienne*, XXXV.)

(7) Reprint of William Caxton's *The History of Reynard the Fox*, 1481, by W. J. Thoms. *Percy Society*. London, 1844, XII. See also *Le roman du renard*, by Ch. Potvin. Paris, 1862.

the single anecdote is replaced by a succession of episodes, in which the stage is crowded with animal actors who mimic the affairs of men. The beasts form a commonwealth, as do the Houyhnhnms, and have their professions, occupations, and amusements. The drama is a farce, a parody on civilization. The satiric method employed is that of ridicule. The beasts represent respectively the various human follies and vices, exaggerated and mildly brutalized. The bestial traits in man are first divorced from his more respectable qualities, and then incarnated in the animals. The total effect is that of caricature; while the comic treatment precludes any very serious inferences. The story of Reynard was popularized in chapbooks of the eighteenth century (8).

In our own time we have a revival of the anecdote of beast life in the negro stories of *Uncle Remus*, and a satiric use of the animal commonwealth in Anatole France's *Penguin Island* (9).

The connexion between the story of the Houyhnhnms and the beast-fable literature is not so significant as it appears, perhaps, at first glance. The essence, nay the *sine qua non*, of the beast-fable, in all of the forms mentioned above, is a reminiscence of the *homo primigenius* with erected ears and hairy hide. It rests its case upon the underlying bond which binds man to his fellow-brutes, and its expression is to make man behave, think, and feel like his unregenerate cousins. It presents a picture of man on a lower plane than the one on which he presumes to stand, but a plane on which it is admitted he once stood. The actors in the play, without exception, stand for types of men. The effect, therefore, is satirical allegory, never a utopian contrast to man. Now it is obvious that in Gulliver's fourth voyage, Swift does not conceive of any underlying blood relationship between the Houyhnhnms and man. The horses are intended to represent horses, and nothing else. The reader and Gulliver as well have no reason at any time to suspect that the Houyhnhnms mirror human character, for the very opposite is expressly stated. It is the Yahoos who here fill the rôle of man's detractors, taken by animals in the fable, and they do not have the bodies of beasts. Certainly the Houyhnhnms are careful to disclaim any relationship here. In short, the Houyhnhnms recall the beast-fable only on the superficial grounds that they are talkative animals. Their life is not a human allegory, and their civilization, unlike that of the animals in the fable, is infinitely

(8) Ashton, *op. cit.*, 95-108.

(9) *Penguin Island*, by Anatole France. Translated by A. W. Evans. London, 1909.

superior to anything evolved by man. The fabulists would drag man down to the level of the beasts; Swift would have man sit at the feet of the Houyhnhnms to learn perfect wisdom.

II.

Indealization of the Beasts—The Tradition of Ulysses and the Beasts.

Nowhere in beast-fable literature is there a hint of the superiority of animals to man. For the contrast between man and beast, resulting in the humiliation of the former, we must turn to other sources for *Gulliver*, to the *Beast-Utopias* and to the tradition of Ulysses and the Beasts.

The latter tradition was based on the incident at Circe's palace in the *Odyssey*, in which Ulysses insists that his companions be restored to their human shape. In the *Odyssey*, however, there is no intimation of the turn the story was destined to take in the hands of subsequent writers. According to Homer, the men are tricked into their bestial shape, and rejoice in their restoration to the "human form divine." The latter is first shorn of its divinity by Plutarch in his dialogue between Ulysses and Gryllus, entitled *That Brute Beasts Make Use of Reason*, included in Plutarch's *Morals,* a work with which Swift was very familiar, and which was translated into English in 1704 (10). The substance of the dialogue is as follows:

> Ulysses demands that Circe restore the Greeks to human form. Circe assures him that this would be a misfortune for them; to which Ulysses replies that she is talking nonsense. Circe agrees to let him make the offer, and even to argue with the beasts, but insists that she will not disenchant them without their own consent. She endows a hog, formerly Gryllus, with the power of speech and leaves Ulysses to converse with him. As the latter commences to pity Gryllus and his companions, Gryllus interrupts him, calling him a fool for refusing to share the enjoyments provided for them by Circe. Gryllus adduces the following arguments to prove that his company are better off as beasts than they were before as men:

> 1. Men win distinction through trickery, artifice, war, faith-breaking, and coney-catching. Beasts are free from craft and deceit, defending their rights by open courage.

> 2. Men make slaves of each other, while beasts prefer death to loss of independence. Constancy in man has to be required by law, it represents only reluctant subservience to edict. Beasts are naturally and voluntarily loyal and trustworthy.

---

(10) *Plutarch's Morals, translated from the Greek by Several Hands.* London, 1704, V, 203-216.

3. The ado made about Penelope's ten year chastity proves how rare the virtue is among men. Beasts are always temperate, and habitually chaste by nature. . Man's intemperance in eating and drinking, as well, makes physicians and diseases necessary; from which misfortunes beasts are exempt.

4. Beasts instruct their young in the necessary arts: Self-preservation, nest-building, physical culture, *etc.*, omitting the vain sophistries in which men waste their time.

(The dialogue ends abruptly at this point.)

Plutarch's dialogue is precisely in the spirit of Swift. A conceited human being attempts to convince an animal of his own superior intelligence. The argument, however, soon passes to the animal, who pours out into his astonished hearer's ears, a withering indictment, not of civilization, but of man's own, inherent nature. The points made by the Governor of the Houyhnhnms include all of the arguments used by Gryllus, and more besides.

In this brief dialogue, twelve pages in length, we have the essence of the more prolix versions that follow. In 1660, James Howell published *The Parly of Beasts . . . in XI Sections* (11), a series of dialogues, this time, in which Ulysses tries his luck with eleven different beasts, but without success. Each beast has his own particular complaint against man. The allusion to Plutarch's essay is unmistakable, though the situation has been superficially altered. Thus Circe is replaced by Morphandra, Queen of the Enchanted Island, and Ulysses has given place to Pererius, a more modern traveller. As there is no new resemblance to *Gulliver* in this version of the Ulysses story, I will omit a synopsis of the contents, confining myself to the barest outline of the scheme on which the work is constructed.

The allegory is a double one. Each beast interviewed represents, first those qualities commonly accorded to him in fable literature, idealized, rather than degraded; and second, each dialogue is concerned with the vices peculiar to a well-known Christian nation. For example: The Ape had once been a preacher in England, carried away by every wind of doctrine and by every new-fangled notion, on which account he had been transformed, with unassailable logic, to the shape of the ape; of all animals, the most capricious and imitative. The ape discourses upon the "sad case and confusion of thought" in England. In like manner the fox, once an unscrupulous Venetian politician, exposes the frightful social morality of Italy. The wolf has been a Swedish robber; the goose, a stupid Scotchman, who had served the interests of the British crown, thinking to secure his country's freedom. The mule, once a Spanish physician, discloses the fraudulent practices of that profession in Spain, *etc., etc.* All of the beasts prefer to bear the ills they have, than return to others that they know too well of.

_____

(11) For complete title, see, above, chapter 3, note 7.

This work is of special interest on several counts: In the first
place it presents a bitter denunciation of human affairs, placed
in the mouths of beasts, in a work written and published in
London, not long before Swift's own time. It is thus a precedent for Swift's use of animals to condemn man, in *Gulliver's*
fourth voyage. Furthermore, there is a hint of the voyage
idea in the general plan. The scene is no longer laid in Circe's
island of the Homeric world, but in the "enchanted isle,"
somewhere in the South Seas in the seventeenth century,
visited by the modern traveller Pererius; and the work, finally,
is filled with allusions to nations and conditions of contemporary Europe.

The Parly of Beasts, as Howell states in the preface, was
based upon the *Circe* of G. B. Gelli, the most significant version of the tradition of Ulysses and the Beasts, and a work
that was translated twice into English during Swift's lifetime (12). The earlier of these translations, the one made
by Tom Brown in 1702, will receive our special attention, as
it seems to have suggested to Swift ideas expressed by the
Governor of the Houyhnhnms.

The *Circe,* which Gelli states in his preface to be "built upon
the plan of the very learned Plutarch," consists of ten dialogues between Ulysses and as many beasts, with occasional
remarks by Circe. The satire, unlike the *Parly of Beasts,* but
like Gulliver's fourth voyage, is aimed at human nature *per se,*
without specific reference to nations or races. Dialogues are
carried on between Ulysses and an oyster, a serpent, a hare, a
goat, a hind, a lion, a horse, a dog, a steer, and an elephant.
Each of the animals, having seen human nature from the
standpoint of his previous profession, delivers himself of a
bitter arraignment of its vices. The sentiments are emphatic,
and the preference for the animal life, vehement. We are not
concerned in this study so much with the work as a whole; it
is little more than an elaboration of the ideas of Plutarch,
with pages and passages which correspond closely to similar
paragraphs in the *Houyhnhnms.* We can pause here to note
but two or three of the most significant parallels. In *Dialogue
III* (Ulysses and the Hare) the Hare recalls his life as a court
parasite as follows:

> "At last, after mature deliberation, I concluded that it wou'd be
> the wisest course for me to place myself in some honourable post
> at court, and to bring this about, employed all my own interest and

(12) *The Circe of J. B. Gelli. Done out of the Italian by Mr. Tho.
Brown.* London, 1702.

*Circe, translated from the Italian of John Baptist Gelli of the Academy
of Florence.* By H. Layng. London, 1744.

that of my friends; for, thought I, where can happiness dwell so properly, as in the magnificence and ease of a palace, near the person of a prince, who can command every thing? But, Good Heavens, how lamentably was I mistaken in my politicks? For besides the slavery of attending a prince and being perpetually about his person, lest someone else shou'd get possession of his ear, or whisper to him some malicious story of you to your ruine; besides your being obliged to flatter all his inclination, though never so unjust and dishonorable, to answer for all his faults, and to stand between him and the ill-humour of his people; besides, these and a thousand other inconveniences you must expect in such a service . . . never suffer'd me to enjoy one minute's happiness."

Speaking of court ministers, Gulliver says to the Governor of the Houyhnhnms,

"He (the courtier) applies his words to all uses, except to the indication of his mind; that he never tells a truth, but with an intent that you should take it for a lie; nor a lie, but with a design that you should take it for a truth; that those he speaks worst of behind their backs, are in the surest way of preferment; and whenever he begins to praise you to others or to yourself, you are from that day forlorn. The worst mark you can receive is a promise, especially when it is confirmed with an oath; after which every wise man retires, and gives over all hopes. There are three methods by which a man may rise to be chief minister: the first, is, by knowing how with prudence to dispose of a wife, a daughter, or a sister: the second, by betraying or undermining his predecessor: and the third is, by a furious zeal in public assemblies against the corruptions of the court. But a wise prince would rather choose to employ those who practise the last of these methods; because such zealots prove always the most obsequious and subservient to the will and passions of their master . . . The palace of a chief minister is a seminary to breed up others in his trade: the pages, lackeys, and porters, by imitating their master, become ministers of state in their several districts, and learn to excell in the three principal ingredients, of insolence, lying, and bribery" (13).

Gelli and Swift agree likewise on the evils of the military establishment and of the spirit of conquest among princes. Alluding to paid troops, the Lion asks Ulysses,

"And pray, what principle of virtue did those rascals in red go upon . . . those valiant plunderers of hen-roosts, those heroic scowrers of hedges, . . . the refuse of goals and gibbets, I mean your half-starved wretches that ventur'd all for two-pence a day, . . . What, they too, I suppose, fought for the liberty of Greece, and Helen's honour, did they not?"

Gulliver explains that

"the trade of a soldier is held the most honourable of all others; because a soldier is a Yahoo hired to kill in cold blood as many of his species, who have never offended him, as he can. There is likewise a kind of beggarly princes in Europe, not able to make

(13) *Houyhnhnms*, 266-268.

war by themselves, who hire out their troops to richer nations, for
so much a day to each man; of which they keep three-fourths to
themselves" (14).

The passages quoted are but a fragment of the anti-military
tirade that covers several pages in each work (15).

A more general accusation of human coveteousness and
pride is made elsewhere by the Lion as follows:

"If we have not reason as you have, that might teach us to overcome them . . . we have not such immoderate, insatiable appetites
as you, because we are ignorant of a thousand things that you
know. Pray tell me, what ambition can possibly have footing
among us, since we are all equal, and none of us despises another;
nay, since we have no such thing as superiority or degree of honour
to tempt us to obtain them by any manner of injustice, as you do
who are so strangely blinded by this lust of sovereignty? . . .
Envy can never find harbour among those of the same species that
are equal . . . Coveteousness also is a vice to which we are utter
strangers, because we have no distinction of *meum* and *tuum*, but
possess all in common. The same may be said of many other
vices, that render your lives unhappy, but never infected our tribes:
upon which consideration, some of our wise Grecians have affirmed,
that if man is the chief of other creatures, 'tis only in respect of
his miseries and troubles."

Quite similar views of European life are held by the Houyhnhnms:

"I was going on to more particulars when my master commanded
me silence . . . He seemed therefore confident, that instead of
reason, we were only possessed of some quality fitted to increase
our natural vices; . . . I was at much pains to describe to him
the use of money, . . . that when a Yahoo had got a store of this
precious substance, he was able to purchase whatever he had a
mind to . . . That the rich man enjoyed the fruit of the poor
man's labour, and the latter were a thousand to one in proportion
to the former. That the bulk of our people were forced to live
miserably, by labouring every day for small wages to make a few
live plentifully. I enlarged myself much on these and many other
particulars . . . but his Honour . . . went on a supposition that
all animals had a title to their share in the productions of the
earth" (16).

The beasts rise to the height of passionate eloquence in de-
nouncing man's intemperance. This is the special and favorite
theme of Gelli's horse (Dialogue VII, Ulysses and the Horse)
as it is also of the Governor of the Houyhnhnms. In the
former, the Horse says to Ulysses,

"But if I should turn the tables upon you, it wou'd make your hair
stand on end, perhaps, to think what wicked and abominable actions

---

(14) *Ibid.*, 255.
(15) *Ibid.*, 254-256.
(16) *Ibid.*, 256, 262.

you men have been guilty of. Consult your own histories a little,
and you will find how much hatred and animosity, how many feuds
and quarrels, how many treasons and murders, as well by sword
as by poison, which is a most execrable barbarity, have ow'd their
original to this disorderly passion (lust). I will therefore drop so
odious a subject, and pass to the pleasures of eating and drinking.
Now pitch upon what beasts you please, either wild or tame, and
you must own that in this respect we are more moderate than you.
I defy you to show me one that at any time either eats or drinks
more than nature requires, or that seeks after any other aliment,
than what she ordained: seed, or grass, or flesh, or fruit; whereas
you are so far from being satisfied with one nourishment, that you
eat everything, almost, search every corner in the universe, and
ransack the four elements to supply your luxury. Nay, not contented with this you employ learned masters in the mystery of
eating, who try a thousand expensive tricks to give a greater *haut
goust* to your food . . . Of drunkenness, your darling sin, that
tempts you for a little delight that you find in the wine to drown
your reason, upon which you value yourselves above all other
creatures, I will say nothing; since you yourselves are so ashamed
of it, that 'tis a common proverb with you, that a drunken man
deserves a double punishment for the crimes he commits in that
disorder . . . Therefore I leave you to judge, whether we are not
much more temperate than you?"

And in *Gulliver*,

"He desired I would let him know, what these costly meats were,
and how any of us happened to want them. Whereupon I enumer-
ated as many sorts as came into my head, with the various methods
of dressing them, which could not be done, without sending vessels
by sea to every part of the world, as well for liquors to drink, as
for sauces, and innumerable other conveniences. I assured him
that this whole globe of earth must be at least three times gone
around, before one of our better female Yahoos could get her
breakfast . . . That wine was not imported among us from foreign
countries to supply the want of water or other drinks, but because
it was a sort of liquid which made us merry, by putting us out of
our senses; diverted all melancholy thoughts, begat wild extravagant imaginations in the brain, raised our hopes, and banished our
fears, suspended every office of reason for a time, and deprived us
of the use of our limbs, till we fell into a profound sleep; although
it must be confessed, that we always awaked sick and dispirited,
and that the use of this liquor filled us with diseases, which made
our lives uncomfortable and short . . ." (17).

The setting used by Swift for the satire of the fourth
voyage is obviously much more closely related to the tradition
of Ulysses and the Beasts than to the beast-fable proper.
Ulysses and Gulliver have these experiences in common: 1.—
Both discourse with beasts whom they have been accustomed
to regard as inferior to man, and much more miserable than
man. 2.—The beasts fail to enthuse over the travellers' boasts

---

(17) *Ibid.*, 263-4.

of human greatness, expressing on the contrary, loathing and horror. 3.—The beasts are represented as less subtle and crafty than man, but much more sensible; they are temperate, healthy, and peaceable, where he is intemperate, vicious, and troublesome. 4.—The beasts do not represent man in an ideal state; they are merely animals, idealized to afford a contrast to mankind. There is no suggestion of the connexion between man and beast, as in the beast-fable. 5.—The faults detected in man are primarily, not faults of civilization and of training, but faults of natural depravity. The degeneracy alleged is applied to the entire race without distinction, and the arguments employed by the beasts in both books, show a striking agreement in expression.

There is still a good deal in *Gulliver* that finds no place in the Ulysses story: there is an animal kingdom on a large scale, composed of a single species, with a constitution and government all its own. For predecessors of the Republic of the Houyhnhnms we must turn to the *Beast-Utopias*.

III.

Beast-Utopias.

Beast-Utopias are not very common in the *Philosophic Voyages*. The fundamental unreality of an animal commonwealth precluded any successful realism in the narrative, and rendered the subject unfit for popular treatment as a part of voyage literature, in the hands of all but a few really great writers, who were able to surmount the obstacle. In fact, d'Ablancourt, Cyrano, and Swift, were the only writers to include *Beast-Utopias* among other less impossible countries visited by their heroes.

Before discussing the *Beast-Utopia* proper, two animal commonwealths of a slightly different type demand our attention. In the fifth book of Rabelais, Pantagruel and his companion Panurge visit the Ringing Island, "Inhabited by large, fine birds, looking for all the world as cunning and as malicious as men." The adventures occupy five chapters, which I have condensed as follows:

> Pantagruel and Panurge arrived at the Ringing Island, inhabited by large, fine birds, looking for all the world as cunning and as malicious as men. Some of them were white as swans, others black as crows, while some others yet were purple and white like pigeons. The males were called Clerghawks, Monkhawks, Abbothawks, Bishhawks, Cardinhawks, and Popehawks, but of the last there was only one. Each has his corresponding female. Yet there was no marriage. The Bishhawks begat Cardinhawks, and the Cardinhawks (if they lived long enough) begat a Popehawk.

Of this last kind there was never more than one at a time, as in our solar system there is but one sun. It is true that about 2760 moons previous there appeared two Popehawks, which resulted in a woeful rout, pecking, and mauling.

The birds spent all of their time chanting and singing, whenever the bells on top of the beautiful cages began to ring. They fed on nothing but fish. Their island is called 'Crooked Isle.' The birds all came from abroad, having been sent away by parents (who had more children than they wanted) to serve the Popehawk. Nine out of every ten among them were crippled, blinking, ill-favoured, deformed, or in some way an unprofitable load on the earth.

Pantagruel with great difficulty managed to catch a glimpse of the Popehawk as the latter knelt drooping in his cage, attended by a brace of little Cardinhawks and six lusty Bishhawks. Panurge was about to strike an insolent Bishhawk, when he was informed that it would constitute the Unpardonable Sin. "Hold, hold, honest friend; wound, poison, kill, and murther all the kings and princes in the world, by treachery, or how thou wilt . . . unnestle the angels from their cockloft, Popehawk will pardon thee all this. But never be so mad as to meddle with these sacred birds" (18).

Now this Ringing Island of Rabelais is a spurious, or false animal commonwealth. The bird disguise is too thin, and the allegory too obvious. There is not even a pretense at the discovery of an actual animal kingdom. Furthermore, the utopian element is wholly lacking from the story; the birds are clergymen in disguise, and a decidedly uncomplimentary disguise at that. The Houyhnhnms are said to be real horses; Rabelais is merely conducting a sort of Halloween joke, in which the actors are cloaked in feathered costumes. The Ringing Island is, therefore, not a real fore-runner of Houyhnhnmland; there is in the latter no genuine animal fable, and certainly no element of the *Beast-Utopia*.

An animal commonwealth figures also in Segrais' *Isle Imaginaire* (19), an abstract of which may be consulted in the appendix to this book. Segrais' Republic of Dogs, however, is not a sincere representation of cultivated animals; it is a burlesque, a deliberate parody on ideal commonwealths. Segrais felt the want of logic and truth in the exaggerated virtue and wisdom attributed to remote peoples by travellers. Why not as well, he implies, attribute utopian government to a race of dogs? Consequently we have represented a Republic of Dogs, but one which is ostensibly a joke. It is not to be supposed that the traveller really discovered these dogs, and the reader is not asked to credit their remarkable virtues. I take it there is a genuine distinction here. The Houyhnhnms are of course fictitious, but the fiction is a serious one. Swift

---

(18) *Op. cit.*, XXVI, 246-274. Bk. V, ch. 1-9.
(19) See the synopsis in the appendix.

implies that their life is a model one, better than man's. Segrais has no such didactic theme. He does not maintain the thesis that a canine republic is either better or worse than a human one. He only pokes fun at those who would have us believe that there is any region of the world where the people are better or happier than in civilized Europe, miserable as these latter may be. In short, Segrais does not create the situation essential to the *Beast-Utopia:* a contrast between man and beast, resulting in the humiliation of man.

The term *Beast-Utopia* is here used to designate an Imaginary Voyage, purporting to be the veritable account of a journey made by one or more Europeans to an ideal commonwealth of animals, whose virtuous and healthful life offers a striking contrast to the comparatively degenerate state of the human race.

(a) d'Ablancourt's, *Isle des animaux.*

A very curious *Beast-Utopia* is visited by the travellers in d'Ablancourt's *Sequel* (20) to Lucian's *True History*, the *Sequel* which I have already shown (21) served as a direct source for *Gulliver's Travels*. The following extract will give the reader a fair idea of the story.

"Toward evening, those who had reconnoitred reported that the land was inhabited by many kinds of animals, several of which were unknown to them. These animals had never before laid eyes on man. They had been most astonished to discover, on one side, lambs feeding with wolves, on the other side, hawks flying in company with doves . . . In the meantime there arrived monkeys in Greek costume, who brought to us the King's invitation to visit him . . . Accordingly, to comply with the orders of the price, we directed our steps toward him, and learned from our guides on the way that we were in the Island of the Animals, which was allied to the vaste Empire of Fables; this island, we were told, was surrounded by the Island of the Magicians, the Island of the Pygmies, the Island of the Giants, and others of like nature, all of which were under the jurisdiction of the poets, whose island was near by . . . Among the poets it was accounted the greatest crime to relate the same incident twice, or to repeat an idea. No one entered this domain without first checking his judgment at the gate, with permission to recover it on his exit; but when reclaimed it was invariably found to be bewildered and corrupted.

The Republic of Animals was ruled by the Phoenix, who was curious to see us, having never laid eyes on man. But for this curiosity we would not have been permitted to linger, because their legislators had prohibited them very strictly from having any commerce with members of our race . . . (Here follows a lengthy account of the various animals, and of their traits. The birds are

----

(20) *Voy. Imag.*, XIII. See above, chapter 5.
(21) Above, chapter 4.

the most intelligent, and the monkeys, the most useless and mischievous.)

The Phoenix had been appointed king because since his life lasted many centuries, frequent changes of sovereign were avoided, together with the attendent revolutions . . . The monkeys acted as orderlies and messengers; the tigers and lions formed the army; the geese and dogs served as footmen and sentries; the parrots were interpreters; *etc.* (Here follows a description of the reception given to the travellers, including games and entertainments at the court.)

The spectacle had only begun, when we saw approaching the talkative swallow, who roused the court to the greatest excitement with news of the revolt of the animals in the antipodes (Europe) against their human, or rather inhuman, masters. The swallow had been sent to the Republic of Animals for help, asking especially for a commander to lead their army, as they suffered from their long servitude, for lack of leaders. Straightway a council of the ruminating animals was held, in which it was determined to send the prime minister to the relief of their oppressed cousins. I secured permission to go along . . . We departed that same night, as circumstances allowed no delay, since all of the brutal races of mankind were up in arms to crush the animals back into slavery. (An exciting journey across the seas is made on the back of whales.) We learned on our arrival, that their revolt was induced by a parrot, who, having been blown by a terrible wind from the Republic of Animals into their country, described to them the peace and security in which the animals lived under their own rule, and encouraged them to throw off the yoke of bondage to humanity.

(A grand battle ensues, in which the animals are victorious.)

Certain rather interesting and unique parallels between this story and Gulliver's fourth voyage are obvious. 1.—In the first place, the animals live under their own rule, with no contact at all with civilized man. 2.—In the antipodes, on the contrary, animals are enslaved by man. 3.—The animals feel strong sympathy for their oppressed relatives, and indignation for their oppressors. 4.—The traveller becomes convinced of the superiority of the beast civilization, or rather their freedom from civilization. There are, on the other hand, fundamental differences in the two accounts. d'Ablancourt's *Isle des animaux* is filled with animals of all sorts, whereas the Houyhnhnms are all horses. There is a similar lack of unity in d'Ablancourt's picture of the animal life; it is one long continuous riot of fun and antics, each animal expressing his own self, with no real agreement in thought and conduct among the various species. It is hard to see just who keeps the peace in this jungle. In contrast to this the Houyhnhnms have a well ordered state, homogeneous in all respects, (though I suppose we should say "equusgeneous"), with all distracting passions properly curbed. d'Ablancourt does little more than assemble the animals and endow them with speech; he does not stamp upon them a super-bestial character. He keeps within the domain of the true fable, in which beasts are beasts and nothing more. It is only in respect to the attitude of the animals toward the injustice imposed upon their domesticated cousins that d'Ablancourt approximates the theme of Swift.

(b) Cyrano de Bergerac's *Histoire des oiseaux*.

Embedded in the *Histoire comique du soleil* of Cyrano de Bergerac is the *Histoire des oiseaux* (22), the birds who inhabit one of the islands in the sun. This story is so important for the understanding of the satire of the Houyhnhnms, that I have decided to resume it here in detail, quoting in the original passages of special importance.

After a three weeks flight we arrived in the Realm of the Birds. A beautiful bird floated down through the air to meet us, greeting us with these words: "You are a stranger here, and have come from a world in which I was born. I understand your language and will serve as your companion. Like other birds in all the planets my ambition was to mount up into the air to enter the Realm of the Birds, which is here located in the sun. The desire is attained by but few of us. In your world I was called the Phoenix." I followed this guide for about fifty miles to a region filled with birds, whose numbers equalled the leaves on the trees. That which pleasantly surprised me was the fact that these birds, instead of shunning me, circled familiarly around me; one whistling in my ear, another perching on my head. Seized by four eagles I was carried a thousand miles to the heart of a great forest, where (so a magpie informed me) their King resided.

Their first move was to throw me into prison, into the hollow trunk of a gigantic oak, on the branches of which the strongest of the birds perched to guard against my escape. Twenty-four hours later these guards were relieved by others, leaving me distracted with the uncertainty of impending disaster. The friendly magpie relieved my curiosity by telling me that the populace resented this prolonged confinement, demanding instead that I be turned over for them to devour, before I should lose my plumpness. The demand of the mob for a lynching verged on a riot. La rumeur pensa s'échauffer en sédition, car, ma Pie s'étant émancipée représenter que c'étoit un procédé barbare de faire ainsi mourir sans connoissance de cause un animal qui approchoit en quelque sorte de leur raisonnement; ils la pensèrent mettre en pièces, alléguant que cela seroit bien ridicule de croire qu'un animal tout nu, que la Nature même en mettant au jour ne s'étoit pas souciée de fournir des choses nécessaires à le conserver, fût comme eux capable de raison. "Encore, ajoutoient-ils, . . . l'Homme, sit sot et si vain, qu'il se persuade que nous n'avons été faits que pour lui; . . . l'Homme, qui soutient qu'on ne raisonne que par le rapport des sens, et qui cependant a les sens les plus foibles, les plus tardifs et les plus faux d'entre toutes les créatures; l'Homme, enfin, que la Nature,

(22) *Histoire du soleil*, 273-297.

pour faire de tout, a créé comme les monstres, mais en qui pourtant elle a infus l'ambition de commander à tous les animaux et de les exterminer." . . .

Ma charitable Pie m'avoit donné auparavant quelques instructions qui me furent trèssalutaires, et, entre autres, que je me gardasse bien d'avouer que je fusse Homme. Je répondis donc que j'etois de ce petit Monde qu'on appeloit la Terre, dont le Phénix et quelques autres que je voyois dans l'assemblée pouvoient leur avoir parlé; que le climat qui m'avoit vu naître étoit assis sous la zone tempérée de pôle arctique, dans une extrémité de l'Europe, qu'on nommoit la France; et, quant à ce qui concernoit mon espèce, que je n'etois point Homme comme ils se le figuroient, mais Singe; que des hommes m'avoient enlevé au berceau fort jeune et nourri parmi eux; que leur mauvaise éducation m'avoit ainsi rendu la peau délicate; qu'ils m'avoient fait oublier ma langue naturelle et instruit à la leur; que, pour complaire à ces animaux farouches, je m'étois accoutumé à ne marcher que sur deux pieds; et qu'enfin, comme on tombe plus facilement qu'on monte d'espèce, l'opinion, la coutume et la nourriture de ces bêtes immondes avoient tant de pouvoir sur moi, qu'à peine mes parens, qui sont Singes d'honneur, me pourroient eux-mêmes reconnoître. J'ajoutai, pour ma justification, qu'ils me fissent visiter par des experts, et qu'en cas que je fusse trouvé Homme, je me soumettois à être anéanti comme un monstre . . . Cette raison, quoique spécieuse, n'étoit pas suffisante; mais la plupart, ravis d'entendre que je n'étois pas Homme, furent bien aise de la croire; car ceux qui n'en avoient jamais vu ne pouvoient se persuader qu'un homme ne fût bien plus horrible que je ne leur paroissois, et les plus sensés ajoutoient que l'Homme étoit quelque chose de si abominable, qu'il étoit utile qu'on crût que ce n'étoit qu'un être imaginaire. (Cyrano, *op. cit.*, 277-280.)

The final trial approaches. The prosecuting attorney's charges place Cyrano in a position much lower than a Yahoo:

"Pour moi, je ne fais point de difficulté qu'il ne le soit (c'est à dire, homme), premièrement, par un sentiment d'horreur dont nous nous sommes tous sentis saisis à sa vue sans en pouvoir dire la cause; secondement, en ce qu'il rit comme un fou; troisièmement, en ce qu'il pleure comme un sot; . . . (*etc.*) Il faut maintenant examiner si, pour être Homme, il mérite la mort . . .

La première et la plus fondamentale Loi pour la manutention d'une République, c'est l'égalité; mais l'Homme ne la sauroit endurer éternellement: il se rue sur nous, pour nous manger; il se fait accroire que nous n'avons été faits que pour lui; il prend, pour argument de sa superiorité prètendue, la barbarie avec laquelle il nous massacre et le peu de résistance qu'il trouve à forcer notre foiblesse . . . Encore, est-ce un droit imaginaire que cet empire se flattent; ils sont, au contraire, si enclins à la servitude, que, de peur de manquer à servir, ils se vendent les uns aux autres leur liberté. C'est ainsi que les jeunes sont esclaves des vieux, les pauvres des riches, les paysans des gentilhommes, les princes des monarques, et les monarques mêmes des lois qu'ils ont établies . . .

Tout le Barreau frémit de l'horreur d'un si grand supplice; c'est pourquoi, afin d'avoir lieu de le modérer, le Roi fit signe à mon Avocat de répondre . . .

"Il est vrai, Messieurs, qu'ému de pitié, j'avois entrepris la cause de cette malheureuse bête; mais, sur le point de la plaider, il

m'est venu un remords de conscience, et comme une voix secrète
qui m'a défendu d'accomplir une action si détestable. Ainsi,
Messieurs, je vous déclare, et à toute la Cour, que, pour faire le
salut de mon âme, je ne veux contribuer en façon quelconque à la
durée d'un monstre tel que l'Homme." . . .

En même temps, l'assemblée se leva, et j'entendis murmurer qu'on
ne s'étoit pas davantage étendu à particulariser les circonstances
de ma tragédie, à cause de l'accident arrivé à un Oiseau de la troupe
qui venoit de tomber en pâmoison . . . On crut qu'elle était causée
par l'horreur qu'il avoit eue de regarder trop fixement un Homme.
C'est pourquoi on donna ordre de m'emporter.
                    (*Loc. cit.*, 286-291.)

In these pages of Cyrano, which have failed to catch the attention of critics, we have the most important source for the
satire in the last voyage of Gulliver. It should be remembered
from chapter four, above, that Swift borrowed heavily and
frequently from Cyrano's *Fantastic Voyages* for the contents
of *Gulliver's Travels*, so that his acquaintance with the Realm
of the Birds is a certainty. We have, to begin with, in both
accounts a sweeping and ruthless condemnation of human
nature, *per se*, pronounced by a tribunal of animals. In both
it is made clear that man, not his fellow creatures, is the real
brute; his crime is simply that he is a human being; it matters
not whether civilized or not. Both writers have the same
cutting wit that gives point and interest to the savage satire.
Then also, the stories correspond. A general assembly is held
in each case to decide the fate of the traveller. The charges
in both cases are precisely the same. The defendant stands
condemned, because, no matter what merits or special abilities
he has, he is a man, and as such is by nature "malicious,
treacherous, libidinous, cowardly, and insolent" (23). Hatred
for him is due largely to his presumption and cruelty in tyran-
nizing over his meeker superiors. The jury in both cases are
more lenient than is necessary, and the just sentence is merci-
fully commuted. Cyrano is here the model for Gulliver in his
adventures among the Houyhnhnms.

IV.

The Houyhnhnms

Swift has been heartily condemned for writing the fourth
voyage, so frequently, that the task of the dispassionate critic
is now extremely hard. For the present, however, let us forget the unpleasant quality of the satire, and confine ourselves
to a consideration of Swift's success in attaining his object.

---

(23) *Houyhnhnms*, 277.

It must be admitted by every thoughtful reader that Swift's
narrative machinery in this voyage is a clumsy and unconvincing vehicle for the satire. The proposition which Swift
attempts to prove is that man is an ungainly, ill-constructed
creature, and the horse a physical paragon. Anyone might
well be excused for failure to demonstrate this postulate satisfactorily, but the blunder of setting up so impossible a theorem remains to plague the inventor. The fictions of *Lilliput*
and *Brobdingnag* are admirably conceived. Beside the dainty
and graceful Lilliputians, Gulliver appears as an awkward,
lumbering Man-Mountain; in the presence of the Brobdingnagians he shrivels to the insignificance of an insect. The
situations are calculated to lead the reader naturally to
acquiesce in the satire.

The same cannot be said for the fourth voyage. The
Governor of the Houyhnhnms repeatedly criticizes the human
form, alleging it to be unfit for the elemental needs of life,
and ill-adapted for the service of reason, but the argument
is absurd.

> "Considering the frame of our bodies, and especially of mine, he
> thought no creature of equal bulk was so ill-contrived, for employing that reason in the common offices of life . . . He said . . .
> that my nails were of no use either to my fore or hinder feet . . .
> That I could not walk with any security, for if either of my hinder
> feet slipped I must inevitably fall. He then began to find fault
> with other parts of my body, the flatness of my face, the prominence of my nose, my eyes placed directly in front . . . That I
> was not able to feed myself without lifting one of my fore feet to
> my mouth . . . That as to myself, (it) was manifest I had neither
> strength nor agility . . . that I walked infirmly on my hinder feet;
> had found out a contrivance to make my claws of no use or defense,
> and to remove the hair from my chin, which was intended as a
> shelter from the sun and the weather. Lastly, that I could neither
> run with speed, nor climb trees" (24).

Passages of this sort tend to disprove the sound common sense
to which the Houyhnhnms lay claim, and serve to discount the
value of their criticism of mankind in general. Swift tells us
that the Houyhnhnms are more reasonable than Gulliver, but
the Houyhnhnms do not bear him out. To me the defect of
the fourth voyage, is not the brutality of the satire, but the
stupidity of the Houyhnhnms, whose judgments of Gulliver
prove nothing beyond their own incompetence to judge. Gulliver is quick to recognize the excellent qualities of the horses.
How is it then that the Houyhnhnms, who we are assured are
so much more sensible, are unable to realize that the human
body is much more suitable than their own for the common

---

(24) *Ibid.*, 250, 270.

needs of life? Someone has blundered, and I fear me it is Swift.

Again, the horses themselves are grotesque, inconsistent creatures. It may be granted to the author of a fable to endow his beasts with reason and speech, but where is the "horse-sense" in a fable that makes horses build houses and lay clay floors, weave mats, excell in pottery, milk cows, build fires, and thread needles (25)? Does not a horse lose some of his dignity when riding in a carriage (26)? The authentication and pseudo-realism of which Swift is elsewhere the perfect master, is conspicuously absent here. The situation is a forced one, the horses are not real horses, and consequently they prove nothing at all about the relative merits of man and horse. It was all very well for Swift to borrow the excellent ridicule of man, expressed by Cyrano's birds, but the latter were only birds, and confined their comparisons to matters of fact. The equine properties of the Houyhnhnms have been reinforced with magical and wholly inexplicable faculties that place them outside of the animal world altogether. The Houyhnhnms voice no plea for a return to nature, since they are themselves extra-natural.

Again, Swift is inconsistent in representing the Houyhnhnms as divided into social castes, that dare not mingle (27). How is it that these "horses" who live in gentle accord, free from all those instincts and institutions which have resulted in inequality among men, have their own aristocracy and their own slaves? The answer is simply that Swift was careless of his story; the fires of misanthropy obscured his judgment, and vitiated his argument. Much may be said for Swift's Yahoo conception of man, but much more against his misconception of the ideal Houyhnhnms. Powerfully as he reiterates and supports his postulate that the horse is the better creature, the Houyhnhnms refute it on every page.

In making this judgment I realize that I am reversing the accepted opinion of most critics, who incline to find fault with the Yahoos rather than with the Houyhnhnms. We may not like the Yahoo, but that is beside the point. The Yahoo is at least a consistent and a conceivable representative of man. Revolting he may seem, but he is physically possible. After all, he is a fair and a rather flattering illustration of man in a state of *complete* degradation, and that is all that Swift implies. The indignant objection, so frequently made, that civilized man is better than the Yahoo, is wholly irrelevant,

---

(25) *Houyhnhnms*, 236, 237, 285, 239, 290, and 285, respectively.
(26) *Ibid.*, 239.
(27) *Ibid.*, 267-268.

since Swift agrees. The Houyhnhnms remark on the fact that Gulliver is cleaner, and more intelligent than the native Yahoo (28). He is admitted by the Houyhnhnms to social privileges never granted to the Yahoos. The latter are Hyde, and Gulliver is Dr. Jekyll.

The Yahoos are Swift's own creation. A hint for them may have been derived from the *Isle des animaux* of d'Ablancourt, in which the animals conquer and enslave the men in the antipodes; or again, from the *Voyage of Gonzales*, in which Gonzales discovers that on the moon, men of his own stature are despised, and assigned to servile tasks (29), but the Yahoo has no real ancestor in literature.

Attempts to evaluate the philosophy of the fourth voyage usually have been ruined by strong prejudice. Thackeray's disapproval, here quoted, is mild for those of his own view.

> "Some of this audience may not have read the last part of *Gulliver*, and to such I would recall the advice of the venerable Mr. Punch to persons about to marry, and say "Dont." When Gulliver first lands among the Yahoos, the naked, howling wretches clamber up trees and assault him, and he describes himself as 'almost stifled with the filth that fell about him.' The reader of the fourth part of *Gulliver's Travels* is like the hero himself in this instance. It is Yahoo language, a monster gibbering shrieks, and gnashing imprecations against mankind—tearing down all shreds of modesty, past all sense of manliness and shame; filthy in word, filthy in thought, furious, raging, obscene" (30).

Few, if any, have lifted their voices in defense of the picture which Swift paints. It would be futile to add, here, another opinion of the justice of the satire. One thing, however, is pretty clear. Whether or not the indictment of the human race be fair, the shot has missed its mark. Relatively few of the readers of *Gulliver* have read the fourth part: it has been excised from the more popular editions; failing in this way for want of an audience. I suppose we may safely say that circulation is essential to the greatness of any book, and no doctoral theses can elevate in our esteem a work which is fundamentally unreadable. Moreover, the best judgment of those who have read it is that the picture is overcharged with nauseating details, that the colors are not sufficiently subdued. The situation created does not warrant the brutal sentiments, however just these may be in and by themselves; the arguments are illogical; and the Houyhnhnms themselves, not

---

(28) *Ibid.*, 267, 276.
(29) See above, chapter 7, 14.
(30) W. M. Thackeray, *The English Humourists*. London, 1911, pp. 23-24. For similar opinions consult Mitford's *Life of Swift*, and Edward Young's *Conjectures on Original Composition*.

wholly admirable. Cumulated invective does not alter the fact
that Gulliver is and remains, throughout, more attractive and
more sensible than the Houyhnhnms. Gulliver may be a
despicable creature, but he meets no superiors in Houyhnhnmland.   In fact Swift fails to show us any better race in the
world about us; he advocates no return to nature, no imitation
of the "noble" savage. The heart of his philosophy is not
original, for it is identical with Christian pessimism. Man
that is born in sin is born a Yahoo; and, unless he be born
again, will live and die a Yahoo.

Part III

The Influence

of

Gulliver's Travels

"Gulliver has been the conversation of the whole town ever since. The whole impression sold in a week . . . From the highest to the lowest it is universally read, from the Cabinet Council to the nursery."

(Letter from Gay to Swift, Nov. 17, 1726.)

CHAPTER 11

Gulliveriana—The Minor Works of Lemuel Gulliver.

In a graduate course in English literature in one of our
Eastern universities the question was raised, not long ago,
"How many books of the eighteenth century (or more exactly,
of that part of the century called "eighteenth" by scholars)
are alive today? In spite of the recent re-discovery of the
interesting world, through which Dr. Johnson and Boswell
moved, the class could agree on less than half a dozen works,
which today are widely read outside of the college campus.
Boswell's *Johnson*, and Gray's *Elegy* were on the list, of course,
with *Robinson Crusoe*, and—by unanimous consent—*Gulliver's
Travels*.

Gulliver is indeed still read, as Gay said in 1726, "from the
cabinet council to the nursery." Like many other writers, the
witty and mendacious captain lives to-day on the reputation
of one famous work; but it was not always so. The collected
works of Lemuel Gulliver (were they collected, and I wish they
were) would occupy several volumes of poetry and prose.
While a large number of his writings are dead, and not to be
resurrected by any amount of labor, many others, though
frivolous and inconsequential, are exceedingly witty, a quality
lacking in much that has survived. The publication of the
most worthless of these, is itself a tribute to Gulliver's fame,
as Lady Bolingbroke once wrote to Swift, "It is at least an
indication of your honest traveller's having had such success
among us, that the name of Gulliver is sufficient to recommend
the most paltry performance to the public" (1).

Swift himself was fearful of the reception which *Gulliver's
Travels* would find in political circles, where he could ill spare
any more favor. To Pope, he wrote, "I have employed my
time in finishing, correcting, and amending my Travels in
four parts, complete and intended for the printer . . . if one
should be found brave enough to venture his ears" (2); to
which Arbuthnot, who saw the letter, replied that, if necessary,
he would set up the type himself. The fears were groundless.
So far from taking offense at the satire, the early readers of

(1) Letter to Swift, Feb. 17, 1727.
(2) Letter to Pope, Sept. 29, 1725.

Gulliver were so completely engrossed with the quaint language, manners, and dress of the strange creatures described, that they ignored the author. Swift wrote to Pope that his purpose in writing the *Travels* was "to vex, rather than to divert the world." The world obstinately chose to be diverted; it forgot Swift, the misanthrope, and gathered about Gulliver, the entertainer.

I.

Sequels and continuations to *Gulliver's Travels* appeared in time, as we shall see later; but at first, the Queen Anne Wits were captured by the grotesque and fantastic manner of the book, rather than by its matter. Swift received letters written wholly or in part in the dialect of Lilliput, Brobdingnag, and Houyhnhnmland. (Laputa was rarely quoted.) The vogue of this new script is confirmed by the following extract from a letter written to Swift by the Earl of Peterborough:

> "I was endeavoring to give an answer to yours in a new dialect, which most of us are very fond of. I depended much upon a lady, who had a good ear and a pliant tongue, in hopes that she might have taught me to draw sounds out of consonants. But she, being a professed friend of the Italian speech and vowels, would give me no assistance, and so I am forced to write to you in the Yahoo language. The new one in fashion is much studied, and great pains taken with the pronunciation. Everybody approves of it, but the women seem most satisfied, who declare for few words and horse performance. It suffices you to know that there is a neighing duet appointed for the next opera . . ." (3).

Mrs. Howard wrote a letter to Swift (4), composed wholly of Gulliverian jargon; its failure may be measured by Swift's reply that he could not understand three words together. Years later, Diderot, in his notorious novel, *Les Bijoux Indiscrètes*, had one of his characters translate the speech of a mare by using *Gulliver's Travels* as a dictionary. Fans were sold in the streets of Paris, painted with scenes taken out of *Gulliver's Travels*, and two burlesque dramatizations (now lost) of scenes from the book were staged in Parisian theatres (5). The enjoyment of the readers was increased by occasional dupes who took Captain Gulliver too seriously. Besides the old gentleman who searched his map for Lilliput, there was a Roman clergyman who warned his congregation against believing what had been written by that heretic

---

(3) Nov. 29, 1726.

(4) Nov. (?), 1726.

(5) Letter from Lady Bolingbroke to Swift, Feb. 17, 1727.

mariner (6). Arbuthnot wrote to Swift, "Lord Scarborough, who is no inventor of stories, told me that he fell in company with a master of a ship, who told him that he was well acquainted with Gulliver" (7). For a brief time, indeed, Gulliver was the conversation of the whole town. Public interest was met with keys and commentaries, including the tract, *"Gulliver Decypher'd* (8), and a voluminous traveller's guide to the topography and customs of the new countries, entitled, *"Gulliver's Travels" Compendiously Methodized. In Four Parts.* What Gulliver's royalties from the Parisian fans and neighing duets in the opera were, we are not told; but, with the entire nation subscribing, it is not strange that he was tempted to take up his pen once more, to silence the insistent publishers.

II.

Of Gulliver's minor writings, which ran over a hundred in all, about sixty titles are preserved. The mythical volume of his verse included everything from street ballads to polished odes. *An Excellent New Ballad on the Wedding of Pretty Miss Sally . . . By Capt. Gulliver, London,* 1730, lacks the virtue of refinement alone to make it thoroughly enjoyable. Gulliver treacherously gave to the press a touching love-poem, which his devoted nurse had slipped into his pocket before he left Brobdingnag, *The Lament of Glumdalclitch for the Loss of Grildrig,* written actually by Gay. Two short poems, by Pope, appeared in 1727, one addressed to Mr. Lemuel Gulliver by a British Houyhnhnm, congratulating him on his enviable sojourn among the horses. The other (an epistle from Mary Gulliver to her husband) expresses her fear lest some amiable Houyhnhnm be preferred to her in his affections. A school of poets flourished over-night to create a new metrical form: the "Lilliputian Ode,"—consisting, usually, of two-stress, three-syllable lines, petty in form and content to conform to the "Tiny race, and nation void of brain," which Swift fashioned in Lilliput. Scores of these *Odes* were printed. As they will never be printed again, the occasion having passed forever, and as most readers have never seen one, I quote here a specimen, written by Henry Carey, 1728, which differs from the norm, only in that it contained two syllables to the line instead of three.

---

(6) See article by W. E. Axon. *Notes & Queries,* 1831, Ser. 6:VI, 128.
(7) Nov. 8, 1726.
(8) The reader is referred, once and for all, to the bibliography of "Gulliveriana" at the close of this chapter.

A Lilliputian Ode on their Majesties' Accession

Smile, smile,
Blest isle.
Grief past
(At last)
Halcyon
Comes on.
New KING
Bells ring;
New QUEEN,
Blest scene.
Britain
Again
Revives
And thrives
Fear flies,
Stocks rise;

Wealth flows,
Art grows.
Strange pack
Sent back;
Own folks
Crack jokes.
Those out
May pout;
Those in
Will grin.
Great, small
Pleased all.
God send
No end,
To line
Divine,

Of GEORGE and CAROLINE.

Another Lilliputian Ode, and about the only one that to-day is accessible to the general reader, may be found in any volume of Pope's Poetical Works, *Ode to Quinbus Flestrin, The Man-Mountain, By Titty-Tit, Poet-Laureate to his Majesty of Lilliput. Translated into English.* The vogue of this abbreviated or "infantine" metre is confirmed by the following statement, quoted from Arbuthnot's *Miscellany*, 1728.

> "Whereas the wits of the town are mightily taken with the Lilliputian measure, and have shrunk their verses to two syllables in a line, the author is preparing for the press an ode which shall contain but a syllable and a half in a line."

Unfortunately, for it would be a rare curiosity, the ode in question, if written, has been lost. Even the university students of the day were writing their class-day poems in the new verse, thereby calling forth King Oberon's edict, which appeared in a volume of trifles, entitled, *Gulliveriana*, 1728, a few lines of which are here quoted:

> "King Oberon's Edict. (On Occasion of the Students of the College of Dublin Continually Writing in the Lilliputian Manner and Measure of Verse.)"

> "Little lads of Dublin town,
> Dangling in a dirty gown;
> On your short iambic feet,
> Through each lane, and through each street,
> Ye bards, by tasting Patrick's spring,
> Who little sonnets learn to sing.
> . . . . .
> To ye, ye pygmy poets, I
> Prince of pygmiest pygmies, hie,
> And command you, quite, to quit,
> This laconic fit of wit,

> For to me, without dispute,
> Appertain all things minute.
> Minute metre, dapper wit,
> Tiny thoughts, which bit by bit,
> Straining through a nutshell brain
> Form the genuine fairy strain.
> Banishing, with all his tricks,
> From my court, (Swift) Dean of Saint Patrick's.
> Who is a mere usurper grown,
> And aims at Oberon's rightful crown."

The Prose writings of Gulliver reveal a surprising variety. *The Fop's Oberservation on Lilliput; The Pleasures and Infelicities of Marriage, Display'd in Ten Books; A Voyage to Locuta;* and, *Gulliver's Last Voyage, Describing Ballymugland,* are but a few titles of a score or more of witty and scurrilous pamphlets to which unknown authors forged the name of Gulliver. One tract is a real curiosity. *The Anatomist Dissected, or The Man-Midwife Finely Brought to Bed. By Lemuel Gulliver. Surgeon and Anatomist to the Kings of Lilliput and Balnibarbi,* 1727, which ran through two editions. This tract is a treatise on obstetrics, exposing the fraud of one, Mary Tofts, who claimed to have been delivered of fifteen rabbits at one confinement. Several physicians wrote stormy refutations of her story, and libels against her attendant physician, who vouched for its truth. These pamphlets are interesting reading, if only because their vehement tone argues for the credulity which seems to have been given to the claims of Mrs. Tofts. Gulliver analyzes the fraud, point by point, in a thoroughly scientific manner, and concludes by asserting that such a miracle, while not uncommon in Balnibarbi, could never occur in conventional London. This tract explains an allusion to Gulliver's connexion with the Toft's case, at the close of a letter from Mrs. Howard to Swift, November 26, 1726, which has escaped the eyes of Swift's editors.

The obvious thing for imitators of Swift to do was to publish pretended sequels to the original *Travels* of Gulliver, which, they alleged, were discovered among Gulliver's papers. In the *Gentleman's Magazine,* volume 3, 1733, some witty and anonymous correspondent recommended to the British Parliament the methods of the projectors of Laputa. Gulliver, it was suggested, should be dispatched to bring back to London a Laputan physician, who should be engaged to attend sessions of Parliament, feel pulses, administer laxatives and corrosives, with the aim of opening a few mouths and closing a great many others. This suggested to the youthful Dr. Samuel Johnson, then a hack-writer in London, the application of the satire in *Gulliver's Travels* to Parliamentary proceedings.

Although few of the readers of Johnson realize it, it is a fact that for eight years he reported these proceedings in the *Gentleman's Magazine,* as, *Debates in the Senate of Lilliput,* purporting to be accounts of Lilliputian politics, given to the public by Gulliver himself. Boswell tells us that some of the names used by Johnson were purely fictitious, while others were anagrams of the names of members of Parliament whose speeches were being reported. For a few months, Boswell says, the public was deceived. In these reports, Lilliput was England, Blefuscu, Ireland; Hurgoes, House of Lords; Clinabs, House of Commons; Milendo, London; Walelop, Walpole; Ptit, Pitt; *etc.* Altogether the debates cover several thousand pages of very dry reading; were it not for the Gulliverian disguise and the famous author, they would never leave our library shelves.

The Abbé Desfontaines, the translator of *Gulliver's Travels* into French, was the only writer to attempt a continuation equivalent to the original in scope and design. *Le Nouveau Gulliver,* purporting to be the travels of John Gulliver, son of Lemuel, appeared in Paris in 1730, and was promptly translated into English by John Lockman in the same year. The *New Gulliver* is inferior to the work of Swift, but that does not mean that it deserves the total neglect into which it has fallen. To invent a series of new adventures equal to those of Lemuel Gulliver could hardly be expected, even of Swift himself, and I think Desfontaines did very well. The first voyage is to Babilary, the land of Amazons. The satiric method here is to attribute to the dominant female sex all the corruption practised in Europe by men, in which light they appear doubly revolting; or at any rate, they appear so to the conventional, double-standard reading public, who have been accustomed to expect a superior brand of virtue from the gentler sex. The reader is informed confidentially, that in reality a few favored males rule Babilary, indirectly; "just as in Europe a courtezan is ordinarily the power behind the throne." The second voyage is to Tilibet, where the natives mature at the age of five. Here babies grow so fast that they have to be measured for new clothes every month. The value of time is appreciated by these people who have so little of it. *Ennui* is unknown, and of course no one has time to make war. Tilibet is a utopia where more progress is made in five years than in Europe in fifty. Altogether the six voyages on which John Gulliver conducts the reader, are conceived and executed with no small degree of ingenuity.

In the latter half of the eighteenth century two imitations of *Gulliver's Travels* appeared, neither one possessing any great merit. *Modern Gulliver's Travels to Lilliput,* is a lengthy account of Gulliver's amorous intrigue with a Lilliputian lady, stated in the preface to be an integral part of the original, omitted by Lemuel through delicacy. Readers will remember that there is a hint of the scandal in the work of Swift itself, a hint which was expanded in the imitation to unnecessary length of indecency. The same theme is the subject of the companion piece, a theatrical farce, written by the famous actor, David Garick, entitled, *Lilliput.* The text is preserved for us to-day in volume 6 of the *Collection of Esteemed Farces,* 1792. Both works capitalize the grotesque nature of the love affair between a giant and a pygmy mistress. It must be admitted that both are amusing; but the humor of Garrick is suited to the drawing room, while the other,—well it could be read in a smoking car, by the members of the Society for the Suppression of Indecent Literature.

In addition to the writings attributed to Gulliver by their authors, the reader will find in the bibliography at the close of this chapter, a number of works of acknowledged authorship, directly inspired by *Gulliver's Travels.* Most of them are unimportant. The two satires on pedantry, written by Swift's friend, John Arbuthnot, *An Account of Learning in the State of Lilliput,* and, *Critical Remarks on Gulliver's Travels,* are exquisite bits of clever satire, equal in every respect to anything that Swift wrote. The *Micromégas* by Voltaire is recommended as an amusing exaggeration of the ridicule heaped upon mankind in *Lilliput.*

III

A close study of the imitations of *Gulliver* makes a few generalizations possible. The source of inspiration in nine cases out of ten was the story, not the philosophy of the book. The fictions and the fancies of *Gulliver* were served up by the press in a hundred or more imitations; the bitter undertone of misanthropy which marked the work of Swift, remained undigested. The pill was taken eagerly because of its sugar-coating. For the most part, the imitations are short and trifling, amusing but not convincing. The contributions of Arbuthnot are classics of literature; and the sequel by Desfontaines is good reading. Nothing else is of more than adventitious interest.

Nine out of ten of the imitations deal with Lilliput. For some reason, the first voyage appealed most strongly to the imagination of readers; perhaps, because it is pleasanter to laugh at the pettiness of mankind, than to enthuse over its grossness or its stupidity.

Looking over the whole field, in England and abroad, we find only scattered traces of the influences of *Gulliver's Travels*. Swift did not found any school, established no new form of satire; nor did his *Gulliver* in any way modify or divert the channel of contemporary literature. *Gulliver* marks not only the high-point in the history of *Philosophic Voyages*, but it stands near to the end of the line.

If the imitations of *Gulliver* were short-lived, yet the book itself lives on; the real measure of its influence is to be found, not in the works of those who mimicked Swift, but in the pleasure of the multitude who read him. In English, the work has been reprinted, time without number; it has been translated into French, Dutch, German, Norwegian, Spanish, Portugese, Polish, Greek, Swedish, and Hebrew. It is true that Swift failed in his hope of vexing the world with *Gulliver*, but he prophesied the truth when he wrote to Abbé Desfontaines:

> "An author who would sit down to write only for a single town, a province, a kingdom, or even a century, so far from being translated, does not even deserve to be read. *Gulliver* will last as long as our language" (9).

---

(9) Letter to Desfontaines, July, 1727.

Gulliveriana

A Chronological List of All of the Imitations of *Gulliver's Travels*, of the 18th Century.

1726

The Blunder of All Blunders; or, The Wonder of All Wonders; or, Gulliver Devour'd by Butterflies; or, The Fop's Observation on Lilliput. Dublin, 1726.

Lemuel Gulliver's *Travels* Into Several Remote Nations of the World, Compendiously Methodized. London, 1726. (Dublin reprint, 1727.)

> (Second · Title Reads: A Key, Being Observations and Explanatory Notes upon the *Travels* of Lemuel Gulliver. By Signor Carolini.)

The Most Wonderful Wonder, That Ever Appear'd to the Wonder of the British Nation . . . With a Dialogue Between the Old She-bear and Her Foster Son. Written by the Copper-farthing Dean. (London, 1726.) Arbuthnot's *Miscellanies*. 2nd ed. Glasgow, 1751, I, 192-193.

1727

The Anatomist Dissected, or, The Man-Midwife Finely Brought to Bed. By Lemuel Gulliver. Westminster, 1727.

Memoirs of the Court of Lilliput . . . By Capt. Gulliver. Containing an Account of the Intrigues and Some Other Particular Transactions of That Nation, Omitted in the Two Volumes of his Travels. London, 1727.

1727

Poems Suggested by *Gulliver*. *Pope's Complete Poetical Works*. Edited by H. W. Boynton. Boston, 1903, pp. 121-5.

> 1. Ode to Quinbus Flestrin, The Man-Mountain. By Titty-Tit, Poet Laureate to His Majesty of Lilliput. Translated into English. (London, 1727.)
> 2. The Lamentation of Glumdalclitch for the Loss of Grildrig. (London, 1727. Attributed also to Gay.)
> 3. To Mr. Lemuel Gulliver. The Grateful Address of the Unhappy Houyhnhnms Now in Slavery and Bondage in England. (London, 1727.)
> 4. Mary Gulliver to Captain Lemuel Gulliver. An Epistle. (London, 1727.)

Poems Occasioned by Reading the *Travels* of L. G. Explanatory and Commendatory. By H. Carey. Dublin, 1727.

Several Copies of Verses on Occasion of Mr. Gulliver's *Travels*. Never Before Printed. London, 1727.

Two Lilliputian Odes: The First, On the Famous Engine with Which Captain Gulliver Extinguished the Flames in the Royal Palace . . . The

Second, Inviting a Bookseller to a Coffee-House, where the Author was. London, 1727. Printed by S. Pigmy for Tom. Thumb.

A Voyage to Cackogallinia, With a Description of the Religion, Policy, Customs,. and Manners of that Country. By Samuel Brunt. London, 1727. Travels Into Several Remote Nations of the World, by Capt. Lemuel Gulliver, Vol. III. London, 1727.

(A forgery, consisting chiefly of a translation of the *Histoire des Sévarambes*, by Denys Vairasse d'Alais.)

1728

The Miscellaneous Works of the Late Dr. Arbuthnot. 2nd ed. Glasgow, 1751. 2 vols.

1. The Masquerade. A Poem Inscribed to C — — t H-D-G-R. By Lemuel Gulliver, Poet Laureate to the King of Lilliput. (London, 1727), II, 6-18.
2. Gulliver Decypher'd, or, Remarks on a Late Book entitled, "Travels into Several Remote Nations of the World, by Capt. Lemuel Gulliver." Vindicating the Reverend Dean on Whom it is Maliciously Father'd, With Some Probable Conjectures Concerning the Real Author. (London, 1728), I, 75-113.
3. Critical Remarks on Capt. Gulliver's *Travels*. By Doctor Bantley. (London, 1728), I, 114-140.
4. An Account of the State of Learning in the Empire of Lilliput, together with the History and Character of Bullum the Emperor's Library-keeper. Faithfully Transcribed out of Captain Lemuel Gulliver's General Description of Lilliput, Mentioned in the 69th Page of the First Volume of his *Travels*. (London, 1728), I, 141-151.
5. The Life and Adventures of Don Bilioso de l'Estomac. Translated from the Original Spanish into French; Done from the French into English. (London, 1728), I, 182-192.
6. The Devil to Pay at St. James's. (London, 1728), I, 213-224.

Gulliveriana. A Fourth Volume of Miscellanies Being a Sequel to the Three Volumes Published by Pope and Swift. (By Jonathan Smedley.) London, 1728.

1730

A Libel on Dr. Delaney. Dublin, 1730. Reprinted for Capt. Gulliver. An Excellent New Ballad on the Wedding of Pretty Miss Sally to Jolly Old J——O. By Captain Gulliver. Dublin, 1730. Le nouveau Gulliver, ou, Voyages de Jean Gulliver, fis du Capitaine Lemuel Gulliver. Par l'Abbé Desfontaines. Paris, 1730.

1731

The Travels of Mr. John Gulliver, Son to Capt. Lemuel Gulliver. Translated from the French, by J. Lockman. London, 1731. 2 vols.

1733

Human Ordure Botanically Considered. The First Essay of the Kind Ever Published in the World. By Dr. S——t. Dublin (Reprinted at London), 1733.

The Maxims of the Laputan Projectors Applied to the British Parliament. *Gentleman's Magazine*, III, 463-465. London, 1733.

1735

Voyage merveilleux du prince Fan-Férédin dans la romancie. Par P. Bougeant. Paris, 1735. (*Voy. Imag.*, XXVI, 68-70.)

1738-1745

Debates in the Senate of Magna Lilliputia. *Gentleman's Magazine*, VIII-XV. London, 1738-1745.

1739

A Defence of Mr. Gulliver's *Voyages*. Truth Asserted, or, A Demonstration that the Relations in Mr. Gulliver's *Voyages* are No Fiction. By Jonathan Wagstaff. *Gentleman's Magazine*, IX, 55-59. London, 1739.

1745

The Pleasures and Felicity of Marriage, Display'd in Ten Books. By Lemuel Gulliver. 2nd ed. London, 1745.

1748

Les bijoux indiscrets. (Paris, 1748), ch. 31. *Oeuvres de Denis Diderot*. V, 178-181. Paris, 1821.

1752

Micromégas. Voyage d'un habitant du monde de l'etoile Sirius dans la planette de Saturne. *Oeuvres Complètes de Voltaire*. XXI, 105-122. Paris, 1879.

1766

Les aveugles juges de couleurs. (Paris, 1766.) *Oeuvres Complètes de Voltaire*. XXI, 245-246. Paris, 1879.

1782

The Lilliputian Library, or, Gulliver's Museum . . . The Whole Forming a Complete System of Juvenile Knowledge. By Lilliputius Gulliver. 10 vols. Berlin, 1782.

1792

Lilliput, A Dramatic Entertainment. By David Garrick, Esq. (Date ?.) *A Collection of Most Esteemed Farces*. VI, 313-332. Edinburgh, 1792.

1796

Modern Gulliver's Travels: Lilliput, Being a New Journey to that . . . Island. Containing a Faithful Account of . . . Those Famous Little People from the Year 1702-1796. By Lemuel Gulliver, Jun. London, 1796.

1797

Gulliver Revived. Containing Singular Travels, Campaigns, Voyages, and Adventures . . . By Baron Munchausen. 5th ed. London, 1797.

1818

Voyage to Locuta. A Fragment with Etchings and Notes. London, 1818.

1825

Gulliver's Last Voyage. Describing Ballymugland, or, The Floating Island. 2nd ed. London, 1825.

Bibliographies and Appendices

Appendix A, *Fantastic Voyages*

1. Lucian, *True History* (*ca.* 170 A. D. The *Dryden Lucian*, London, 1711, III, 122-186).
   (Synopsis given in chapter 1.)

2. Lucian, *Icaromennipus, or A Voyage to Heaven.* (*Ibid.*, I, 304-326.)
   (Synopsis given in chapter 6.)

3. Rabelais, *Voyages of Pantagruel to the Queendom of Enthelechy, Lanternland, etc.* (Books 4-5, *ca.* 1550. *Tudor Translations*, 1900, Reprint of translation by Motteux, 1694.)
   (Synopsis given in chapter 1.)

4. Ariosto, *Voyage of Astolpho to the Moon.* (*Orlando Furioso*, Bk. XXXIV-XXXV. Published, 1532.)

   Astolpho rides in a chariot to the moon, which he finds like our own world in appearance, with the same oceans, rivers, fields, cities, and castles, lovely woods peopled with nymphs and satyrs, etc. To his wonder he learns that everything that is wasted on earth is safely treasured up in the moon. Wealth, time, and opportunity, which have been thrown away by mortals are there utilized to the full. A deep valley is filled with the surplus refuse of the world. In this pile Astolpho recognizes unnumbered prayers and unfulfilled vows, lover's sighs, days spent in gambling and in dissipation, etc., etc. There also are heaps of gold and silver treasure bestowed by slaves upon their princes, in the vain hope of reward. Ruins of empires lie strewn across the valley. The moon-people place a true valuation upon wit, the divine gift abused upon earth. (Leaving Astolpho on the moon, the poet turns to the story of Bradamant and Flordelis.)
   (Based on the translation by John Hoole, London, 1799, IV, 209-220.)

5. Thomas Artus, *Description de L'Isle des Hermaphrodites, nouvellement découverte, contenant les Moeurs, les Coutumes, & les Ordonnances des Habitants de cette Isle . . .* (Paris, 1605. This study based on edition, Cologne, 1724.)
   1 vol. in-12, 119 pp.

   The traveller, with a companion, embarks for Lisbon after a sojourn in one of the *terres nouvelles découvertes*. The inevitable storm occurs, in which the ship is dashed into a thousand pieces. The traveller and two others are the only ones to escape. As they are about to drown, they see a skiff near at hand, in which they make their way to land. They are again thrown into a panic when they discover that the land floats about "vagabond upon the ocean." On the island is a beautiful palace of marble, jasper, gold, and many other gems.
   The description of the customs of the inhabitants is a savage satire on the French Court. The effeminacy and immorality of the courtiers are elaborately set forth. Adultery is an achieve-

ment, not a disgrace. The laws of the land are the reverse of the Ten Commandments. Sex perversions are the vogue. The result of this moral hermaphroditism is the lack of any virility or manliness whatsoever.

6. Joseph Hall, *Mundus Alter et Idem.* (*Ca.* 1610. Edition, 1643.) 1 vol. in-16. *Ca.* 99 pp.
(Synopsis given in chapter 3.)

7. Bishop Francis Godwin, *The Voyage of Domingo Gonzales to the Moon, ca.* 1603. First edition, 1638. (Reprinted in *Anglia*, X, 428-456; and in the *Harleian Miscellanies*, XI, 511-534.)
(Synopsis given in chapter 1.)

8. N. Perrot d'Ablancourt, *Supplément de l'histoire véritable de Lucien.* (*Ca.* 1648. *Lucien, de la traduction de N. Perrot d'Ablancourt*, 1707, III, 461-522.)
(Synopsis given in chapter 4.)

9. Cyrano de Bergerac, *Histoire comique de la lune.* (1657.)

10. Cyrano de Bergerac, *Histoire comique du soleil.* (1657.)
(Synopses of both, given in chapter 1.)

11. Jean de Segrais, *L'ile imaginaire*, 1658. (*Oeuvres* de Segrais, 1723, and, 1755, II, 177-206.)

Returning from Madagascar, the ship is attacked by pirates, the pilot killed, and the rest left to drift about, helplessly. A storm drives them upon the shores of an island, which has no name and no human inhabitants. This island is one-hundred leagues in circumference, and is surrounded by a marble wall, in which there are two openings that serve as gates. There are groves of oranges, pomegranates, olives, prunes, pears and cherries. Many-colored animals are to be seen in the woods. Of these the aristocrats are the dogs, a very intelligent race forming a republic of their own. Their chief, a sheep-dog, is revered by all. Their government is excellent; dissention is unknown. In fact, no race so remarkable nor so ideal has ever been discovered. It would be a good thing if all Jesuits could be sent thither, for they would fit nicely into this commonwealth.

The *Ile Imaginaire* is a parody on works of the *Utopia* type.

12. Joshua Barnes, *Gerania, or News from the Pygmies.* 1675.
(Synopsis given in chapter 5.)

13. Defoe, *The Consolidator.* 1705.
(Synopsis given in chapter 1.)

14. Laurent Bordelon, *Mital, ou, avantures incroyables . . . contiennent quinze relations d'un voyage rempli d'un très-grand nombre de différentes sortes de prodiges.* 1708. Paris. 1 vol. in-12. 450 pp.

In the cumulation of prodigies, *Mital* is like Lucian's *True History.* Employing many modes of travel, the voyager visits fantastic countries. He finds societies of animals that are intelligent, others that can tell the time of day, cats that fly. In one place a man gives birth to a child from the thigh. Elsewhere, fishes live on land, chickens wear hair instead of feathers, men possess four eyes, and women wear beards. He finds, in one place, that the snow which falls in the winter is red, not white. Human varieties are numerous. There is a race of men with

one arm and one leg, others are all hunchbacks. One race of
men do not walk, but glide on their bellies like serpents. Unicorns, Siamese twins, and centaurs, fill out the list. The narrator
tabulates 650 customs he has observed; ranging from the land
where the children are never weaned from their nurses, to the
land where the inhabitants possess the power of speech, only
between noon and one o'clock of each day.

In all this there is no didactic element apparent. The author
concludes by asking whether the reader is inclined to credit his
story. Assuming the negative, he then discloses the fact that
his marvels are all gathered from works of history or science
which are taught with authority as reliable. *La Clef des Aventures de Mital*, appended, is an index to the works from which
the marvels have been copied. The Mital is thus a satire of the
same kind as the *True History*.

14. Laurent Bordelon, *Gomgam, ou, l'homme prodigieux, transporté dans
l'air, sur la terre, et sous les eaux.* Paris, 1711. 1 vol. in-12. 325 pp.

Early chapters are devoted to the education of Gomgam, the
avarice, ignorance, cruelty, and immorality of his preceptors.
On leaving college he makes a fool of himself by thinking he is
well informed. Soon finds out that he is not so wise as he
thought. He spends mornings studying up articles in encyclo-
pedias, and then discourses on those subjects in the afternoons.
Decides to turn his academic education to good account by writing. He outlines the contents of 100 books, all on trifling subjects, including, "Occupations for the Idle," "Personal Attire,"
"The Art of Speaking Without Saying Anything," etc., etc. A
queer little old man makes his acquaintance, exposes the pedantic
and impractical nature of his education, and offers to reveal to
Gomgam the truths he has failed to get from his books. By
magical means, Gomgam is transported over the earth; up into
the air where he examines the rainbow and finds that it has no
colors. Visits the Red Sea, which turns out to be not at all red.
Finds in the ocean no Tritons, Sirens, Naiades, and no Neptune.
He unlearns all that he had learned from his classical texts, and
devotes himself to exposing the deceits of scholastic tradition.

16. Baron Lewis Holberg, *Journey of Klimius to the World Underground.*
(*Ca.* 1720-1732. See English Translation, 1828.)
(Synopsis given in chapter 1.)

17. *Wasobiyoe* (?). Published, 1774, in 4 vols. Japan.
(Synopsis given in chapters 7 and 10.)

18. *Gulliver's Travels.*

Appendix B, *Realistic Voyages*

1. *Les avantures de Jacques Sadeur,* by Gabriel Foigny. (1676.)
Voyages Imaginaires, vol. 24.

2. *Histoire des sévarambes*, by Denis Vairasse d'Alais. (1677-9.) *Voyages
Imaginaires*, vol. 5.

3. *Aventures de Télémaque*, by Fénelon. (1699.)

4. *Histoire de Calejavo ou l'isle des hommes raisonnables.* 1700, by
Claude Gilbert.

5. *Voyages et avantures de François Leguat en deux isles désertes des Indes Orientales*, by F. M. Misson, 1708.

6. *Voyages et avantures de Jacques Massé*, by Simon Tyssot (de Patot), 1710.

7. *La vie les aventures et le voyage de Groenland du révérend pére cordelier Pierre de Mésange, avec une relation bien circonstanciée de l'origine, de l'histoire, des moeurs & du paradis des Habitans du pôle arctique*, by Simon Tyssot (de Patot), 1720.

Appendix C

The following is a list of some philosophical works closely related to the *Philosophic Voyage*, having for the most part the same general didactic content, and partaking of the elements of a voyage.

I

Ideal Commonwealths

Plato, *The Republic*.
  Atlantis (Described in the *Timaeus* and the *Critias*. *Works of Plato*, translated by Henry Davis, 1894, II, 325-9, and 420-9.)

More, Sir Thomas, *Utopia, The Communication of Raphael Hythloday, Concerning the best state of a commenwelth*, (1516).

Andreae, Johann Valentin, *Christianopolis, An Ideal State of the Seventeenth Century*, (1619). Translation by F. E. Held, 1914.

Bacon, Sir Francis, *The New Atlantis*, (1622-4). Edition by G. C. Moore Smith, 1900.

Gott, Samuel, *Nova Solyma*, 1648.
Campanella, Thomas, *Civitas Solis*, (ca. 1632).
Harrington, James, *The Commonwealth of Oceana*, 1656. (Morley's *Universal Library*, vol. 53.)

Morley, Henry, *Ideal Commonwealths*, 1896. (Contains the works mentioned above of More, Bacon, Campanella.)

II

The Oriental Traveller in Europe

Marana, G. P., *L'Espion du grand seigneur*, 1684. (English translation by W. Bradshaw, 8 vols. London, 1687-1693.)

Du Fresne, C. R., *Amusements sérieux et comiques*. Paris, 1699.
Brown, Tom, *Amusements Serious and Comical*, 1700.

Montesquieu, *Lettres Persanes*, 1721. (English translation by Ozell. London, 1730.)

Addison, Joseph, *Spectator*. (Nos. 50, written 1711; and 557, written 1714.)

Lyttelton, George, *Letters from a Persian in England to his friend
at Ispahan.* London, 1735.

Goldsmith, Oliver, *The Citizen of the World.* London, 1762.

Conant, M. P., *The Oriental Tale in England in the Eighteenth
Century.* New York, 1908.

III
Voyages of Abstract Allegory
(No geographical setting what-so-ever)

Fontaines, Louis, (Sieur de Saint Marcel) *Relation du pays de
Jansenie.* Paris, 1664, 1 vol. in-12.

D'Aubignac, Abbé, *La relation du royaume de coquetterie.* Paris,
1663. (*Voyages Imaginaires*, vol. 26, pp. 308-335.)
   Macarise, ou la reine des isles fortunées. Paris, 1664, 2
vols. in-8.

Tallemant, Abbé, *Le voyage de l'isle d'amour.* Paris, 1664.
(*Voyages Imaginaires*, vol. 26, pp. 233-306.)

Lesconvel, Pierre, *Voyage du prince de montberaud.* Cazères, 1703,
1 vol. in-12.

Bibliography of Source-studies

The following is a list of all the writings that are primarily
concerned with the sources of *Gulliver's Travels.* The list does
not include the remarks found in the standard biographies of
Swift and in various introductions to editions of *Gulliver.*

Borkowsky, Th.
   Quellen zu Swift's *Gulliver. Anglia*, XV, 1892. (Reprinted as
   monograph, Halle, 1893.)
Conant, M. P.
   Influence of "The Turkish Tales" upon "Lilliput." (*The Oriental
   Tale in England.* New York, 1908, pp. 259,262.)
Eddy, William A.
   D'Ablancourt's "Sequel" to Lucian's "True History,"—A Source for
   Gulliver's Travels. (*Mod. Lang. Notes*, XXXVI, 419-422. Nov.,
   1921.)
   Lucian's *Icaromennipus, or A Voyage to Heaven,*—A Source for
   Lilliput. (*Mod. Lang. Notes*, XXXVII, June, 1922.)
   Cyrano de Bergerac's *Histoire comique du soleil,*—A Source for
   Gulliver's Travels. (*Mod. Lang. Notes.* Accepted but not yet
   published.)
   Rabelais—A Source for *Gulliver's Travels.* (*Mod. Lang. Notes.*
   November, 1922.)

Firth, C. H.
The Political Significance of *Gulliver's Travels*. (*Proceedings of the British Academy*, IX, 1920.)

Hanford, J. H.
Plutarch and Dean Swift. (*Mod. Lang. Notes*, XXV, 181-4, 1910.)

Hönncher, E.
Quellen zu Dean Swift's *Gulliver's Travels*. *Anglia*, X, 1888.

Hübener, Gustav.
Die Entstehung von *Gulliver's Travels* und die 'Curiosity' Kultur. (*Neophilologus*, VII, 1921.)

Poll, Max.
The Sources of *Gulliver's Travels*. (In *Bulletin of the University of Cincinnati*, No. 24, 1909.)

Reed, Edward Bliss.
Tom Brown and *Gulliver*. (*Mod. Lang. Notes*, XXXIII, 57-8, 1918.)

Thierkopf, Paul.
Swift's *Gulliver* und seine französische vorgänger. (Monograph, Magdeburg, 1899.)

Thompson, Elbert N. S.
Tom Brown and *Gulliver's Travels*. (*Mod. Lang. Notes*, XXXII, 90-94, 1917.)

Toldo, Pietro.
Les voyages merveilleux de Cyrano de Bergerac et de Swift, et leur rapports avec l'oeuvre de Rabelais. (*Rev. des Etudes Rabelaisiennes*, vols. 4 and 5, 1906-7.)

Bibliography—General

The bibliography here listed does not repeat the titles of works already included in the classified lists that precede.

Ablancourt, Nicolas Perrot d'
Lucien de la traduction do N.Perrot d'Ablancourt. Paris, 1707. 3 vols.

Addison, Joseph
Poems. (Edited by H. G. Bohn.) London, 1913. 2 vols.

Arbuthnot, John
Miscellany. London, 1751. 2 vols.

Aristotle
The History of Animals. (Translated by R. Cresswell.) London, 1897.
Poetics. (Translated by Daniel Twining.) London, 1812.

Ashton, John

Chapbooks of the Eighteenth Century. London, 1882.
Social Life in the Reign of Queen Anne. London, 1882.

Ashton, W. G.

History of Japanese Literature. New York, 1899.

Atkinson, Geoffroy

The Extraordinary Voyage in French Literature before 1700. New York, 1820.
The Extraordinary Voyage in French Literature from 1700 to 1720. Paris, 1922.

Banier, Abbé

La légende des pygmées. (In appendix to his translation of Ovid. Paris, 1732. 2 vols.)

Barni, J.

Histoire des idées morales et politiques en France an XVIIe siécle. Paris, 1865.

Bayle, Pierre

Dictionnaire critique et historique. Rotterdam, 1715. 4 vols.

Beattie, James

Poetical Works. London, 1864. (*Aldine Poets*, X.)

Benjamin (of Tudela)

Travels. (Translated by M. N. Adler. *Jewish Quarterly Review*, XVI-XVIII, 1904-6.)

Berkeley, George

A New Theory of Vision. London, 1709.

Besant, Walter

The French Humorists. New York, 1877.

Biron, C.

Curiosités de la nature . . . apportées dans deux voyages des Indes . . . Paris, 1703.

Bordelon, Abbé Laurent

Histoire des imaginations extravagantes de M.Oufle. Paris, 1710.

Boswell, James

Life of Samuel Johnson. London, 1887. 6 vols.

Bougeant, Abbé

Voyage merveilleux du Prince Fan-Férédin dans la Romancie. Paris, 1735.
History of the Reign of Queen Anne. London, 1853.

Burton, J. H.

Burton, Richard F.
The Book of the Thousand Nights and A Night. London, 1897.
12 vols.

Brown, A. C. L.
Gulliver's Travels and an Irish Folk-tale. (Mod. Lang. Notes,
XIX, 45-6. 1904.)

Brown, Tom
Works. (Ninth edition.) London, 1760. 4 vols.

Brun, Pierre
Savinien de Cyrano Bergerac. Paris, 1909.

Campbell, J. G.
Waifs and Strays of Celtic Tradition. Edinburgh, 1895.

Carey, Henry
Poems on Several Occasions. London, 1729.

Carré, Abbé
Voyage des Indes Orientales, mêlé de plusieurs histoires curieuses.
Paris, 1699. 2 vols.

Cauche, F.
Relations véritables et curieuses de l'Isle de Madagascar et du
Brésil. Paris, 1651.

Chamberlain, Basil Hall
A Japanese Gulliver. (Journal of the Asiatic Society of Japan,
VII. London, 1879.)

Chinard, Gilbert
L'Amérique et le rêve exotique dans la littérature française au
XVIIe et au XVIIIe siècle. Paris, 1913.

Conant, Martha P.
The Oriental Tale in England in the Eighteenth Century. New
York, 1908.

Collins, J. Churton-
Jonathan Swift. London, 1902.

Craik, Henry
Life of Swift. London, 1882.

Croly, George
Salathiel, The Immortal. Philadelphia, 1827. (Reprinted with the
title, "Tarry Thou Till I Come." New York, 1900.)

Cyrano (de Bergerac)
Oeuvres. Paris, 1858.

Dampier, William
A New Voyage Round the World. (Sixth edition.) London, 1717.
2 vols.

Dargan, H. M.
The Nature of Allegory as Used by Swift. (*Studies in Philology*, XIII, July, 1916.)

Davenant, William
Madagascar, With Other Poems. London, 1638.

Davis, Henry
Works of Plato. New York, 1894. 6 vols.

Defoe, Daniel
The Life and Surprising Adventures of Robinson Crusoe. Oxford, 1910.
The Life, Adventures, and Piracies of the Famous Captain Singleton. London, 1720.

Desfontaines, Abbé
Les voyages de Gulliver, traduites de l'Anglais. Paris, 1727.

Dixmerie,
L'Isle Taciturne, & l'isle Enjouée. Amsterdam, 1663.

Dunlop, John
History of Prose Fiction. London, 1911. 2 vols.

Eddy, William A.
Gulliveriana. The Anatomist Dissected, by Lemuel Gulliver. (London, 1727.) *Mod. Lang. Notes*, 1922.

Fénelon, François de S.
Aventures de Télémaque. Paris, 1859.

Ferriar, John
Illustrations of Sterne, With Other Essays. London, 1812. 2 vols.

Fontaine
Fables. Paris, 1779. 3 vols.

Fontenelle, Bernard le Bovier, Sieur de
Oeuvres. Paris, 1790. 8 vols.

France, Anatole
Penguin Island. (Translated by A. W. Evans.) London, 1909.

Fuller, Thomas
History of the Worthies of England. London, 1662. 3 vols.

Furetière, Antoine
Furetiriana. Lyons, 1696.

Gelli, Giovanni Battista
Circe. (Translated by Tom Brown.) London, 1702.

Godwin, William
St. Leon, A Tale of the Sixteenth Century. London, 1799.

Goldoni
Memoirs. (Translated by John Black.) London, 1814.

Gossouin, Maître
L'Image du monde de Maître Gossouin. Lausanne, 1913.

Gould, S. Baring-
Curious Myths of the Middle Ages. London, 1869.

Greene, H. E.
The Allegory as Employed by Spenser, Bunyan, and Swift. (Publ. of the Mod. Lang. Soc. of America, IV. 1888-9.)

Gulliver, Lemuel (pseud.)
(See writings attributed to Gulliver in appendix to chapter 11, above.)

Hakluyt
Voyages. (Reprint.) Glasgow, 1904. 20 vols.

Harleian
Miscellanies, London, 1808-11. 12 vols.

Hawkesworth, J.
Life of Swift. London, 1765.

Hazlitt, William
Collected Works. London, 1902. 6 vols.

Herbert, Thomas
Some Yeares Travels into Africa and Asia. London, 1638.

Herodotus
Works. (Translated by Henry Cary.) London, 1898.

Hime, H. W. L.
Lucian,—The Syrian Satirist. London, 1900.

Hoffman, David
Chronicles Selected from the Originals of Cartaphilus, The Wandering Jew. London, 1853. 6 vols.

Holberg, Lewis
Memoirs. (Anonymous translation.) London, 1827.

Howell, James
The Parly of the Beasts, or, Morphandra, Queen of the Enchanted Island. London, 1660.

Hunt, Robert
Popular Romances of the West of England. London, 1865.

Jacobs, Joseph
More Celtic Fairy Tales. London, 1895.

Justel, P.
Recueil de divers voyages faits en Afrique et en l'Amérique, qui n'ont point esté encore publiez. Paris, 1674.

Keidel, G. C.
A Manuel of Aesopic Fable Literature. Berlin, 1896.

Keightley, Thomas
Fairy Mythology. London, 1853. 2 vols.

Kircher, Athanasius
Mundus Subterraneus. Amsterdam, 1665. 2 vols.

Kirk, Robert
The Secret Commonwealth of Elves, Fauns, and Fairies. London, 1691.

Köerting, Heinrich
Geschichte des französische romans im 17 jahrhundert. Oppeln, 1891. 2 vols.
Fahrten nach Mond und Sonne. Leipsic, 1887.

Lane, E. W.
The Thousand and One Nights. London, 1859. 3 vols.

Lang, Andrew
The Homeric Hymns (translated). London, 1899.

Lanson, Gustave
Manuel bibliographique de la littérature française moderne. Paris, 1914. 4 vols. in 1.

Le Blanc, Vincent
Les voyages fameux du Sieur Vincent Le Blanc. Troyes, 1658.

Lichtenberger, A.
Le socialisme utopique. Paris, 1898.

Lotheissen, Ferdinand
Geschichte der französischen literatur im 17 jahrhundert. Berlin, 1877.

Lucian
Works. (Dryden translation.) London, 1711. 4 vols.

Macaulay, Thomas B.
Works. New York, 1860. 5 vols.

Mandeville, John
Adventures and Travels. London, 1895.

Manley, Mrs. Mary de la Rivière
Secret Memoirs and Manners from the New Atalantis, An Island in the Mediterranean. (Sixth edition.) London, 1720. 4 vols.

Mardus, J. C.
Livre des mille nuits et une nuit. Paris, 1917. 16 vols.

Martino, Pierre
L'Orient dans la littérature française au XVIIe et au XVIIIe siècle. Paris, 1906.

Maturin, C. R.
Melmoth, The Wanderer. London, 1892. 3 vols.

Merriman, H. S.
In the Track of the Wandering Jew. (In *Tomaso's Fortune*. New York, 1904.)

Meyer, Richard M.
Jonathan Swift und G. Ch. Lichtenberg. Berlin, 1886.

Michel, F. Xavier-
Les voyages merveilleux de Saint Brandan. Paris, 1878.

Microphilus, (pseud.)
The New Year's Gift, Presented at Court from the Lady Parvula
to the Lord Minimus. London, 1630.

Morley, Henry
Ideal Commonwealths. London, 1896.

Mouhy, Chevalier de (Charles Fieux)
Lamékis, ou les voyages extraordinaires d'un Egyptien dans la
terre interieure. Paris, 1735.

North, Thomas
The Morall Philosophie of Doni. London, 1570.

O'Grady, Standish H.
Silva Gadelica. London, 1892. 2 vols.

Orrery
Remarks on the Life and Writings of Dr. Jonathan Swift. London, 1751.

Palissot, Charles
Memoires pour servir à l'histoire de la littérature française.
Paris, 1771.

Perrault, Charles
Les Contes des fées. Lyons, 1865.

Pinto, F. M.
Voyages in China, Tartary, etc. (Translated by H. Cogan.) London, 1663.

Plutarch
Morals. Translated from the Greek by Several Eminent Hands.
London, 1704. 6 vols.

Polo, Marco
The Book of Ser Marco Polo. London, 1871. 2 vols.

Potvin, Ch.
Le roman du Renard. Paris, 1862.

Psalmanazar, George
Memoirs. London, 1765.

Purchas, Samuel
Hakluytus Posthumous, or, Purchas His Pilgrimes. Glasgow, 1906.
20 vols.

Quatrefages,
Pygmies. (Translated by Frederick Starr.) Chicago, 1895.

Revue des Etudes Rabelaisiennes. IV, V. Paris, 1906-7.

Rabelais, François
Works. (In Tudor Translations. London, 1900.) Oeuvres. Paris,
1858. 2 vols.

Relation du monde de mercure. (Anonymous.) Paris, 1750.

Rohde, Erwin
Der griechische roman und seine vorläufer. Leipsic, 1876.

Roumier, Marie Anne de
Les voyages de Milord Céton dans les sept planettes. Paris, 1765.

Saturday Review, LXII. London, 1886.

Scott, Temple
Bibliography of Swiftiana. (*Prose Works of Swift*, XII.) London, 1899.

Spindler, Heinrich
Der gigantenmythus in seiner älteren überlieferung. Leipsic, 1888.

Stephen, Leslie
Jonathan Swift. London, 1882.

Sterne, Lawrence
Works. London, 1873. 4 vols.

Sturmy, Samuel
Mariners' Magazine. London, 1684.

Süe, Eugène
Le juif errant. (English translation. Boston, 1899.)

Taylor, W. Cooke-
Gulliver's Travels. Philadelphia, 1864.

Thackeray, W. M.
The English Humourists. London, 1911.

Thoms, W. J.
The History of Reynard the Fox. London, 1844.

Tyson, Edward
Essay Concerning the Pygmies of the Ancients. London, 1699.

Voltaire, (François-Marie Arouet)
Oeuvres complètes. Paris, 1879.

Voyage du pôle arctique au pôle antarctique. (Anonymous.) Paris, 1723.

Voyages Imaginaires, (Bibliothèque des.) Paris, 1787, 39 vols.

Wallace, Lewis
The Prince of India. New York, 1893.

Wells, J. E.
A Manual of the Writings in Middle English. New Haven, 1916.

Waller, Edmund
Poems. London, 1784. 2 vols.

Waller, J. F.
Gulliver's Travels. London, 1865.

Wonderart, Hermann
Mythologo Graecorum de Pygmaeis. Leipsic, 1714.

Wood, E. J.
Giants and Dwarfs. London, 1868.